STUDENT WRITING

Student Writing presents an accessible and thought-provoking study of academic writing practices. Informed by 'composition' research from the US and 'academic literacies studies' from the UK, the book challenges current official discourse on writing as a 'skill'. Lillis argues for an approach which sees student academic writing as 'social practice'.

The book draws extensively on a three-year study with ten 'non-traditional' students in higher education and their experience of academic writing. Using case study material – including literacy history interviews, extended discussions with students about their writing of discipline-specific essays, and extracts from essays – Lillis explores the following three issues surrounding individual student writing.

- **Access** to higher education and to its language and literacy representational resources
- **Regulation** of meaning-making in academic writing
- **Desire** for participation in higher education and for choices over ways of meaning in academic writing

Student Writing raises questions about why academics write as they do, who benefits from such writing, which meanings are valued and how, on what terms 'outsiders' get to be 'insiders' and at what costs.

Theresa M. Lillis is Lecturer in Language and Education at the Centre for Language and Communications at the Open University.

D0161894

LITERACIES
Series Editor: David Barton
Lancaster University

Literacy practices are changing rapidly in contemporary society in response to broad social, economic and technological changes: in education, the workplace, the media and in everyday life. The *Literacies* series has been developed to reflect the burgeoning research and scholarship in the field of literacy studies and its increasingly interdisciplinary nature. The series aims to situate reading and writing within its broader institutional contexts where literacy is considered as a social practice. Work in this field has been developed and drawn together to provide books which are accessible, interdisciplinary and international in scope, covering a wide range of social and institutional contexts.

CITY LITERACIES
Learning to Read Across Generations and Cultures
Eve Gregory and Ann Williams

LITERACY AND DEVELOPMENT
Ethnographic Perspectives
Edited by Brian V. Street

SITUATED LITERACIES
Theorising Reading and Writing in Context
Edited by David Barton, Mary Hamilton and Roz Ivanic

MULTILITERACIES
Literacy Learning and the Design of Social Futures
Edited by Bill Cope and Mary Kalantzis

GLOBAL LITERACIES AND THE WORLD-WIDE WEB
Edited by Gail E. Hawisher and Cynthia L. Selfe

STUDENT WRITING
Access, Regulation, Desire
Theresa M. Lillis

STUDENT WRITING

Access, regulation, desire

Theresa M. Lillis

London and New York

First published 2001 by Routledge
11 New Fetter Lane, London EC4P 4EE

Simultaneously published in the USA and Canada
by Routledge
29 West 35th Street, New York, NY 10001

Routledge is an imprint of the Taylor & Francis Group

Typeset in Baskerville by Keystroke, Jacaranda Lodge, Wolverhampton
Printed and bound in Great Britain by St Edmundsbury Press,
Bury St Edmunds, Suffolk

British Library Cataloguing in Publication Data
A catalogue record for this book is available from the British Library

Library of Congress Cataloging in Publication Data
Lillis, Theresa M., 1956–
Student writing: access, regulation, desire / Theresa M. Lillis.
p. cm. – (Literacies)
Includes bibliographical references (p.) and index.
1. English language–Rhetoric–Study and teaching–Social aspects.
2. Report writing–Study and teaching (Higher)–Social aspects.
3. Minority women–Education (Higher) 4. Nontraditional college students.
5. College prose–Evaluation. 6. Motivation in education.
I. Title. II. Series.

PE1404 .L525 2001
808'.042'071'1–dc21   00–051706

ISBN 0–415–22801–8 (hbk)
ISBN 0–415–22802–6 (pbk)

To Jean and Noel Lillis
Thank you for all the many Scarlet Ribbons

CONTENTS

FIGURES AND TABLES

Figures

Tables

PREFACE
Why write this book?

As somebody from a working-class background and a member of the first generation in my family to go to university, I experienced a range of contradictory emotions in my steps towards, and later my participation in, higher education. In the institutional spaces leading to entry in higher education – studying at school for state exams – and later sitting in seminars and lectures, I felt a strong sense of being an outsider, hating this 'place' as well as loving the possibility of learning that it promised to offer up. Language was often at the centre of these emotions, conscious as I was of not having the 'right' language to express myself in speech and in writing. Whilst fiercely proud of my own background – my family, my local working-class English community on the council estate, my wider Irish community – I knew that these were the 'wrong background' and that I risked publicising my membership of the wrong communities every time I opened my mouth. I had a strong fear of being 'found out', a fear that although I had passed the official tests of the time – state exams at 11, 16 and 18 – I wasn't really good enough to be at university. At the same time I had a strong sense of the injustice of the power wielded by those who possessed what I would later come to call the 'appropriate linguistic capital', that is, the ways with words that the institution values. Later, as a tutor working with adults studying on undergraduate courses, I witnessed similar struggles, fears and hopes. I also became aware of how many of these tensions centred on academic writing as the students attempted to write within the rules of the game without knowing what the rules were. At the same time, students were often dissatisfied with the kinds of meaning making in which they felt they were expected to engage. This book is my attempt at making publicly visible what many, like myself, from backgrounds traditionally excluded from higher education, know intuitively at some level.

There are good reasons for thinking that such an attempt is timely. In recent years participation in higher education, in the UK as in many parts of the world, has grown significantly, now involving greater numbers of students from social backgrounds previously excluded. Within this reconfigured space, the experiences explored in this book are not peripheral but central to the new project of higher education, raising questions not only about the nature of such participation but also about the nature of higher education, about what it is and does, and to what end. This book is therefore intended as a contribution to the much larger debate about what we want from higher education at the beginning of the twenty-first century.

ACKNOWLEDGEMENTS

I would like to thank the many people who helped and encouraged me while I was writing this book and doing the research on which this book is based. I would especially like to express my sincerest thanks to the following people.

The student-writers who gave so generously of their time, patience and ideas. Without you, this book would not exist.

To Peter Ashworth, Asher Cashden, Karen Grainger and the Learning and Teaching Institute at Sheffield Hallam University who funded my research studentship and encouraged the research on which this book is based. Thank-you also to the many people who made my time at the LTI pleasurable, in particular, Shauna Morton, Iain Garner, Chris Glover, Li Wang, Lyndsay Aitkenhead, Kerry Cripps, Meg Handscombe and Mark Neath.

To David Barton, the editor of the Literacies series for taking time to offer critical comments on earlier drafts.

To colleagues at the Centre for Language and Communications at the Open University where I now work, especially those of you who read and commented on parts or wholes of draft chapters- Joan Swann, Pam Burns, Libby Brill, Fulden Underwood, Cathy Lewin and Mary Jane Curry.

To Mary Scott and the Academic Literacies Research Group at the Institute of Education, London, for welcoming me to their regular meetings – providing me with a 'home' for my interests, worries and ideas. Mary's flowers and coffee have brightened many a tired and grey Saturday morning trip to London.

To Mary Scott and Joan Turner for finding time in your busy teaching lives to read earlier versions of chapters.

To Roz Ivanic for constantly demonstrating that it is possible to share in the world of academia.

To Barry, Jim and Dee for growing up with me. Merthyr Road taught us a lot.

Y como siempre a Guillermo, Liam y Carmen. 'A esta cita, sólo faltan las gaviotas'.

INTRODUCTION
Focus and research background

What is this book about?

This book is about student writing in higher education. It sets out to explore academic writing practices in higher education with particular reference to the experience of so-called 'non-traditional' students in the United Kingdom, that is, students from social groups who have historically been largely excluded from higher education. (A range of terms is used to refer to such students in different higher education contexts; for example, 'educationally disadvantaged' in South Africa, 'disadvantaged minorities' in North America.) The principal arguments in this book are as follows:

1 Current ways of thinking and talking about student writing in official discourse are limited, working against the more recent aim of widening access to students from social groups historically excluded.
2 Recent theory and research emerging from what can be broadly described as a *social practices* approach – within linguistics, composition and literacy studies – need to be brought into current discussions about written communication in higher education. This theory and research provides a powerful framework for defining the nature of institutional literacy practices as well as for our understanding about what may be at stake for individuals as they engage in these practices.
3 Students' written academic texts and their accounts of the production of these texts need to be at the centre of any attempt to explore what's involved in student academic writing.
4 Current pedagogic practice surrounding student writing needs to be critically reviewed; in particular, the dominant practice of tutor 'feed-back' needs to be transformed by a more dialogic approach to students' construction of meaning in written texts.

In making these arguments, I put the experience of student-writers centre stage. In doing so, I'm conscious of the danger of constructing an 'other', an 'outsider' who is somehow fundamentally different from those who are

1

already insiders, or who are most likely to become insiders, in higher education (henceforward HE). Constructed as already outside of academia, it's easy to represent any struggles students face as 'their' problem. But this is not an 'us' versus 'them' debate. A key argument in this book is that detailed attention to specific instances of students' writing helps to illuminate the nature of the writing practices within the academy and, consequently, to raise important questions for all of us who engage in them. So, whilst the focus of this book is the production of written texts by 'non-traditional' students, it is also a book about us, you and me, and all those who read and write academic texts. Why do we write as we do? Who gets to write in these ways? Who benefits from such writing? What meanings are we valuing and how? Who does the academy construct as belonging, and how? On what terms do 'outsiders' get to be 'insiders' and at what costs? How do we want to write, and why?

The tensions surrounding these questions – and possible answers to these questions – are explored across three key dimensions in this book, as indicated by the subtitle: *access* to HE and to its representational resources, that is, the language and literacy resources for meaning making that are available in higher education; *regulation* of meaning making in academic literacy practices; *desire* for participation in HE and for choices over meaning making.

> ### *Connections . . .*
>
> One way of attempting to break down the 'us' versus 'them' split is to recognize that I'm one of 'them'. This is not an autobiography – my story alone would not be important enough, I think. Where it is important, is in the way it connects with the lived experience of the student-writers who shared their views, their texts and their time with me. I make connections at different points in the book by bringing in some of my particular experiences, past and present, of being and writing in academia. In doing so, I'm attempting to avoid constructing an 'other', to emphasise that the reasons why we engage in academic endeavour are often (always?) connected implicitly to our own experiences and desires; to point to the constructed nature of knowledge making – there is a person writing this book with her own history and interests.

Who is this book for?

In writing this book, a key aim has been to bring together the ideas, concerns and positions from three broad, often quite distinct, communities in HE; these are student-writers, practitioners in HE (whether teachers or policy makers) and academic literacy researchers. These often exist as separate constituencies, failing to engage actively with each other's understandings about student writing. My aim is to bring together these constituencies, both as the sources and the readers of this book, in an attempt to construct a framework we can share for thinking about students and their writing in HE.

If you're a student, particularly from a so-called 'non-traditional' background, I hope that you'll find this book useful at a personal level in validating, perhaps, some of your experiences – 'I've felt like that too' – and, more importantly, in making visible some of the ways in which institutional practices work. If you are a tutor with an interest in, or responsibilities relating to, student writing, I hope that you'll find the student-writers' perspectives useful to your practice, as well as to your theorising about what's involved in student writing in HE. The insights from the student-writers' experience challenge the official discourse on writing as a 'skill' and raise questions about current institutional practices. They thus provide a critique which can contribute to a wider debate about student writing and student writing pedagogy in HE.

If you are interested in teaching and learning in HE more generally, the close attention paid to specific instances of written texts, alongside the student-writers' perspectives, will illustrate the value of such analysis for documenting the 'student experience', a relatively recent interest in the UK context. If you are an educator and/or policy maker committed to widening participation in HE, this book should be of interest in that it links the problematics of access (to what? and by whom?) to questions about academic language and literacy practices in HE.

As well as being of relevance to those primarily concerned with teaching and learning in HE, this book will be of interest to those working in the growing field of literacy studies in the UK and in the research domain of student academic writing more specifically, in the following ways: by making available substantial case study material drawn from a specific group of students in higher education; by making connections between current work on student writing, particularly 'non-traditional' students and their writing, from two distinct contexts, the UK and the US; by foregrounding the relevance of a New Literacy Studies' perspective to researching student writing in HE; by exploring connections between the dominant literacy practice in HE, essayist literacy, and gender.

In thinking of all these potential readers, I have tried to write in ways which will not drive people away: I do use terminology which may be new to some readers but I have tried to explain such terms rather than take them for granted (or see them as your problem). In writing about academic writing I am acutely aware of the ways in which particular uses of language may serve to exclude, rather than include, particular readers. But I have also learnt enough to know that I cannot know how different readers will respond to, or 'read', me and this text. In writing this book, it has helped me to think of readers who will accept this book as an inevitably flawed, yet honest, attempt to contribute to an understanding about students and their writing in HE.

The research on which this book is based

This book constitutes a critique of current official discourse on student writing. This critique is informed by socially oriented theory and research emerging from a number of disciplinary and geographical contexts, but is driven by my understandings generated from a research project spanning some four years. This project focuses on the experience of ten 'non-traditional' students as they engage in academic writing during their first years of undergraduate study in the UK. The value of such case study research is that it offers up the possibility of 'thick description' (Geertz 1973) which facilitates insights into the nature of the phenomena being explored: in this instance, detailed attention to specific instances of student writing tells us about individual student experiences, as well as about the nature of academic literacy practices in higher education.

Brief profiles, drawn from literacy history interviews and ongoing conversations of three of the student-writers, are provided on pages 5, 7 and 8 as a way of beginning to introduce the student-writers to you. Further profiles are offered throughout the course of this book, with brief overviews of the student-writers' educational background in Appendix 1.

There are obvious differences between the three student-writers, Amira, Bridget and Siria, not least in terms of age, ethnicity and linguistic backgrounds. But their profiles also illustrate experiences that are common across all the students' experiences: all of them have been through the compulsory schooling system in England, but their route towards higher education has not been smooth; none went from school to university at 18; most were unsuccessful at secondary school, and even those who were successful, in that they passed several GCSEs/O levels (national examinations at age 16), did not think of university as a realistic option; they all describe themselves as being from working-class backgrounds; seven of the ten student-writers are the first in their families to go to university; they have all worked in paid employment; all have had (and most continue to have) substantial family responsibilities to parents and/or children. Their pathways through higher education are not straightforward in that only three of the student-writers have managed to sustain continuous participation in higher education over a three/four-year period (see Chapter 5).

It is important to note that I don't see the student-writers' literacy/life-history accounts as 'background information', but rather as central to any attempt to understand their specific experiences of engaging in academic writing in HE. Thus, although throughout the book I refer to them as 'student-writers', it is important to recognise that, firstly, and like increasing numbers of participants in higher education, they are 'students' for only a part of their lives. They are also, not least, workers, mothers and daughters. Secondly, as 'students', they are not a homogeneous group: they are Black, white, working-class, bilingual, monolingual, Muslim. Language is central to

Amira[1]

Amira is a 21-year-old woman from a Yemeni background. She is married and has one young child. She was brought up in a bilingual household where Arabic and English were spoken on a daily basis and where much codeswitching between languages went on. She remembers from an early age being told stories both in Arabic and English. She feels equally comfortable when talking Arabic and English, but feels that she is more competent in reading and writing in English than in Arabic.

Amira went to a white monolingual primary school, which she loved, and where she remembers doing well, receiving many certificates for her success in different subject areas. She also attended Arabic classes for two years but feels she didn't learn much. Her mother taught her how to read and write in Arabic at home. She would like to improve her written Arabic but currently does not have the time.

Her success at school changed when she moved to the *posh* white secondary school.

> At primary school they were always encouraging you. But at secondary, I don't think they were bothered. There were too many pupils anyway.

Although at third year (Y9 – aged 14) it was estimated that she was heading for good grades in all her GCSEs,[2] she passed only Maths and English.

> I never used to go to school, I was a nut! I used to go to my friend's house which was up the road. And the teachers, I don't think they cared, because everybody was wagging it, so they never used to check. I mean, they knew I was never in a lesson. I think the school should have taken more care. At 15 or 16, you don't realise what you're doing. I think they should have rung my parents up. At least that would have made me go to school. But they didn't do anything.

On leaving school she *just passed* her BTEC in social work; she was still spending a lot of time *messing about*. She then got married in Yemen where she planned to live but, due to illness, returned to England. She decided to return to formal education and, on advice from the community centre where she then worked, joined a level 1 higher education course in Language Studies. However, Amira was unclear as to where such a course might lead her.

Amira expressed concern about having to write *more academic English*, which she felt was at a *higher level* than the English she would normally use. In her first year in higher education, she said she was trying to deal with this by looking for more formal words from the course books she was reading, as well as using a thesaurus and a dictionary.

the many activities and corresponding identities that make up their daily lives, and concerns about the status of such language(s) in an academic context are often at the forefront of their minds as they engage in academic writing. So, for example, monolingual student-writers feel that the type of English language that they use is not good enough for academia, whilst some bilingual student-writers worry about what they feel to be the negative effect of being brought up bilingually in two 'non-standard' languages. The kinds of meanings that the student-writers make in their academic texts and their feelings about what they do/don't mean in their writing are bound up with ongoing aspects of their identities in the many dimensions of their lives, both inside and outside the world of academia.

This is an obvious but important lesson for academia to learn: that students bring a whole range of cultural and social experiences to their acts of meaning making in academic writing and, as I argue in this book, these need to be brought into our thinking about teaching and learning in HE.

Moreover, such life and language experiences are central to any exploration of meaning making in academic writing. I start from the premise that in order to understand what is involved in students' writing, it is important to have a sense of who the student-writers are and the representational resources they are potentially drawing on, that is, the language resources that they draw on for their meaning making (Kress 1996: 18; see Chapter 2). I am not suggesting that it is possible to link, in any straightforward way, all specific instances of meaning making in academic writing with aspects of a student-writer's life and habits of meaning. However, coming to know something of the student-writers' lives has been central to my understanding of their experiences of engaging in academic writing, as is evident in discussions in Chapters 4, 5 and 6.

The importance I attach to the student-writers' literacy/life histories, my stance as a participant-observer of their experience of engaging in academic writing alongside the collection and analysis of numerous kinds of texts related to their writing (course guidelines on essay questions, departmental feedback and advice sheets, tutors' written comments) locates this study within ethnographic approaches to language and literacy where the emphasis is on exploring literacy in real-world settings, through a range of methods (see for examples, Baynham 1995; Barton and Hamilton 1998; Ivanic 1998). However, the principal methodological tool used in this project was that of 'talk around texts', carried out over a period of between one and four years. Details of the data collection are provided in Appendix 3. Briefly, the student-writers and I met at regular intervals to discuss drafts of assignments they were writing for their courses of study, which included Language Studies, Law, Educational Studies and Women's Studies.

Given our, often, quite different interests for meeting to talk about texts, it was important to find ways of practically engaging in two principal types of

6

Bridget

Bridget is a 47-year-old white woman from a working-class background. She lives with her husband and daughter who is 17 years old. Before beginning her BA course in Social Work Studies, she had successfully completed an Access course.

Bridget remembers little about her primary schooling except that her older brother encouraged her to read and write and, unlike their parents, thought highly of studying. Bridget unexpectedly failed the 11-plus examination[3] and, although initially disappointed, was pleased to be going to the brand new secondary modern school. She enjoyed English and was interested in learning in general. However, continuing education after 16 was never an option, and university was well out of sight:

> It never came into it. For a start, my parents couldn't afford it. And also, girls just weren't pushed to go into university. And if you went to secondary modern it wasn't mentioned. *No* possibility at all.

On leaving school at 16 with three O levels, Bridget went to secretarial college for a year and then began work in a chartered accountant's office. She was pleased to get this *decent job*. After marrying, she and her husband ran a small business successfully. During this time she had a daughter and, as well as having the main responsibilities for house and children, she did the administrative work for the business. After twelve years, when her husband became ill, they abandoned the business. This left Bridget to make a decision about looking for paid work elsewhere. She decided to go to college. Although she had an idea about studying social work from the moment she thought of returning to study, she only considered this a realistic proposition towards the end of the Access course:

> The time came to fill in these UCAS forms and I thought, what am I doing here? . . . And then I thought, well nothing to lose, why not?

To a large extent, university was still a distant place:

> I think, because before university always seemed so far off, you always thought that the standard was way above your head and you could never get to that standard.

Although uncertain of her capabilities, Bridget, like others, talks of her desire for learning:

> the more you do, the more you want to do.

Bridget felt that her writing in HE was not *academic enough* for higher education, even though tutors on the Access course had reassured the students that it would be acceptable to use language that they felt comfortable with:

> They [tutors on the Access course] always said to us, 'Just try and use simple language. Don't try and use words you don't understand.' But I always thought that the way I wrote was not what they expected, not the academic standard.

Siria

Siria is a Sylheti-Bengali and English speaker from a Bangladeshi family. She has lived in England since she was 2 years old.

From when Siria came to England, Sylheti was, and continued to be, the language of the home and her local community. Siria attended Bengali classes for three evenings a week from the age of 7–14 years, as well as learning Arabic for religious purposes.

Siria remembers doing a lot of reading and writing:

> By the time I was 8, there was a vast amount of reading and writing going on. And I didn't really enjoy so much of it because there was so much time involved, reading and writing three languages. It was quite intense.

Whilst *doing quite well* at primary school, things changed for Siria in secondary school:

> I'd say I didn't really enjoy school [secondary]. I used to hate going to secondary school. I think it was the atmosphere, I didn't think it was a nice atmosphere, whereas in primary school, I think the children . . . it was a lot more supportive. Whereas in secondary, it was cold, not very welcoming, the children used to be very sarcastic. They weren't exactly friendly. Because of all that, I never used to ask for extra help if I didn't understand anything. I just used to keep quiet, never put my hand up and say I don't understand, in case somebody said, 'oh dummy'.

She did not think of herself as being good at school, and certainly never thought of university as an option.

> I always felt as if university was something well out of reach. But now I'm sort of thinking, well, things can't be too difficult! Okay, I haven't done so well in the past. That doesn't mean to say I can't do well in the future.

After leaving school, Siria began a BTEC course in social work. She did not complete the course because of plans for an arranged marriage, which she challenged and, after much stress, left home to start her life alone. Having taken this major decision in her life, she felt quite confident about pursuing her interests in education.

One of Siria's concerns about studying in HE was the problem she felt she faced in getting ideas down on paper:

> I'd say, as a writer I can write quite well, but I think the only problem I'd tell you with my writing is sometimes I have a very good idea and I think, right, this is what I'm going to write about and I've already got it mapped in my head. But when I actually come to writing, I can never get the same phrase or the same definition of what I want to talk about. So the great idea that I have in my head turns out a mess on paper.

talk: talk to get on with the 'business as usual' (Ellsworth: 1994) of HE, that is, talk aimed at teaching and learning how to write in the ways required by the academy, and a key concern of the student-writers; and talk to engage in an exploration of the students' experiences of engaging in academic writing practices. This first type of talking space, with the conventionally prescribed talking roles of student and teacher, was easy for us to occupy. The second type of space had to be more consciously constructed. For whilst I was not always the tutor-assessor at the times of our discussion about texts, that is the assessor of the writing assignments, with all the student-writers I have always been the 'knowledgeable insider' (Harris 1992: 379), that is, viewed by the student-writers as someone who knows more about the conventions that they are expected to write within than they do. As the powerful participant within this context, I attempted to move us away from the conventional teacher-dominated talking space. The most obvious way of doing this was to ask open questions in order to move away from my role as talker to that of listener. Examples of these questions are given below:

Example 1[4]

T: Do you think it's harder for you than others. Do you think it's hard for everybody?

M: I don't know. Maybe other people will experience it as well, but, say, I don't want to use anybody as an example, but say for instance, somebody in our class, like G——— can speak his first language very well, that's the impression I've been given, so maybe he can speak English very well as well. He can write it very well, maybe, that's the impression I get, I might be wrong. But because I can't speak either language very well, I probably, that's probably why I find it so difficult to write standard English. Because I've got like a mixture of dialects, haven't I? The Yorkshire dialect and I've got no standard in a sense. So when I use standard English I find it very difficult to get ideas down properly. I know I can do it and if I hear something that's ungrammatical in English, I can pick it out. But to produce it, get it down in a quick time, takes a very long time. It takes a long time, I have to think about it as well. At one time I used to have problems with the past and present tense. I didn't see it as important because in Creole they don't stress tense. So I used to have a problem when I wrote in English. I'd write *wasn't* there and *is* in the middle of a paragraph when I was talking about the same subject when I should use the same tense all the way through. But I don't have that problem so much now. I've conquered that. But it's like each time I start a course or I do some kind of written work I conquer something . . .

Example 2

T: Do you think the English you use is different from academic English?

K: Definitely. Fancy words for a start, erm . . . very, I don't like using the word . . . I don't see why not. I tend to write from a personal point of view. I never see academic writing as personal. It's cold. That's how I feel.

T: Do you feel under pressure to make your writing cold?

K: I don't know, I haven't been here long enough [six weeks into the course].

Although the student-writers and I here are still occupying the conventional roles of teacher-as-questioner, student-as-respondent, the above questions/ answers move us a little away from what I refer to as the institutional 'space for telling', in that there is some space for the student-writer to talk of her views and experiences. But what is more important about these questions and answers is that they are not one-off exchanges between us but, over time, become part of shared strands of meaning across our talk; in Maybin's terms, they are part of a 'long conversation' (1994).

In order to facilitate this more exploratory and extended type of talk, I made 'talkback', in contrast to 'feedback', notes, as an attempt to construct an agenda aimed at opening up discussion and at foregrounding the student-writer's interests and concerns. The differences between 'talkback' and 'feedback' are briefly illustrated in Table I.1 below. The comparisons are based on an early example of feedback and talkback notes (see Appendix 4).

There are overlaps between the 'feedback' and 'talkback' sheets: in both there is a focus on the text as a final product, through my references to paragraphs, sentence structure, cohesion and grammar. However, it is also possible to see significant differences. In the 'feedback' sheet the emphasis is on the student-writer's text as final product which the tutor is evaluating through the comments exemplified in Table I.1. In the 'talkback' sheet, the text is treated as something which is provisional, in the making, aspects of which are thus still to be explored. The predominant focus and discoursal features in both indicate my attempts to both work within, and to move away from, a tutor-directed talking space.

Figure I.1 illustrates how we organised our meetings to talk around the individual student's writing of a particular text. Thus at stage 1, we met to talk either about a draft or an idea that the student-writer was working on for a course essay. For example, the student-writer might talk about how she was thinking of approaching the writing of an essay. This stage might be repeated several times, up to four times in one instance in this research project, or happen only once, depending on the individual student-writer's decision to meet or not with me. At stage 2, the student-writer handed me a final draft. At stage 3, I would read the final draft and make comments (if

10

Table I.1 Differences between 'feedback' and 'talkback'

	Assessment feedback sheet	**Talkback notes sheet**
Focus	• Text as finished product • Draws on tutor's implicit understanding of conventions	• The making of the text • Draws on what the student-writer said about aspects of text
Discoursal features	• Evaluative language: examples – *good, well done, very good*	• Questions about future actions: examples – *Would you use it again? How will you use them [commas] in future?*
	• Directives (direct and indirect): examples – *I'd like us/you could have/see notes/ more examples would have enhanced/we need to discuss/to discuss*	• Exploratory questions: examples – *Do you feel confident? Do you feel that you understand this? Are you using any new words in this essay? Where will you fit yourself, your personal experience, in?*

Source: Based on specific instance – see Appendix 4

I was also the assessor) or read the comments made by the tutor. At stage 4, we discussed the assessment feedback. Stage 5 involved me listening to all of our tape-recorded talk and then making talkback notes. These sheets were based on points that the student-writers had raised in previous talk but which we hadn't had time to consider, as well as involving an attempt to open up our talk more generally for exploration. The emphasis in stages 1–4 was therefore predominantly on getting on with business as usual of student academic writing, whereas the aim of stages 5 and 6 was to engage in more exploratory and problem-posing talk. Working at constructing opportunities for this kind of cyclical talk was initially, and primarily, a research-oriented

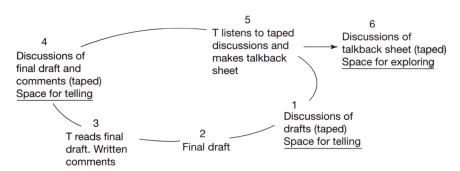

Figure I.1 Talking about one writing task

activity: the ways in which such talk might be viewed as a valuable pedagogical tool are discussed in Chapter 6.

Participation, interests and knowledge making

The content of this book is bound up with my own experiences, interests and beliefs. This is signalled throughout the book; for example, in the Preface and in the brief sections throughout the book, entitled 'connections'. My commitment to a more inclusive higher education is signalled in several chapters (for example, Chapters 1, 3, 4 and 5) as is my belief that the dominant discourse on language in higher education works against the possibilities for greater participation in HE, as well as diversity in meaning making (for example, Chapters 1, 4 and 5). Whilst acknowledging these personal interests, I have not sought simply to confirm what I already knew, but rather constantly to scrutinise my understandings at every stage of research and writing. A key way in which this has been done is through the active involvement of the participants in the discussion of ideas and in the reading of my written analyses and interpretations of their experience. In part, such involvement amounts to 'member checks' (Guba and Lincoln 1981) and these have varied across individuals and specific moments in time: some student-writers wanted to comment on everything, as well as elaborating on, and being critical of, my drafts; others simply confirmed what they had previously said. However, the active involvement of participants in research has a more fundamental effect on the ways in which we construct knowledge, helping to guard against any easy categorising of the 'other's' experience. This occurs for two reasons: firstly, because the participants, or 'others', are actively involved in the construction of that experience in the most obvious sense of contributing, checking, critiquing the researcher's perspectives; secondly, and less obviously, because the participants and their perspectives become part of the researcher's internal dialogue about what it is she is looking at and why. This last point illustrates the importance of the notion of *addressivity* for exploring meaning making, which is discussed in Chapter 2 and throughout the book.

A further way in which I have sought to problematise my knowledge-making throughout the research and writing processes, is to draw on Lather's exploration of how researchers can engage in openly committed research (see Lather 1986, 1991, 1995). She describes the processes that a researcher must engage in, as a three-way conversation between empirical data, self and theory: 'Empirical evidence must be viewed as a mediator for a constant self and theoretical interrogation between self and theory' (Lather 1991: 62).

I suggest that the understandings presented in this book are the result of a three-way conversation: between the data-experience, that is, the students' written texts and the taped discussions around the texts; the literature, that is, published works of writers whose voices were significant before I began work on this project, as well as the voices who have more recently become significant for my understanding of student writing in higher education; and me, that is, my interests as described above, and my evolving understanding and experience of the relationship between language, learning and self in formal institutions of learning. In the 'textual staging of knowledge' in this book (see Lather 1991: chapter 7), I have attempted to make all dimensions to this three-way conversation available to the critical gaze of the reader by doing the following: textually locating my self, stating the theoretical positions (in)forming the arguments, and offering the analysis of the data-experience up for scrutiny.

How this book is organised

In Chapter 1, I bring together debates around widening access and the 'problem' of student writing in higher education in the UK. I point to the recent expansion of higher education in the UK, in terms of overall student numbers and the social diversity of the student population. I argue for the need to explore the ways in which 'non-traditional' students experience conventional higher education practices; this book focuses on the literacy and pedagogical practices surrounding student academic writing. The student-writers' experiences tell us about the nature of these practices, as well as about what is involved for them, as 'non-traditional' students participating in HE. Drawing on research from the US and UK contexts, I contrast the official discourse on writing as a skill with recent approaches to writing as social practice. I argue that the former limits our understanding about the nature of language and communication and hence our under-standing of the highly publicised 'problem' of student writing.

In Chapter 2, I explore in more detail what it means to understand student writing as a social practice. I outline key ideas from New Literacy Studies and critical discourse analysis which connect closely with the student-writers' experiences, focusing in particular on works by Fairclough, Scollon and Scollon, Gee, Bakhtin and Ivanic. I draw on their ideas, to offer an alternative frame to that currently available in official discourse for understanding what is involved in student writing in academia, and in order to construct a heuristic; that is, a tool for helping us to ask questions about what student-writers are doing in their writing, and why.

The aim of Chapter 3 is to focus on the pedagogic practices surrounding student writing and, in particular, to signal the ways in which specific practices work against facilitating access to the privileged literacy practice of academia, essayist literacy. A common theme emerging from talk with the student-writers is their confusion about the nature of the academic conventions they are expected to make meaning within. To illustrate how this confusion is routinely enacted, I trace specific attempts by several student-writers to make sense of the 'essay question'. I argue that confusion is so all-pervasive a dimension of their experience as a group of 'non-traditional' students in higher education that it signals the need to look beyond a notion of individual confusion, towards an ideologically inscribed institutional practice of mystery.

In Chapter 4, I turn to explore the ways in which particular meanings, and relationships around meaning making, are privileged in essayist literacy. I illustrate how this regulation occurs by focusing on a common tension across the student-writers' experience; that is, a tension between what they feel they want to say and what they feel they are allowed to say in their academic writing. By analysing extracts from student-writers' texts and their talk about their texts, we glimpse the ways in which regulation works in relation to individual meaning making, at the levels of *context of situation* and *context of culture*. I discuss how specific instances of regulation relate to specific areas of social experience and identity, notably social class, 'race' and ethnicity.[5]

In Chapter 5, I focus on student-writers' desires. In particular, I explore the ways in which students historically excluded from higher education negotiate their desires around access to the institution of higher education and their desires around meaning making in essayist literacy. I argue that gender is a significant, although backgrounded, dimension to the student-writers' shifting desires to participate in higher education and in their meaning making in essayist literacy practice. By focusing on extracts from the students' written texts and their talk about these texts, I illustrate how, in their desires for meaning making, the writers problematise the fundamental binary framing evident in essayist literacy practice.

My aim in Chapter 6 is to engage with the principal criticisms that I make throughout this book of the current pedagogy surrounding student academic writing in HE in the UK. I argue that the participation of 'non-traditional' students in essayist literacy, and hence in higher education, can be enhanced through sustained dialogues between students and tutors. I draw on extracts of student/tutor talk around texts to illustrate four key types of dialogue which are necessary to fulfil the student-writers' desires to learn essayist conventions, as well as providing them with the opportunity for taking greater control over their meaning making.

In the final chapter, I propose a different starting-point for considering the 'problem' of student writing from that available in official discourse, discussed in Chapter 1. I focus on understandings emerging from an 'academic literacies' research approach to student writing, and to which this book contributes, in order to offer a frame for reconsidering the ways in which student writing pedagogy is conceived and enacted. I summarize the specific directions offered in this book for developing an 'academic literacies' writing pedagogy and point to questions which need further exploration.

Notes

1   These are not the student-writers' real names. Most of the names here have been chosen by the student-writers themselves. Throughout the accounts, I use the present tense to indicate information (for example, age) and comments (feelings about education, language) which were correct/valid at the time of our meetings. Most of the information presented in the accounts is drawn from the literacy history interviews, carried out during the first year of our meeting together. Although an interview schedule was drawn up and followed (see Lillis 1998), the profiles inevitably vary depending on the type of information and comments offered by each participant.

    The student-writer profiles here are edited versions of slightly longer profiles, which all the student-writers read and commented on (see Lillis 1998). On reading the accounts, most of the student-writers accepted the profiles as 'true accounts'. But we also made some changes, by adding comments, which they felt explained more fully their experience. We also chose to exclude information of too personal or painful a nature.

2   For details of UK examinations, qualifications and courses mentioned throughout the book, see Appendix 2.

3   See Appendix 2.

4   See Appendix 3 for transcription conventions.

5   I use the term 'race' to foreground the specific experience of the students who are socially marked as 'non-white' and the racism that such marking ensures. Ethnicity is used to signal membership of particular cultural, religious and linguistic groups, such as Pakistani, Yemeni.

1

LANGUAGE, LITERACY AND ACCESS TO HIGHER EDUCATION

Introduction

In the UK, as in many parts of the world, there has been a significant change in higher education in recent years, in terms of the overall increase in the number of students and the social diversity of the student population. In particular, there are increasing numbers of 'non-traditional' students, that is, students from social groups historically excluded from higher education: these include students from working-class backgrounds, those who are older than 18 when they start a university course and students from a much wider range of cultural, linguistic and religious backgrounds. The relevance, in this changed context, of conventional higher education institutional and pedagogical practices has yet to be fully explored. The dimension to be explored in this book is that of student writing.

The aim of this chapter is to bring together current debates around access to higher education and the 'problem' of student writing. In the first part of the chapter, I point to the increasing numbers of students participating in higher education whilst also signalling the tensions surrounding such participation. These are evident in the continued underrepresentation of particular social groups in higher education in general, and the obvious stratification across higher education sites. I argue that it is against this backdrop, of diversity against stratification, that the practice of student writing needs to be explored. In the second part of the chapter, I discuss the current emphasis on student writing as a 'problem'. In contrast to the official discourse on student writing as a skill, I draw on research in the US and UK contexts to argue for the need to conceptualise student writing as social practice. I argue that the former limits our understanding about the nature of language and communication, and hence our understanding of the highly publicised 'problem' of student writing.

Access to higher education

At the end of the 1930s only some 2 per cent of the population participated in HE in the UK,[1] yet by the end of the 1990s more than a third of the traditionally eligible age group gained entry. There has been huge growth particularly in the last decade, with a twofold increase in young people (aged 18 on entry) and an even greater increase in adult students (aged over 21). Actual student numbers have risen from 700,000 to around 2 million and government expectations are that, within the coming years, 50 per cent of people will go into higher education by the age of 30 (see Robertson 1997; DFEE 1998; HEFCE 1999).

The student population is not only larger but is also certainly more diverse. The number of women participating in HE has risen from around 0.5 per cent in the late 1930s to around 50 per cent in 1999/2000; by 1992 older students were outnumbering traditional-age entry students; and by 1997 the proportion of students classified as belonging to 'ethnic minorities' was greater than their ratio to the population as a whole, with 8.2 per cent of students entering higher education at the age of 18 (see Blackburn and Jarman 1993; Halsey and others 1997; National Committee of Inquiry into Higher Education/Dearing Report 1997 – henceforward referred to as Dearing 1997).

Whilst the student population has grown in both size and diversity, there are important questions to be asked about the nature of this participation, not least in terms of who is gaining access, and to what. In relation to the former, continued underrepresentation of individuals from particular social groups has been acknowledged to some extent in recent major policy reports relating to post-compulsory education. Specifically relating to higher education, Dearing states:

> Increasing participation in higher education is a necessary and desirable objective of national policy over the next 20 years. This must be accompanied by the objective of reducing the disparities in participation in higher education between groups and ensuring that higher education is responsive to the aspirations and distinctive abilities of individuals.
>
> (Dearing 1997: 101)

Concern about the non-participation of specific social groups is echoed in the government consultative paper, *The Learning Age* 1998, which states as follows:

> We must bridge the 'learning divide'- between those who have benefited from education and training and those who have not – which blights so many communities and widens income inequality.
>
> (*The Learning Age* 1998: 11)

Exactly who the non-participants are deemed to be, however, varies across official reports. In the specific context of HE, social class continues to be a major determining factor, with people from socio-economic groups 4 and 5 (partly skilled/unskilled) being far less likely to be involved in formal education after 16 years of age than those from other socio-economic groups. Recent statistics indicate that young people from wealthy areas are ten times more likely to enter HE than those from poorer backgrounds (HEFCE 1999). The possibility of engaging in HE study varies significantly; the notion that certain social groups are 'underrepresented' may, in some instances, be a euphemism for non-existent. As Robertson (1997) has pointed out, a school leaver in particular inner city areas of Liverpool is 250 times less likely to reach a university than a school leaver in Richmond on Thames (in the south of England), where 50 per cent of 18 year-olds go to university (see also recent report by Knowles 2000).

Connections . . .

One boy was famous on our council estate – he went to university. I remember hearing people talk about it when I was little. It didn't really seem possible – he was ordinary enough. He lived round the corner from us, one of twelve children, his dad worked in the local shoe factory, his mum was always busy cleaning, knitting, cooking, ironing.

He worked as a delivery boy for the butchers, on Saturdays and during school holidays. I used to wonder whether the big black bike he used to bring us our meat on had anything to do with him being special, different. It was all a bit of a mystery really.

And what about the kind of HE that different groups are accessing? Whilst women now constitute about half the student population, they are still less likely to study particular subjects, for example engineering and technology (Dearing 1997). Women are also far more likely to be part-time students; during the period 1970–89 there was a 620 per cent increase in part-time women students, as compared with a 67 per cent increase in men (Blackburn and Jarman 1993). The type of HE institution that students are likely to gain access to also varies significantly across social groups. For whilst the binary British education system was abolished in name in 1992 – polytechnics could now claim university title – institutions differ significantly in terms of status and resources. The current diverse range of HE provision includes the system of Oxford and Cambridge which serves as the gateway to powerful positions within British society, the 'old' universities, the 'new' universities and colleges of higher education. The status of the degree qualifications from these different institutions differs markedly: a first-class degree from a college of higher education amounts to considerably less cultural capital than a third-class degree from Oxford. Students from social groups previously excluded – women, older students, part-time students, working-class students, students from minority ethnic groups – are more likely to be found in these newer, and for the most part less prestigious, HE contexts (see Dearing 1997; see also HEFCE 1999 for currently evolving patterns of participation).

Thus, whilst there is, at one level, official support for expansion and inclusion, there are continuing tensions surrounding the democratisation of higher education. There is also fundamental resistance to extending access to higher education from some quarters, as is evident in press reports[2] and which is manifested in the current obsession with 'quality' and 'standards'. This emphasis on quality often only superficially conceals the ideological nature of current debates about higher education, not least the unstated perspectives on who should participate, how and to what end. It is particularly ironic that the calls for 'maintaining standards' should be paralleled by a marked decrease in funding; funding per student in HE has fallen since 1976 by more than 40 per cent (see Dearing 1997; Newby 1999).

Given the range of institutions described above, we could ask whether it's meaningful to talk of 'higher education' in the UK in general terms at all. My answer is that we need to recognise the diverse and stratified nature of HE whilst acknowledging that HE continues to exist as a social institution, with both a history and a specific current context. The social institution of HE has a long historical tradition relating to what counts as legitimate knowledge: such knowledge is constructed and maintained through particular teaching and learning practices. This history continues to exert influence on all HE institutions. By the same token, all institutions are bound to current developments and initiatives. Most recently, the 1992 Education Act created a single system, which ensures that different institutions are funded by a single agency (in broad terms), governed by the same regulatory bodies and have the same degree awarding powers. In curriculum terms, for example, and of particular relevance to this book, is the current, official emphasis on the teaching and learning of 'key skills' in HE. In relation to pedagogy, there is considerable similarity across institutions with an emphasis on particular practices, such as lectures, seminars, written course work and examinations. In relation to the specific focus of this book, student writing, a very particular type of literacy practice, informed by a particular perspective on language, continues to hold sway across HE, as I discuss below.

To summarise the points made so far in this section:

- In recent years, the student population has increased significantly.
- The current student population is more diverse, culturally, linguistically and socially.
- HE continues to be a stratified social space, in terms of who is gaining access and to what: a key example is that 'non-traditional' students are more widely represented in 'newer' institutions of HE.

19

However:

- It is meaningful and important to talk of HE in general terms, as a social institution with its specific socio-cultural history and its particular range of practices.

It is against this backdrop of stratification and diversity that the practices which have historically come to constitute HE as a particular and powerful social institution, and the ways in which these impinge on student participation, need to be explored. The particular HE practices at the centre of this book are the literacy and pedagogical practices relating to student academic writing.

Student writing in higher education

Student writing is at the centre of teaching and learning in HE in the UK, being seen as the way in which students consolidate their understanding of subject areas, as well as the means by which tutors can come to learn about the extent and nature of individual students' understanding. However, the principal function of student writing is increasingly that of gate keeping. Writing is a key assessment tool, with students passing or failing courses according to the ways in which they respond to, and engage in, academic writing tasks.

Whilst there have been some changes to the kinds of written tasks that students are expected to carry out, a very particular type of writing continues to be the mainstay within many subject areas. Such writing, institutionally labelled as the 'essay', is at the centre of practice in the Social Sciences/ Humanities (Liberal Arts) but, surprisingly perhaps, is also referred to as a key assessment tool in subjects such as Medicine, Dentistry, Sciences, Law, Languages, Creative Arts and Education, as well as in the increasing numbers of inter- and multidisciplinary courses (see Dearing 1997, Report 2, table 3:1). Given its prevalence, Womack refers to the essay as the 'default genre' indicating its taken-for-granted place within formal institutions of schooling (see Womack 1993).

However, it would be wrong to think of the 'essay' as a clearly defined genre if by 'genre' we mean something like a text type.[3] For 'essay' (and hence the scare quotes) is really institutionalised shorthand for a particular way of constructing knowledge which has come to be privileged within the academy. In order to signal this broader notion of a particular way of making meaning in texts, it is more useful to talk of a particular academic literacy practice, *essayist literacy*, which I explore in more detail in Chapter 2.

Success in writing within this practice has a very real impact on the nature of students' participation and success in HE and hence, potentially, of their life chances post HE. Attempting to tease out what's involved for students as they engage in writing is therefore of considerable importance, particularly in relation to those students who are least familiar with the practices of HE.

This teasing out is particularly important at the current time, when student writing is increasingly represented as a 'problem'. The idea that students can't write is central to official, public and pedagogic discourse in many parts of the world (see, for example, discussions in Rose 1989; Horner 1999 for the US; see Angelil-Carter 1998 for South Africa). In the UK, this 'problem' is implicit in official education reports, such as Dearing, where there is a call for greater emphasis to be placed on developing communication as one of several key skills, building on some twenty years of skills-focused initiatives (for overview, see Drew 1998). The 'problem' is explicitly signalled in some research (see for example, Lamb 1992; Winch and Wells 1995) and emphasised in the press (see discussion in Creme and Lea 1999). A comment in a recently instituted 'Agony Aunt' column for lecturers in the *Times Higher Education Supplement* gives a flavour of this stance. A tutor wrote: 'The standard of written English among some of my new undergraduates is truly awful. Is there a simple way of tackling this?' (*THES* 15/10/99), echoing much informal tutor/lecturer talk about student writing in HE (see also Clark and Lorenzini 1999).

Complaints about student writing in the academy are of course taking place within a more general, and continuing, outcry against literacy standards across the age range, and a high-profile concern about standards in education more generally, illustrating the 'literacy crises' documented by Graff (1987). Graff argues that such crises are often indications of wider social and economic problems within society. The current 'crisis' in the UK, for example, is powerfully linked to questions of national economic success or otherwise, where blame for poor economic success has long been, and continues to be, laid at the door of formal institutions of schooling (see Holland, Frank and Cooke 1998). More specifically in relation to student writing in HE, the current 'crisis' can be linked to the widening of access to students from social groups previously excluded. Although explicit causal links are not usually made, there is often an implied deficit model at work: more students from social groups previously excluded accounts for the fact that there are more problems in writing. In North America, where 'open admissions' policies have been in operation since the early 1970s such links have often been far more explicitly made (see discussion in Horner 1999).

The response to this 'problem' in a number of parts of the world has been to focus on additional support for student writing in various forms. In the US, the main provision comes in the form of 'composition' classes aimed at teaching the 'general writing skills' demanded by the academy (see Petraglia 1995; see also Crowley 1998 for a historical account of shifts in approaches to writing provision), and 'basic writing' courses aimed specifically at students identified as having problems with Standard (American) English in grammar, syntax, spelling (see Shaughnessy 1977; see also Horner and Lu 1999 for a

21

critical review of 'basic writing'). Such classes often exist alongside writing centres, which are also a main form of support in other parts of the world, such as Australia and South Africa. In these centres, students seek tutorial advice on texts they are currently writing for their courses. In the UK, where an elite system of higher education is still in the early stages of opening its doors to greater numbers of diverse student populations, there is only fragmented and limited additional provision. Where there have been initiatives, to date these have been predominantly characterised by the teaching of particular features of academic writing as part of a more general concern with 'study skills'. This approach exists, for example in the form of foundation or introductory modules in specific discipline areas, in which first-year undergraduate students may be offered guidance on essay writing as one of the several 'study skills' they need for HE. Such an approach is more often to be found in the 'new universities' where there are, as mentioned above, greater numbers of 'non-traditional' students (see Goodwin 1998).

Whilst differing in detail, the above institutional responses in composition, basic writing, writing centres and study skills, share a common (albeit contested) frame of reference which has three prominent characteristics. Firstly, both the 'problem' and the 'solution' are constructed/perceived as being overwhelmingly textual. That is, they are construed as being locatable and identifiable in the written texts that students produce, rather than in any broader frame of reference which includes, for example, questions about contexts, participants and practices. This is manifested not least in the continuing widespread belief in the possibility of teaching writing skills or 'good academic writing' outside mainstream disciplinary courses. This 'textual bias' (after Horner 1999) is evident in approaches to student writing which at first sight seem very different – whether texts as instances of genre (as exemplified in the work of Swales 1990 and Martin 1993), particular traditionally demarcated rhetorical modes (see discussion in Petraglia 1995) or common sense notions of text which can be broadly referred to as a 'skills' approach. In the British context, pedagogical approaches working with the notion of writing-as-skill can be characterised by advice on surface language features such as spelling, a cluster of features labelled 'grammar' and the most visible of academic conventions, such as simplified representations of text structure and citation practices.

The second characteristic is what can be referred to as the institutional claim to transparency; that is, whilst the language of students is made visible and problematised, the language of the disciplines and the pedagogic practices in which these are embedded usually remains invisible, taken as 'given'. I explore this more fully in the section below.

Thirdly, given the textual bias in this framing, both the 'problem' and the 'solution' are conceived as being, whilst annoying, relatively straightforward to identify and resolve. As Goodwin states in her overview of current language and study support in HE, there is an assumption, particularly in the increasing use of web pages, that 'it is quick and easy to produce a simple set [of guidelines] on essay writing' (1998: 12). Thus advice, in the form of 'handy tips' in booklets and on web pages, is the order of the day. In some institutions, students write what is termed a 'diagnostic essay' in their first semester of study, on the basis of which tutors are expected to diagnose errors and, presumably, provide a quick 'cure'.

All three characteristics signal the implicit model of language informing the discourse on communication and, our principal focus here, student writing in higher education. For, although theories of language are rendered invisible in official discourse, there is an implicit theory at work.

The model of language in official discourse

What is the model of language at work in official discourse relating to student writing? The first point to make is that there is a notable lack of any explicit attention to language in official reports and much writing related to the broad area of communication in HE in the UK, from either a theoretical or an empirical base. In order to tease out the model of language informing current official discourse, we have to look instead towards discussions on 'communication' and on teaching and learning more generally.

The dominant discourse on teaching and learning can be characterised by two main features: an emphasis on the individual and an emphasis on learning as acquiring a set of discrete, autonomous skills. At least since Callaghan's famous 'Great Debate' speech in 1976, where clear links between education, individual employment and national economic success were made, the development of individual 'skills' has been central to educational discourse in the UK. Callaghan, the then prime minister, set up a distinction between the broad aims of liberal education and employability, by stating:

> There is no virtue in producing socially well-adjusted members of society who are unemployed because they do not have the skills.
>
> (Callaghan 1976)

These 'skills' have come to include any number of things, not least the following: organisation, management, numeracy, literacy, information technology, as well as personal, interpersonal and learning how to learn skills. Within the specific context of HE, communication, and hence implicitly writing, is currently one of the four key/transferable skills identified as being essential to student learning and as being of relevance to the world of work. The others are numeracy, information technology and learning how to learn (see Dearing 1997; CVCP 1998).

What is important for the discussion here is that language, implicitly through the category of communication, is classified as a 'transferable skill', which presupposes the following. Firstly, that language is something that individuals possess; consider, not least, the prevalence of the metaphor of possession in official discourse, for example, 'equipping people with skills' (Training Agency 1990), 'the acquiring of skills' (National Council for Vocational Qualifications (NCVQ) 1995), 'possessing skills' (Dearing 1997). Secondly, that given the claim of transferability, the context in which such skills are used is given minimal importance, implicitly signalling a split between language, user and context.

This 'commonsense' split can be linked to a powerful dichotomy in traditional linguistic theory, notably Saussure's distinction between *langue* – language as system – and *parole* – instances of language use (see Saussure 1966). This dichotomy not only justifies what Saussure saw as the discipline of linguistics proper but is itself powerfully bound up with the division between language and meaning, emphasised in the tradition of Western rationality. By arguing that *parole* (language use) was not the concern of linguistics, the work of Saussure advanced the notion that language was in a fundamental way separate from use, hence reinforcing what has been referred to critically by numerous writers as the *conduit* metaphor of language. This metaphor signals the following common sense notions about language: that language serves as a conduit, conveying thoughts from one person to another; that language is a transparent medium, reflecting rather than constructing meanings; that language is an autonomous system independent of social context (see discussions in Reddy 1979 and Wertsch 1991). Intrinsic to this model of language as an idealised system is the notion of the individual as a rational user of this system, who, like language, is independent of society and socio-cultural practices, including language practices (see Wertsch 1991: 70–1).

Within this framing, homogeneity, of both users and system, is emphasised. This does not mean that diversity is totally ignored. For example, in some statements about student writing in HE there is an acknowledgement of the need to vary communication depending on audience and purpose, according to a notion of 'appropriateness'. However, this notion of 'appropriateness', as Fairclough has argued, presupposes 'clearly distinguished contexts, according to clear-cut conventions, which hold for all members of what is assumed to be a homogenous speech community' (Fairclough 1995: 243). Any struggles and tensions within and across contexts, tutors and disciplines are effectively silenced. For whilst students are expected to tailor their communication according to context and audience, these contexts and audiences are represented as fixed and homogenous. Likewise, the writer herself is constructed as an autonomous and socially neutral, or empty, subject. Yet particular identities are privileged in particular practices. As is discussed in Chapters 2, 4 and 5, it is in relation to the privileged literacy practice of higher education – essayist literacy, and the identity that it invokes – that student-writers construct both their texts and their selves (see Chapter 2 for fuller discussion of practices and identity/subjectivity). The tensions surrounding meaning making in essayist literacy raise questions about the kinds of identities, and participants, that HE wants to encourage and discourage.

The dominant theory of language implicit in a skills approach to communication, and briefly outlined here, ignores more recent thinking on the nature of the relationship between language, user and context which fundamentally challenges the Saussurean dichotomy referred to above. In recent work within critical linguistics in particular, emphasis has been on acknowledging, rather than dismissing, the significance of social context in and for communication, and on framing language as discourse practices, rather than language as a set of discrete skills. In broad terms, this involves acknowledging that language is fundamentally linked with action – what people do – and that language as action is socially situated in powerful ways. Fairclough states:

> Linguistic phenomena are social in the sense that whenever people speak or listen or write or read, they do so in ways which are determined socially and have social effects. Even when people are most conscious of their own individuality and think themselves cut off from social influences – they still use language in ways which are subject to social convention.
>
> (Fairclough 1989: 23)

Fairclough proposes a three-dimensional framework for analysing any specific socio-discursive event: 'Any discursive "event" (i.e. any instance of discourse) is seen as being simultaneously a piece of text, an instance of discursive practice, an instance of social practice' (1992a: 4).

Within this framing, discursive events are viewed as sites of tension at various levels, not least in terms of the differential positions of power between actual participants. In contrast to dominant approaches to language and literacy which ignore issues of power and identity, work in critical linguistics and New Literacy Studies seeks to make such dimensions visible. In Chapter 2 I discuss in detail the relevance of key ideas from these studies for exploring specific instances of student writing. In the following section, I want to turn to recent research on student writing and, through a brief overview, signal the ways in which such research challenges the official framing of the 'problem' of student writing in HE.

Significant shifts in research on student writing

Just as there is little evidence of interest in recent theorisations of language in the official discourse on communication, little attention has been paid to insights from research on student writing. In this section, I will briefly foreground such insights, by making connections between research from two distinct geographical areas: the substantial field of writing research from

25

the US and the relatively smaller field emerging out of the British context within which I locate my own work. It is possible to discern significant and parallel shifts in writing research, which are important to bring in to any discussion on student academic writing in HE.

The institutional contexts, both in terms of pedagogy and research, differ significantly in the US and the UK. In North America, unlike in the UK, there is widespread institutional consensus within HE that undergraduate student-writers need to be taught how to write academic texts, which is manifested in the universal requirement of writing courses (see Crowley 1998 for a historical account of the development of this requirement). This is indicated by two principal types of institutional provision, already mentioned above: 'freshman composition', where undergraduates spend time in learning to write (see Parker and Campbell 1993 for an overview of a variety of practices); and 'basic writing' courses, which were introduced at the time of open admissions policies to HE in the late 1960s and are aimed at those students considered to have problems with Standard (American) English in grammar, syntax, spelling, punctuation. A third and less widespread type of provision is 'writing across the curriculum' initiatives (WAC), which are much influenced by the work of Britton, Barnes and others in England (1975) and where the aim is to teach writing within subject areas, with an emphasis on learning through writing (see Ackerman 1993 for a review of effectiveness of WAC programmes; see also Russell 1991). This substantial pedagogical activity around student writing in the US has led to a vibrant and complex research field. There are different accounts of the emergence of student writing research as a field of study, but that a research field exists is well acknowledged; the powerful presence of a writing research community is reflected not least in the existence of a number of academic journals, such as *Written Communication, College Composition and Communication, Journal of Advanced Composition, Rhetoric Review, Journal of Basic Writing*; there are also established Ph.D. programmes in rhetoric and composition.

In England, the institutional contexts of both research and pedagogy surrounding undergraduate academic writing differ significantly from those in North America. Entry to HE has been severely restricted until recent years to a small and predominantly privileged part of the population. Where attention was paid to student writing pedagogy within this context, it was very much a case of individual/small group tutoring. Within the current growing and more diverse context of HE in the UK, the teaching of writing continues neither to be formalised through specific provision nor, indeed, until recently, to receive explicit pedagogical attention. Research on student writing emerging from this context is therefore comparatively recent and small in size when set against the North American context.

However, it is possible to identify parallel shifts across these contexts, of both a methodological and epistemological nature, and which I want to outline here.

26

Student-writers' texts and perspectives are a worthy topic of research

It may seem obvious that if your interest is student writing then you need to treat students' texts as a worthy research focus, rather than start from some idealised notion of what the written text should be. But this has not always been the case.

The work of Shaughnessy in North America in the 1970s was particularly significant in signalling the need to explore actual student-writers' texts. In her book *Errors and Expectations* (1977), based on the scripts of some 4,000 students and substantial student and tutor commentary, she set out to explore why so-called 'ineducable students' write as they do. Whilst fundamental criticisms of her work have been made (see for example Lu 1991), the importance she attached to actual student-writers' texts and their perspectives on these texts has been taken up by many researchers in the North American context, for example by Rose (1989), Lu (1994) and Canagarajah (1997). A similar stance has developed from different educational contexts in the UK; witness the work of teacher-researchers in adult education, for example Gardener (1992), Mace (1992), Hamilton (1994); and the work of teacher-researchers in HE, for example Ivanic (see Ivanic 1998: see also Ivanic and Roach 1990, Ivanic and Simpson 1992), Lea (1995) and Scott (1999).

Focusing on student-writers' texts has inevitably led to an interest in student-writers' perspectives on their texts. Flower, working in the North American context, refers to this as paying attention to uncovering 'the hidden logic' (Flower 1994: 51) of student writing, signalling a need to move away from the practice of tutors and researchers claiming to know the reasons why students' texts are written as they are. This is a key dimension to the work of the writers I've already referred to in North America and in the UK. Hamilton, in the introduction to *Worlds of Literacy*, a book exploring literacy practices within academia as well as in other social domains in the UK, refers to this approach as 'putting the insights and perspectives of literacy users at the centre of research about literacy' (1994: 3). In the study on which this book is based, the attempt to make visible, and work with, the perspectives of the student-writers was central to the research process.

Writing is meaning making

Focusing on what actual writers do in texts constitutes a methodological/ epistemological shift. It leads, not least, to a challenging of the idea that writers' problems are predominantly to do with language as surface features, grammar, syntax and punctuation, and brings to centre stage the complicated history of writers' intentions around meaning making in texts. Shaughnessy's work, referred to above, exemplifies the beginnings of this shift. Here she is pointing to the pedagogical implications of her research:

> He [the tutor] needs to remember, too, that his purpose is to recommend or prescribe *in the interest of the student's purpose and intent* – to be wary of substituting his stylistic preferences for those of his students, riding (and writing) roughshod over the student's meaning in the interest of grace or economy or ferreting out errors without commenting upon or even noticing what the writer is getting at, as if thought were merely the means for eliciting grammatical forms.
>
> (Shaughnessy 1997: 84; emphasis in original)

This shift signals the limitations of viewing writing as a technology, that is, as a tool for encoding meanings, towards a central interest in writing as meaning making. Other researchers in the North American context and working out of different theoretical positions, began to explore student writing as meaning making along a cognitive–social continuum. Whilst earlier works emphasise meaning making as a cognitive activity, that is, a process of the individual mind, later works point to meanings as a social phenomenon (for examples of the former see Emig 1971; Flower and Hayes 1977). Thus, more recently, Flower has been working within a socio-cognitive approach, (Flower 1994). Bizzell and Lu are examples of writers who place meaning making as a social phenomenon at the centre of discussions about student writing. Bizzell has focused in particular on the meanings privileged through the dominant conventions of the academy (see for example Bizzell 1982a, 1982b, 1990, 1997); Lu has foregrounded the ways in which historically marginalised students write at a 'site of conflict', that is, at a site of struggle between familiar, yet marginalised, discourses and the dominant discourses within the academy (see for example Lu 1987, 1990).

In the UK, a focus on meaning making as a social phenomenon has been pushed to the fore, predominantly by tutor-led research in both adult education and HE. An important early work in this respect is that of Gardener in 1985 (see Gardener 1992). Gardener's principal aim was to examine tutors' theories of writing development but she also situates students' writing and reading within the context of their life histories and the context of the institution they are writing in and towards. She signals issues which are particularly relevant to students writing in HE: a critique of the essay as the privileged text type in formal education; the exclusive nature of academic language; the learning of academic discourse as involving questions about personal and social identity. More recently, similar interests are to be found in practitioner-led research in the specific context of HE, as indicated in Street's conversations with other academic-practitioners about student academic writing generally (see Street 1999), as well as in some writings within the specific area of English for Academic Purposes (see, for example, English 1999; Turner 1999). The small number of research studies which specifically aim to explore the experience of 'non-traditional' students' writing in higher education in England, all place meaning at the centre of their focus. This includes work by student-writer researchers (Karach 1992; Benson and others 1993; Karach and Roach 1994); work by tutor-researchers with student-writers (Clark and others 1990; Ivanic and Roach 1990; Ivanic, Aitchison and Weldon 1996); and work by tutor-researchers (Clark and Ivanic 1991; Ivanic 1993, 1998; Lea 1995).

In the research on which this book is based, I was working within this tradition of the tutor-researcher who seeks to explore students' experiences of making meaning in academic writing.

Academic practices/discourses should be explored rather than taken as 'givens'

The idea that academic practices/discourses should be explored, rather than taken as 'given' is a more recent focus in both North America and the UK (for discussion of practice and discourse, see Chapter 2). This has been explored at several interrelated levels: generic academic practice/discourse; discipline-specific practice/discourse; and pedagogical practice/discourse.

The notion of a generic academic practice/discourse has been explored from the perspective of literacy practices (see for example Gee 1996), rhetorical practices (see for example Bizzell 1982a, 1994), linguistic features (for example, Corson 1985; Halliday 1993; Ivanic 1998) and ideology (for example Berlin 1982, 1988; Bizzell 1990, 1994; Ivanic 1998). Writers have sought both to describe and theorise the ways in which available academic discourses enable particular ways of meaning in the academy, as well as foregrounding their ideological nature, to which I return below.

An increasing interest is in the discipline or field-specific nature of academic practices/discourses. Examples of writers working within this approach, albeit in different ways, are Bazerman and Myers who have explored rhetorical differences across academic disciplines (see for example Bazerman 1981, 1988; Myers 1985). Thus, for example, Bazerman (1981) offers a framework for analysing the range of distinct discursive features associated with writing in the different academic fields of literature, biochemistry and sociology. Of growing interest are the historical roots of disciplinary discourses, as indicated in the work of Bazerman (1988), Russell (1991) and Berkenkotter (1999). Geisler (1994) and Prior (1998) have been particularly interested in the ways in which students become more closely involved in these historically situated disciplinary practices/discourses; Geisler in philosophy, Prior in a number of disciplines, including sociology, language education, geography.

A pedagogical interest permeates many of the above-cited works and is the central focus of work by writers particularly interested in 'conferencing', that is, tutor–student spoken interaction around writing, such as Harris (1992, 1995) and Patthey-Chavez and Ferris (1997). This interest in actual instances of pedagogical practice, as well as in the ways in which these reflect and instantiate particular theories of language and learning, is echoed in the

29

work in the UK by Clark and Ivanic (for example 1997) and Lea and Street (1998, 1999).

All the above writers clearly challenge the notion of language as a transparent medium of communication. They signal, rather, the ways in which language constructs meanings within particular academic fields/disciplines and pedagogical practices in the academy in specific ways.

In this book I foreground the significance of an overarching literacy practice in academia, referred to throughout as 'essayist literacy', and focus on the pedagogy in which such a practice is embedded. This is not to deny the significance of disciplinary difference nor to deny the importance of exploring student experiences situated within specific disciplines. But rather this framing is used to emphasise that a very particular kind of literacy practice holds sway in higher education which contrasts with other language and literacy practices in the lives of many 'non-traditional' students (for further discussion, see Chapter 2).

Academic practices/discourses are about social identities and social relationships

The idea that academic discourses are principally about propositional content, that is, about conveying information, as distinct from particular kinds of social relationships, has been challenged in writing research. One way in which this has been done is through the notion of 'discourse communities' (Bizzell 1982b), echoing the socio-linguistic notion of 'speech communities' (see Hymes 1977) and Fish's 'interpretive communities' (Fish 1980). Within this framing, student writing is problematised as the process of learning the conventions of a particular discourse community, and student-writers are viewed as apprentices to these discourse communities. Studies of students writing within this frame involve questions about how they become, or don't become, socialised into particular practices/discourses (see Bartholomae 1985; Bizzell 1982a, 1982b; Berkenkotter and Huckin 1995). In Prior's words this involves studying 'the processes whereby an ambiguous cast of relative newcomers and relative old-timers (re) produce themselves, their practices and their communities' (Prior 1998: xii).

Researchers have foregrounded the ways in which particular identities are privileged within different academic discourses, both in generic and disciplinary specific terms, as well as emphasising the importance of student-writers' sense of identities as they engage in academic writing. Examples of writers pursuing the significance of identity in student writing from the North American context are Lu (1987), Brooke (1988) and Cherry (1988). A major work in the British context is that of Ivanic (1998), who has sought to explore at both theoretical and empirical levels links between literacy, identity, and discourse in the specific context of 'non-traditional' students and academic writing.

30

Throughout this book, I foreground the importance of identity in student academic writing.

Challenging the 'textual bias'

The above interconnected strands constitute a challenge to the textual bias framing official discussions about student writing and signal a shift towards writing as social practice, which can be distinguished from the current emphasis, in the UK context, on writing as a skill. In broad terms, what this means is that student academic writing, like all writing, is a social act. That is, student writing takes place within a particular institution, which has a particular history, culture, values and practices. It involves a shift away from thinking of language or writing skills as individual possession, towards the notion of an individual engaged in socially situated action; from an individual student having writing skills, to a student doing writing in specific contexts. What the student writer does in her academic writing is shaped both by her understanding of the specific socio-discursive contexts she is studying within and also by what she brings to the act of writing, her 'habits of meaning' (Halliday 1978) from her different life experiences. Academic writing within this frame is viewed as being ideologically inscribed at a number of levels, not least in terms of its distribution as 'cultural capital' (Bourdieu 1984, 1991) – who gets to use this valuable resource – and relatedly, in terms of the particular meanings and identities it privileges. I discuss this further in Chapters 2, 4, 5 and 6.

Making a distinction between writing as a discrete skill and writing as social practice is not simply an intellectual exercise. What's at stake is the nature of students' participation in HE, and their subsequent life chances. The main argument in this book is that the notion of writing as social practice, in broad terms, offers a way of exploring the complexities involved in the production

Table 1.1 Comparing a 'skills' with a 'practices' approach to student writing

A skills approach emphasises	A practices approach emphasises
• student writing as primarily an individual act • the individual as an autonomous, socially neutral, subject • language as a transparent medium of communication • literacy as autonomous and universal • the 'appropriateness' of essayist literacy in HE	• student writing as a social act • language as constructing meanings/identities • literacies as numerous, varied and socially/institutionally situated • the socio-historically situated nature of essayist literacy • the privileged status of essayist literacy within academia • the contested nature of dominant academic conventions

of student academic texts. It can help us to see what is involved for student-writers as they attempt to participate in higher education, particularly for those who are the main focus of this book, 'non-traditional' students.

In the following chapter I discuss in more detail what it means to understand student writing as social practice.

Notes

1 I use UK throughout to signal key similarities across HE in England, Wales, Northern Ireland and Scotland, for example, in relation to student numbers and diversity. This is not to deny significant differences across the regions. For example, see National Committee of Inquiry into Higher Education: Report of the Scottish Committee 1997.

2 See, for example, comments by Chris Woodhead, former chief inspector of schools, in the *Guardian* 5/10/99.

3 By referring to genre as text type here, I'm thinking of work within the Australian genre tradition (for example, see Martin 1993), which differs significantly from work by other genre theorists (for example, Berkenkotter and Huckin 1995).

2

STUDENT WRITING AS SOCIAL PRACTICE

Introduction

Official discourse on the 'problem' of student academic writing in higher education ignores much recent thinking on language and literacy generally and research on student writing more specifically. In broad terms, as argued in Chapter 1, the dominant official approach is to frame student writing as a skill, drawing implicitly on notions of language as transparent and of both language and user as independent of each other, and of context. An alternative perspective can be described as that of writing as social practice, which was outlined in broad terms in Chapter 1. However, there is much diversity in the research writings that take a social practice approach, and include not least the following overlapping perspectives: socio-cognitive (for example Flower 1994); socio-rhetorical or 'new rhetoric' (see for example, albeit with different interests, Bizzell 1990, 1997; Bazerman 1981, 1988; Berlin 1988), activity theory (see for example Russell 1997), some genre approaches (see for example Berkenkotter and Huckin 1995) and cultural studies (Horner and Lu 1999). My own perspective, reflecting in many ways the local institutional and research contexts in which I study and work, draws mainly from New Literacy Studies and critical discourse analysis (for New Literacy Studies, see Baynham 1995; Barton and Hamilton 1998; Ivanic 1998; Lea and Street 1998; Barton, Hamilton and Ivanic 2000). It is a developing perspective, which informs, and is informed by, student-writers' accounts of their engagement in academic writing.

The aim of this chapter is to outline a theoretical framework for thinking about student writing, and to offer a heuristic for exploring specific instances of individual meaning making in academic writing. The principal writers whose work I refer to are Fairclough, Scollon and Scollon, Gee, Bakhtin and Ivanic. In discussing their work, I focus on dimensions that are central to any attempt to explore what is involved in student academic writing: the notion of language and literacy as discourse practices; the nature of the specific literacy practice of higher education, essayist literacy; the significance of addressivity in and for meaning making; the centrality of writer identity in student writing. In the final section, I draw these notions together in order to outline a heuristic for exploring specific instances of meaning making: that is, a tool for helping us to ask questions about what student-writers are doing in their writing, and why. At different points throughout this book, I refer the reader back to the ideas and heuristic discussed in this chapter.

Language and literacy as discourse practices

Language practices

Language as discourse practice provides a powerful challenge to the notion of language as a transparent and autonomous system, which is implicit in official discourse on communication in HE. Practice offers a way of linking language with what individuals, as socially situated actors, do, both at the level of context of situation and at the level of context of culture. Whilst 'practice' is used in various nuanced ways, I think it is useful to hold on to three meanings.[1] Firstly, and at the most concrete level, language as discourse practice signals that specific instances of language use – spoken and written texts – do not exist in isolation but are bound up with what people do – practices – in the material, social world. Secondly, what people do with language tends to be repeated, practised, so that particular practices, ways of doing things with texts, become part of everyday, implicit life routines both of the individual – 'habitus' in Bourdieu's terms (Bourdieu 1991) – and of social institutions. Specific instances of language use – texts – involve drawing on these existing available resources: 'members' resources' (Fairclough 1992a: 80) or, as I prefer to use throughout this book, 'representational resources' (Kress 1996: 18). Indeed, language might best be understood as practice-resource. For, by engaging in an existing practice we are maintaining a particular type of representational resource; by drawing on a particular type of representational resource, we are maintaining a particular type of social practice. At this third and most abstract level, and in specific relation to literacy, the notion of practice 'offers a powerful way of conceptualising the link between the activities of reading and writing and the social structures in which they are embedded and which they help to shape' (Barton and Hamilton 1998: 6).

This approach involves acknowledging that particular practices have become dominant within particular domains of social life, and that these involve and invoke particular values, beliefs and identities, all of which contribute to the maintenance of particular social structural relations. This is indicated in Chapters 4–6, where I discuss how the dimensions of social class, ethnicity/'race' and gender are implicated in the student-writers' struggles around constructing texts in academia.

Fairclough offers a framework for thinking about specific instances of language use whether written or spoken – *texts* – which emphasises the significance of the three notions of practice outlined above. He argues that in order to understand the construction and interpretation of a specific text, we need to acknowledge the ways in which it is situated in a specific *context of situation*; that is, we need to explore the immediate context in which an instance of language use occurs by looking at, for example, the place, the participants and the actual time. But Fairclough also argues for considerable attention to be paid to the *context of culture*; this is a much broader and more abstract notion of context that involves considerations of institutions, social structures and ideologies, all of which impinge on the nature of the language in use at the level of context of situation.[2] In Fairclough's framework, these two levels of contexts are connected through a notion of discourse, for which he draws on a more traditionally narrow intra-textual, or linguistic, focus with a broader socio-discursive approach drawn from Foucault, where the emphasis is on acknowledging and exploring socially constructed sets of meanings (see Fairclough 1989, 1992a, 1995). Acknowledging the lack of analysis of actual texts in Foucault's work, Fairclough's aim is to construct a framework for analysing instances of socio-discursive practices, whilst drawing on Foucault's broader philosophical explication of domains of knowledge. This is what he refers to as text-oriented discourse analysis (see Figure 2.1).

Whilst a focus on discourse signals an interest in ways of meaning/wording, and practice signals an interest in ways of doing, these are not independent phenomena, as is signalled in Fairclough's wording *discursive practices* (see Fairclough 1992a: chapter 3). Likewise, Gee's formulation of Discourses

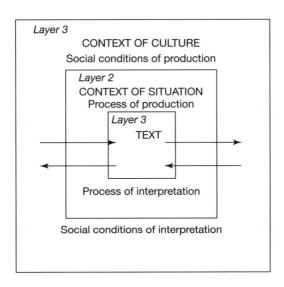

Figure 2.1 A framework for *text-oriented discourse analysis*

Sources: after Fairclough 1989: 25 and Clark and Ivanic 1997: 11

signals the interdependence of these notions when he refers to Discourses as 'ways of being, doing, reacting, using space, thinking and using language' (see Gee 1996 for discussion of his use of d/Discourse). In this book, drawing on these writers, a focus on discourse always implies a focus on practice and vice versa.

Fairclough's elaboration of the second level of context, the context of culture, involves an explicit elaboration of power in relation to texts and practices. Significant dimensions to this elaboration are three important, albeit more abstract, notions: 'orders of discourse', 'ideology' and 'hegemony' (see Fairclough 1992a: chapter 3). Orders of discourse are configurations of discourse practices, which are particular to, and constitutive of, different social domains. Thus, for example, the institutional order of discourse which is of concern in this book, is that of higher education (HE), where the range of discursive practices includes, among others, seminars, lectures, essayist writing. Although distinct practices, they are interrelated through the underlying conventions governing the institution of HE which regulate both the objects and subjects of discourse; that is, the rules governing what can be known about, and who can know it.

Ideology and hegemony are key to understanding the social status and function of these practices and their underlying conventions which, whilst they are neither neutral nor fixed, often appear as if they were. Fairclough defines ideologies as

> Significations/constructions of reality (the physical world, social relations, social identities), which are built into various dimensions of the forms/meanings of discursive practices, and which contribute to the production, reproduction or transformation of relations of domination.
>
> (Fairclough 1992a: 87)

Discursive practices are ideological in the ways in which they serve to maintain existing social relations of power, most obviously in terms of social class, gender and 'race'. Fairclough, like Foucault, highlights the need to focus on power in discourse but, unlike Foucault, he locates power with specific dominant social groups within a social system, which is capitalist 'and dominated by – but not reducible to – relations of class' (1995: 18). In the context of higher education, there is a need to explore the ways in which the existing institutional discursive practices are ideologically motivated, by exploring, for example, the ways in which they serve to exclude and include individuals from particular social groups. The accounts of 'non-traditional' students are important in this respect in that, as participants who often most strongly experience a sense of dissonance with prevailing practices, they are easily able to problematise the 'given' status of such practices, and make visible both the nature of such discourse practices and their ideological force.

However, it is important to note that dominant practices and conventions, whilst powerful, are not fixed, but rather they are the result of hegemonic struggle at any one moment in time; the struggle is between, and across, alliances of social groups around maintaining or contesting dominant orders of discourse. Orders of discourse, their constitutive conventions and practices are always 'the product of the struggles over meaning that have taken place in the recent socio-political history of particular institutions' (Clark and Ivanic 1997: 129–30).

Thus, whilst current discourse practices in higher education appear immutable, they are the outcome of struggles over hundreds of years to privilege particular ways of meaning: most obviously, in the Anglo/Western HE tradition, current 'common' discourse practices embody an overriding commitment to rationality and empiricism.[3] I return to this below. The question as to whether such commitment should continue to be maintained in higher education in the twenty-first century, and the extent to which alternative discourse practices should be adopted, requires considerable thought and discussion. In a more immediate sense, the question raised at various points throughout this book is whether student-writers are to be involved in such discussions.

Literacy practices and essayist literacy

Implicit in a practices approach towards language is a practices account, and theorisation of, literacy. In writings often referred to currently as 'New Literacy Studies', the notion of litera*cies* and literacy practi*ces*, rather than literacy has come to reflect a growing understanding of literacies as multiple and socially situated. This contrasts with a dominant perspective on 'literacy' as a unitary, universal phenomenon. Street has critiqued this last perspective on literacy, with its claims of alleged universal cognitive as well as economic benefits, which he calls an 'autonomous' view. He argues instead for what he calls an 'ideological model' of literacy, whereby the focus is on acknowledging the socio-culturally embedded nature of literacies (see Street 1984, 1995). Ethnographic work carried out by Scollon and Scollon (1981), Scribner and Cole (1981), Heath (1983), Street (1984, 1993) and, more recently, by Barton and Padmore (1991), Barton (1994), Baynham (1995), Barton and Hamilton (1998) and Barton, Hamilton and Ivanic (2000) highlights the range of practices within and across societies where individuals and groups engage in a range of different literacy practices consonant with their socio-cultural histories, beliefs and interests.

An early example of work within the new literacy tradition, and which is of particular significance to our interest here in student academic writing, is the work of Ronald and Suzanne Scollon. Through their comparative work on English-speaking Canadian/North American peoples and the Athabaskan communities of Alaska, they foreground essayist literacy as the dominant literacy practice of schooling in the Western world (see Scollon and Scollon 1981). Echoing much of Olson's description of what he calls the 'essayist technique' (Olson 1977), they point to the ways in which essayist literacy is a particular way of being as well as knowing, which is consonant with notions of Western rationality:

> The ideal of essayist literacy that all meaning resides in the text is of course impossible to achieve. As an ideal, however, it expresses a view of the world as rational and of an identity between rational knowledge and linguistic expression (Foucault 1973). The ultimate knowability of the real world is matched by the assumption of its complete expressability in text. One has only to observe clearly and think clearly, and clear expression will follow automatically.
>
> (Scollon and Scollon 1981: 49)

They contrast the ways of knowing and being associated with essayist literacy with the Athabaskan way of being and knowing. A significant difference is the centrality of decontextualised display in essayist literacy: that is, the writer is expected to show knowledge, regardless of who the writer is writing to/for. This sharply conflicts with Athabaskan cultural practices, where display is only appropriate where the person doing the displaying is in a position of dominance in relation to the audience. Where the relationship is unknown, the Scollons suggest, Athabaskans prefer silence. Given that the fictional-isation of self (as writer) and audience is a central feature of essayist literacy, as is further discussed below, writing for Athabaskans within essayist literacy presents significant problems.

More recently, Gee draws on the work of Ronald and Suzanne Scollon to further elucidate the ways in which essayist literacy is privileged in formal schooling and thus privileges the practices of particular social groups over others. Throughout his book, *Social Linguistics and Literacies* (1990, 1996), Gee outlines the nature of this literacy practice, in terms of its specific features as a culturally available resource and in terms of its enactment in the school classroom. He summarises the features of essayist literacy as follows: such writing (or talking based on similar practices) is linear, it values a particular type of explicitness, it has one central point, theme, character or event at any one time, it is in the standard version of a language. It is a type of writing which aims to inform rather than to entertain. Important relation-ships are those between sentence and sentence, not between speakers, nor between sentence and speaker. The reader has to constantly monitor grammatical and lexical information and, as such, there is a need for the writer to be explicit about logical implications. There is a fictionalisation of both writer and reader, the reader being an idealisation, 'a rational mind formed by the rational body of knowledge of which the essay is a part'. The author is a fiction 'since the process of writing and editing essayist texts leads to an effacement of individual and idiosyncratic identity' (Gee 1990: 63). Gee exemplifies the nature of this practice – both what it is and the ways in which its privileging is maintained – by contrasting the stories of two 7-year-olds: an African-American girl and an Anglo-American white girl in a 'sharing time' session in a primary school. The example is drawn from Michaels (1981). Whereas the story of the Anglo-American girl is considered successful, the African-American girl's story is not. One significant reason for the failure, in school terms, of the African-American girl's story relates to her purpose in telling it. As Gee states, her purpose is not primarily to 'make a point' but is rather to engage in making meaning through patterns of language in which she invites the participation of the audience .The Anglo-American girl, by contrast, and through the careful guidance of the teacher, engages in meaning making in a way which is consonant with essayist literacy. This is done by working at constructing a particular type of unity, that is, one teacher-sanctioned focal point, with limited assumed shared knowledge between speaker and listeners. Other talk, such as talk about a particular feature of the objects under discussion, such as the colour of the candles – which perhaps would be more obvious given that the child is holding these candles for the rest of the children to see – is diverted. Instead, the teacher, working with the child, constructs one principal, and predetermined, focus on the making of the candles (see Gee 1996: 103–21 for full discussion, including the deeper meanings of the texts).

Such a practice-resource is ideologically inscribed at the most obvious level. It privileges the discursive routines of particular social groups whilst dismissing those of people who, culturally and communally, have access to and engage in a range of other practices. The significance of continuity/discontinuity between home and school practices for student success in schooled practices has been foregrounded by many writers.[4] I return to a discussion of the potential effect of such discontinuity in Chapter 3.

The practice of student writing

A central argument in this book is that it is both possible and necessary to talk of a dominant literacy practice-resource within HE which can usefully be called essayist literacy, after the work of Scollon and Scollon, and of Gee. Whilst there is clearly diversity across literacy practices within HE,[5] the notion of essayist literacy is important for exploring student-writers' experience of meaning making in academic writing in several respects. Firstly, it indicates that student academic writing constitutes a very particular kind of literacy practice which is bound up with the workings of a particular social institution. Acknowledging the specific nature of the practice in which students are expected to engage challenges the common deficit approach towards student writing. Whilst people may be unfamiliar with the privileged literacy practice within academia, there is no justification for constructing them as 'illiterate', or by associating use of this literacy with cognitive development, construing them as intellectually inferior in some way. Secondly, and relatedly, the term 'essayist literacy' is useful for signalling that this particular practice involves and invokes particular ways of meaning/wording, and can consequently serve to exclude others. Thirdly, by foregrounding, in general terms, that current student writing is part of a particular tradition of literacy and knowledge making, essayist literacy serves to mark out the socio-historical, rather than any presumed universal, nature of such writing (for further discussion see Lillis and Turner 2001). In brief, essayist literacy provides a way of talking about student writing which acknowledges the relationship between literacy practices and knowledge-making practices whilst situating both within a specific socio-historical tradition. The ways in which the student-writers experience and negotiate essayist literacy practice is the main focus in Chapters 3–6.

When a student-writer sits down to write an essay, even the first time she does so, she is taking part in a particular discursive practice which is bound to a particular social institution. This, in turn, is embedded within wider social practices. In exploring the student-writers' experiences in this book, I draw on this critical perspective to argue that the conventions surrounding the production of student academic texts are ideologically inscribed in at least two powerful ways: by working towards the exclusion of students from social groups who have historically been excluded from the conservative-liberal project of HE in the UK (see Chapter 3) and by regulating directly and indirectly what student-writers can mean, and who they can be (see Chapter 4).

Figure 2.2 locates individual acts of student meaning making in writing within the contexts of situation and culture in HE. It also foregrounds the

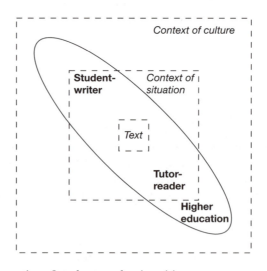

Figure 2.2 The practice of student academic writing

40

particular institutional context of culture within which the writing takes place: that is, the institution of HE and its dominant order of discourse. The particular element of the order of discourse which is the focus in this book is essayist literacy.

However, there is a danger that, in talking of essayist literacy, we construct it as a completely discrete phenomenon. We need a framework that works with the existence and privileging of such a practice but also acknowledges the ways in which discourse practices jostle within and across domains of use. Here the work of Bakhtin is useful, emphasising as he does the tensions in language use at every turn.

Dialogicality, addressivity and meaning making

Bakhtin's key notions are both descriptive as to the nature of language as he understands it and idealised as to how he thinks language, that is, human communication and activity, should be. In this sense his is a critical project, setting out to explore both what is and, potentially, could be in changed socio-political circumstances.

Dialogicality

The notion of dialogicality is central to Bakhtin's view of language. In contrast to much linguistic tradition, Bakhtin's focus is not on language as system but language as utterance, thus challenging the dominant Saussurean gaze in linguistics (see discussion in Chapter 1 on the distinction between *langue* and *parole*). The nature of language as utterance is fundamentally dialogical; utterances are neither unitary in meaning nor can be fixed (as is suggested for example by a dictionary or a traditional grammar) but, embedded as they are in sociocultural practice, are dynamic in their contribution to meaning making. Of the utterance Bakhtin states:

> It is entangled, shot through with shared thoughts, points of view, alien value judgements and accents. The word, directed toward its object, enters a dialogically agitated and tension-filled environment of alien words, value judgments and accents, weaves in and out of complex interrelationships, merges with some, recoils from others, intersects with yet a third group: and all this may crucially shape discourse, may leave a trace in all its semantic layers, may complicate its expression and influence its entire stylistic profile.
>
> (Bakhtin 1981: 276)

This notion of the living, social utterance emphasises the notion of wording-as-meaning, that is, the notion that words construct rather than simply convey meaning. For Bakhtin emphasises not only the socio-culturally situated, but also the socio-culturally saturated, nature of language:

41

The living utterance, having taken meaning and shape at a particular historical moment in a socially specific environment, cannot fail to brush up against thousands of living dialogic threads, woven by socio-ideological consciousness around the given object of an utterance; it cannot fail to become an active participant in social dialogue.

(1981: 276)

Bakhtin's utterance, anticipating Fairclough's focus on texts as discourse practices, problematises the nature and possibility of individual control over meaning making. Given that words carry with them their own histories of meanings, Bakhtin signals the tensions surrounding any attempt to take control over them. Given that utterances are always half someone else's,

it [language] becomes 'one's own' only when the speaker populates it with his own intention, his own accent, when he appropriates the word, adapting it to his own semantic and expressive intention. Prior to this moment of appropriation, the word does not exist in a neutral and impersonal language (it is not, after all, out of a dictionary that the speaker gets his words!), but rather it exists in other people's mouths, in other people's contexts, serving other people's intentions: it is from there that one must take the word, and make it one's own.

(1981: 293–4)

To take control over wordings, given their dynamic nature, is not an easy task:

not all words for just anyone submit equally easily to this appropriation, to this seizure and transformation into private property: many words stubbornly resist, others remain alien, sound foreign in the mouth of the one who appropriated them and who now speaks them; it is as if they put themselves in quotation marks against the will of the speaker. Language is not a neutral medium that passes freely and easily into the private property of the speaker's intentions; it is populated – overpopulated – with the intentions of others. Expropriating it, forcing it to submit to one's own intentions and accents, is a difficult and complicated process.

(1981: 294)

Bakhtin's emphasis on the struggles and tensions involved in individual meaning making is particularly important for understanding student-writers' experience in academic writing; the difficulties surrounding taking control over instances of meaning making are emphasised in Chapters 4, 5 and 6. Here I want to outline another key Bakhtinian notion related to these tensions and of central importance in student writing; that of addressivity.

42

Addressivity

The notion of addressivity is a key dimension to dialogicality. At its most straightforward, it signals that utterances, spoken and written, are addressed to someone, and thus foregrounds the ways in which this addressivity contributes to the shaping of what will be said/written. At another level, addressivity encapsulates a fundamental aspect of language; that is, in making meaning in language, whether in dialogue with someone else or thinking alone, we are always addressing, explicitly and implicitly, a person or people, a question or comment.

> An essential (constitutive) marker of the utterance is its quality of being directed to someone, its addressivity. As distinct from the signifying units of a language – words and sentences – that are impersonal, belonging to nobody and addressed to nobody, the utterance has both an author (and, consequently, expression, which we have already discussed) and an addressee. . . . *Both the composition and, particularly, the style of the utterance depend on those to whom the utterance is addressed, how the speaker (or writer) senses and imagines his addressee, and the force of their effect on the utterance.*
>
> (Bakhtin 1986: 95; my emphasis)

Furthermore, Bakhtin's notion of the living utterance is one in which meaning comes into being between participants rather than being transmitted from one to another (see Holquist 1981: 63). In this framework, the real or potential addressee contributes to what can be meant as much as does the addressor. To acknowledge the centrality of addressivity, in and for meaning making, is to challenge the dominant way in which the writer/reader relationship's impact on the construction of texts is often construed, in several ways. Firstly, addressivity challenges the conduit model of language in use; that is, that individuals convey meanings to each other in a straightforward way. Secondly, and relatedly, it problematises the way in which the addressee is often conceptualised as an additional factor, giving instead the addressee a central role in and for meaning making: Flower exemplifies this 'additional' approach in talking of 'adapting your writing to the needs of the reader' (1985: 1).

In order to exemplify why these interrelated dimensions need to be explored, consider briefly the following three different teaching/learning contexts surrounding the making of meaning; that of the child/adult; adult/adult education tutor; and student/university tutor. In the context of child meaning making, Wells talks about the child 'breaking into' the adult language through the active efforts by the adult to ascertain the 'child's meaning intention' (1994: 52); that is, the adult works at seeking out what it is the child wants to mean and helps her towards wording/meaning. A similar type of meaning making relationship is a prominent feature of adult education. As Gardener points out, adult education tutors working with adults who are learning to write are often 'closer to the struggle to write'. By this she means that tutors are not interested solely in the final written product, but rather direct their energies towards helping the adult student to bring such a product into being (1992: 10). This type of addressivity stands in contrast, I would suggest, to the type of meaning-making relationship in HE between student-writer and tutor-reader. As is discussed in Chapters 3–5, the emphasis is predominantly on the tutor evaluating the student's text as finished product, rather than on the tutor engaging in the construction of text as meaning making in progress.

Thirdly, and at a more abstract level, addressivity refers to the way in which all meaning making involves drawing on the meaning making of others: that is, the voices in terms of wordings, beliefs, knowledge and ideologies that are available within any given socio-cultural context. Thus, in any instance of meaning making, addressor and addressee are to be viewed as being involved in a much broader, historically situated 'chain of speech[6] communication' (Bakhtin 1986: 91). This second more abstract level animates in a more complex way the first level of addressivity, by challenging any straightforward relationships between addressor-addressee and utterance at the level of context of situation, and locating all three – addressor, addressee, utterance – within a context of culture.

> The topic of the speaker's speech, regardless of what this topic may be, does not become the object of speech for the first time in any given utterance; a given speaker is not the first to speak about it. The object, as it were, has already been articulated, disputed, elucidated, and evaluated in various ways. Various viewpoints, world views, and trends cross, converge and diverge in it. The speaker is not the biblical Adam, dealing only with virgin and still unnamed objects, giving them names for the first time.
>
> (Bakhtin 1986: 93)

Addressivity and student writing

Addressivity is a key notion for exploring what's involved in student writing in HE as indicated in Figure 2.3.

The central oval in Figure 2.3 signals the significance of the particular nature of addressivity in and for meaning making in student writing, at the levels both of the context of situation and the context of culture.

Individual student acts of meaning making in writing are embedded within actual relationships at the level of context of situation. Thus, typically, student writing in HE in the UK involves a tutor setting a writing task, in response to which the student must write. In writing, the student-writer must work out the

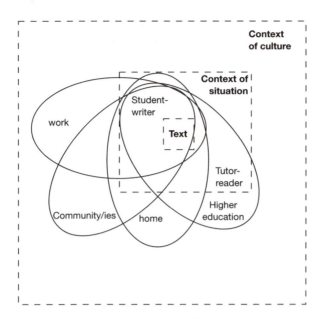

Figure 2.3 Addressivity and student writing in HE

tutor's expectations in order to establish the meanings which she is to make. The student-writer does this in a number of ways, including talking with the tutor, listening to particular lectures and reading written, often departmental, guidelines. The question of how this actual addressivity at the level of context of situation contributes to the student-writers' meaning making is discussed in subsequent chapters in relation to three dimensions. Firstly, I focus on the ways in which the dominant type of monologic addressivity in student/tutor relations, as currently configured, contributes to the nature of the students' learning (or not) of the conventions of essayist literacy (Chapter 3). Secondly, I focus on the ways in which this dominant addressivity contributes to the meanings that the students (don't) make (Chapter 4). Thirdly, I explore the ways in which a more dialogic type of addressivity might significantly enhance students' learning of essayist conventions, as well as facilitating greater control over their meaning making (Chapter 6).

However, what I have described above as addressivity at the level of context of situation is only one dimension of addressivity which impinges upon student meaning making in academic writing. Actual addressivity at the level of context of situation is also bound up with addressivity of a more abstract nature, at the level of the context of culture which contributes significantly to individual student meaning making. This includes the voices, that student-writers bring with them to their specific acts of meaning making in writing, as well as the voices they feel they must respond to within the context of culture in HE.

Whilst such voices are multidimensional, as signalled by Bakhtin, it is possible to conceptualise them in broad terms in the context of student academic writing, in the following ways: voices-as-experience and voices-as-language. Voice as experience refers to the configurations of life experiences that any one individual student-writer brings with her to higher education. Three obvious contexts for such experiences – home, work, community(ies) – are signalled by the ovals in Figure 2.3. Thus, a student-writer may bring to her writing in HE her experience and understanding of being Black, working-class, a woman, a Pakistani. In talking about voice-as-experience, it is important to stress both commonality and difference amongst 'non-traditional' students'. One obvious example of commonality, relating to the focus of this book, is that the student-writers share a sense of never having expected to study in higher education. Difference between the student-writers is also important. Feminist and post-structuralist writers, in particular, have highlighted the multiplicity of our voices as experiences (see, for example, Weedon 1987; hooks 1994; Griffiths 1995): a mature woman student may have, amongst a multitude of voices, several significant voices at a particular moment in time, for example those of student, mother and worker. Each of these carries different meanings for the individual at any one time and she may draw on each of them for her meaning making in academia. Another example relates to political-ethnic identity. 'Non-traditional' students are from a range of social and linguistic backgrounds and may wish to claim different dimensions of their identities at different moments in time: thus, some students at times refer to themselves as 'Black',[7] but at other times wish to emphasise their religious or specific ethnic background, such as Pakistani, Welsh or Yemeni, and/or Muslim.

In talking about voices-as-language I am drawing principally on the ideas of Fairclough and Bakhtin, discussed above, who reject the binary position of language as either transparent or constitutive, and work with the intermediate position of the 'individual-operating-with-mediational-means' (see Wertsch 1991: 96). The mediational means which are important here in exploring students' writing are the specific wordings – words, phrases – drawn from the student-writers' habits of meaning, 'habitus' (see page 34), and which they bring into academia.

Student meaning making in academic writing, however, as indicated by the figures, is not only shaped by the voices the student-writers bring to a specific act of writing, but also by the voices they are attempting to respond to. This dimension of addressivity links with Bartholomae's notion (1985) of student-writers 'inventing' the university. That is to say, in order to work out which meanings to make in their writing, particularly as outsiders to the institution, student-writers often have to invent the voices that they have to respond to: these are the voices as institutionally acceptable content and wordings. This is necessarily a complex activity, given the denial of real participants within essayist literacy practices where, as I explore in detail in

Chapter 4, 'invention' rather than negotiation is often central to the student-writers' meaning making in writing. In 'inventing' the institutional voices they are attempting to respond to, the student-writers draw on the voices they bring as language and experience from the many socio-cultural domains of their lives, as indicated by the numerous ovals in Figure 2.3.

Moreover, the overlapping ovals in Figure 2.3 signal the complex way in which the voices, which student-writers draw on and respond to, interact and collide in meaning making. As Gee points out, discourses 'are always jostling against each other, there are few pure instances' (1996: 164). Exploring the experience of meaning making of student-writers involves, not least, acknowledging the jostling of privileged discourses with marginalised, oppositional discourses, aspects of all of which may constitute the voices that the student-writer draws on and responds to. As will be evident in subsequent chapters, jostling is a useful way of thinking about how student-writers work at making meaning, and links with the way in which Bakhtin elucidates the dynamic nature of language.

To make meaning in academic writing, the student-writer:

- draws on and responds to voices, as language and experience, from different domains of her socio-cultural life world.
- draws on and responds to voices within the university, as understood through addressivity at the levels of context of situation and culture.

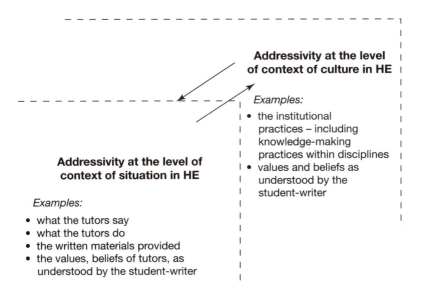

Figure 2.4 Addressivity and meaning making in student academic writing

The making of texts, the making of self(ves)

Agency, identification and becoming

Thus far, the discussion has focused primarily on situating the making of specific texts within social practices. Within this frame, the significance of personal and social identity in the making of texts has been signalled several times: for example the Athabaskan sense of identity clashing with the particular conventions of essayist literacy practice. Such an example points to the importance of an individual's habits of meaning, Bourdieu's habitus, for the construction of any text. It also signals the potential influence of the use of language, as practice-resource, on the shaping of the individual. The fundamental relationship between individual and language, as practice-resource, is signalled throughout Bakhtin's work in his emphasis on struggle in meaning making. This is echoed by Clark and Ivanic (1997) and Fairclough (1992a, 1995), all of whom point to the tensions around meaning making and the potential for transformation as well as reproduction:

> Subjects are ideologically positioned, but they are also capable of acting creatively to make their own connections between the diverse practices and ideologies to which they are exposed, and to restructure positioning practices and structures.
>
> (Fairclough 1992a: 91)[8]

'Actively creating' involves becoming aware of our tacit habits of meaning and making choices about the ways in which we wish to mean. In this process, meaning making is not just about making texts, but is also about the making of our selves, in a process of becoming.[9]

'Becoming' is a central notion in Bakhtin's work:

> The tendency to assimilate others' discourse takes on an even deeper and more basic significance in an individual's ideological becoming, in the most fundamental sense. Another's discourse performs here no longer as information, directions, rules, models and so forth – but strives rather to determine the very basis of our behaviour; it performs here as *authoritative discourse*, and an *internally persuasive discourse*.
>
> (Bakhtin 1981: 342; emphasis in original)

Briefly, authoritative discourse connects with the more current postmodern notions of dominant discourses and available subject positions. Authoritative discourses seek to impose particular meanings and are therefore monologic in nature. These stand in contrast to 'internally persuasive' discourses, which are ways of meaning with which the individual has dialogically engaged, that is, questioning and exploring, in order to develop a newer way to mean (Bakhtin 1981: 346):

> nothing conclusive has yet taken place in the world, the ultimate word of the world and about the world has not yet been spoken, the world is open and free, everything is still in the future and will always be in the future.
>
> (Bakhtin 1984: 166)

Bakhtin argues that dialogue is the means through which newer ways to mean, and to be, can come into being and, as such, stands in contrast to monologue. Dialogue is central to his critical project of rejecting the imposition of any one truth.

Fairclough has explicitly taken up this Bakhtinian postmodern theme of the making of the self as dialogic project:

> It is now a commonplace that a person's social identity is not unitary but a configuration of identities; so that we can see the external negotiation of difference with others as continuous with – and rooted in – the internal negotiation of difference in the struggle to constitute the self.
>
> (Fairclough 1996: 8)

Such struggle is evident in the student-writers' accounts of engaging in academic writing and is signalled throughout subsequent chapters. How best to explore the relationship between identity and specific instances of meaning making in academic writing is discussed in the following section.

Identity and student writing

Ivanic has put writer identity at the centre of our gaze on student writing in HE in the UK (see Ivanic 1993, 1998). She argues that the word 'identity' is useful because it is the everyday word for people's way of describing their sense of who they are. However, in using this wording, she emphasises that she is not focusing only on publicly socially defined roles – such as teacher, farmer, mother – but rather is using it to include both a public and private sense of self(ves). She also draws into her use of identity the notion of subjectivity/ies from postmodern discourse (see discussion in Ivanic 1998: introduction) because this signals

> both that the socially available resources for the construction of identity are multiple, and that an individual's identity is a complex of interweaving positioning.
>
> (Ivanic 1998: 10)

As she points out, although the notion of identity is common in discussions about writers of fiction, it is not usually discussed in relation to student academic writing. Yet, as she argues from an exploration of mature students' experience of academic writing (1993, 1998), student-writers' sense of personal/social identity is a significant dimension to their experience of meaning making, influencing, as it does, what student-writers (don't) write and (don't) wish to write within academia. Her work on identity in academic writing connects with Fairclough's more recent focus on identification, discussed briefly above, where the production of texts is also about the pro-duction – reproduction, transformation – of the self (Fairclough 1996).

Ivanic has elucidated three dimensions for exploring the relationship between identity and authoring in student writing: these are authority, authorship and authorial presence (see Ivanic 1995). Whilst not precisely equivalent, these dimensions map on to Clark and others' three key questions about how students can('t) write in academia (1990) and powerfully connect with the experiences of the student-writers discussed in subsequent chapters. Thus, I have linked Ivanic's notion of authority with Clark's question, 'Who can you be?', as these both foreground the significance of the writer's feelings of control about the type of person she can be in her academic writing. Who the writer is in her text is, in turn, bound up with what we tend to think of as the content of academic writing and which seems to be encapsulated in Ivanic's notion of authorship and Clark's question, 'What can you say?' The content, 'what you can say', is both reflected and constituted in the writer's wordings. It is through such wordings – Clark's 'How can you say it?' – that the writer's presence (authorial presence in Ivanic's terms) comes into being.[10]

I use these three dimensions to construct a heuristic, that is, a tool for exploring questions about why students write as they do, as I outline below.

A heuristic for exploring student writing

In exploring the student-writers' experiences of engaging in academic writing, I have worked with a heuristic constructed from key ideas discussed earlier in this chapter: Fairclough's three-dimensional framework for analysing any discursive event; the notion of literacy practices, and in particular essayist literacy as the element of the order of discourse in higher education with which student-writers have to grapple; Bakhtin's notions of addressivity at the levels of context of situation and context of culture; Ivanic's and Clark and others' work on authoring in student academic writing, particularly the dimensions of authority, authorship and authorial presence (see Ivanic 1995).

The three questions/dimensions shown in Figure 2.5, situated within the contexts of situation and culture, provide us with a useful framework for exploring specific instances of student meaning making in academic

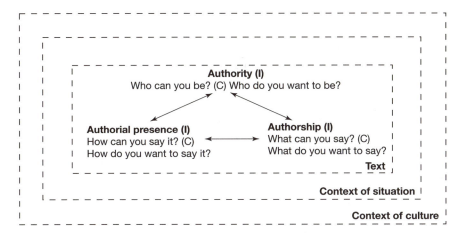

Figure 2.5 Exploring student meaning making in writing

Sources: after Ivanic 1995 (I), Clark and others 1990 (C) and Fairclough 1992a

writing, as I illustrate in Chapters 3 and 4. They thus help to uncover the 'hidden logic' (Flower 1994: 51) of student writing. They also enable us to explore potential choices about meaning making in writing, that is, what the individual student-writers might want to mean in a transformed socio-discursive space.

Notes

1 For discussion of practice, see, for example, Baynham 1995: chapter 1; Barton and Hamilton 1998: chapter 1; Clark and Ivanic 1997: introduction; Chouliaraki and Fairclough 1999: chapter 2.
2 Of course, Halliday (1978) famously invokes Malinowski's notion of context of culture. However, unlike Fairclough, Halliday tends towards a normative stance at the level of a context of situation with the significance of the context of culture often minimised. For example, when analysing interaction in schools, he suggests the primacy of the context of situation in terms of his own interest:

> in describing the context of situation, it is helpful to build in some indication of the cultural background, and the assumptions that have to be made if the text is to be interpreted – or produced – in the way the teacher (or the system) demands.
>
> (Halliday and Hasan 1989: 47)

For further discussion see Lillis 1998.
3 Within rationalist and empiricist approaches to knowledge making, 'language is seen as a necessary adjunct, the means whereby knowledge, which is discovered and stored in the mind, is represented and communicated to other minds' (Lillis and Turner 2001). The discourse practices, which have come to be valued within higher education, reflect and constitute this tradition.
4 For substantial work on links between social class and literacy practices within

the home and school, see Wells 1985, 1986; see also Heath 1983 for continuity/discontinuity between home and school in literacy practices in working-class and middle-class communities in North America.

5 See Chapter 1.

6 Bakhtin stresses throughout that in talking of speech genres he is referring to both spoken and written utterances.

> Special emphasis should be placed on the extreme *heterogeneity* of speech genres (oral and written). In fact, the category of speech genres should include short rejoinders of daily dialogue – everyday narration, writing (in all its various forms).
>
> (Bakhtin 1986: 60; emphasis in original)

7 'Black' here indicates a political stance, signalling, in particular, recognition of Britain as a racist society, which discriminates against minority ethnic groups.

8 Fairclough points to the possibility of transformation, but he has been criticised for being overly deterministic in his approach – see Widdowson 1995, 1996; Stubbs 1997.

9 'Becoming' is of course a key theme in the work of Freire 1985, 1996, on which Fairclough, Clark and Ivanic draw.

10 I am not suggesting that Clark's questions and Ivanic's dimensions are equivalent in any straightforward way. Ivanic in her writings to date has reserved her three dimensions for referring to the self as author, as compared with the discoursal construction of self (see Ivanic 1995; see also Clark and Ivanic 1997); this distinction is not apparent in Clark and others' writing (1990). Moreover, in writings to date, Ivanic's dimensions refer to quite specific aspects of authoring, whereas Clark's terms are significantly broader. For example, Ivanic 1995 uses her notion of authorial presence to refer to two aspects of authoring: authoritativeness and the presence of the first person, 'I'.

3

RESTRICTED ACCESS TO A PRIVILEGED PRACTICE

Introduction

Essayist literacy is the privileged literacy practice within Western societies, constituting considerable cultural/linguistic capital; that is, it is a socially valued and valuable practice, conferring prestige on its users (see Bourdieu 1991, 1994). The practice of essayist literacy is enacted and maintained through formal institutions of schooling and in many ways is synonymous with formal schooling: to do schooling successfully means doing essayist literacy successfully. The further up the schooling ladder you go, the closer you are expected and presumed to come to the ideals of essayist literacy. Whilst essayist literacy is the dominant literacy practice within schooling, it becomes the central action of higher education (after Womack 1993): the highest certification is a Ph.D., which is awarded on the basis of a written thesis (and its defence). In order to be successful in HE, students must gain access to, that is, learn the conventions of, essayist literacy.

In this chapter, I problematise current pedagogy surrounding essayist literacy, questioning its capacity to facilitate access to this privileged literacy practice in HE. In particular, I argue that confusion is so all-pervasive a dimension of the experience of 'non-traditional' students in higher education that it signals the need to look beyond a notion of individual confusion, towards an institutional practice of mystery. This practice of mystery is ideologically inscribed in that it works against those least familiar with the conventions surrounding academic writing, limiting their participation in HE as currently configured.

I begin this chapter by first outlining the ways in which the distance between tutors' and students' understandings of the essayist conventions has been explored in research and practice. Secondly, I problematise the current response to this distance, as enacted in official discourse and in much pedagogy. Thirdly, and in the main section of this chapter, I illustrate how the institutional practice of mystery works, by using extracts from spoken and written texts to trace attempts by several student-writers to make sense of the 'essay question'. The examples show that the practice of mystery is not made up of a discrete list of actions but is enacted in different ways, at the levels of the contexts of situation and culture of higher education. I close the chapter by arguing that current pedagogic practice is characterised by a monologic addressivity (see discussion in Chapter 2) in tutor–student relations. This works against the student-writers' learning of dominant conventions as well as their desire for a different kind of relationship around meaning making in academia.

The gap between tutors' and students' understandings of academic writing conventions

Problematising teaching/learning as implicit induction

The teaching of disciplinary knowledge and academic literacy practices in the traditionally elite system of HE in the UK, has been built on the notion and practice of inducting small numbers of privileged students into the ways of the academy. Teaching-as-induction, in this frame, is of an implicit nature, occurring through close and regular contact between teachers and students, within the context of a relatively small and homogeneous social and cultural community. Metaphors of secrecy and ritual signal the nature of this teaching context: Barnett refers to HE institutions as traditionally performing 'the ceremonial functions of an elite clergy' (1992: 215); Mathews says, of university teaching, 'it is practised as a secret rite behind closed doors' (Mathews, in Layton 1968: vii). Student learning, within such a frame, is akin to a notion of 'environmental osmosis' (see discussions in Wyatt 1990), amounting to breathing in education through the atmosphere (Newman 1959).

This model of learning as implicit induction continues to be pervasive in the UK, in some instances in terms of actual practice – many 'old' universities with relatively privileged student groups continue to maintain small tutorial sessions – but across all institutions as a cultural framework implicitly informing pedagogy. Wyatt (1990: 31) signals the continuing appeal of Newman's ideal of HE, built on the notion of a small academic community and the Oxford college tutorial system; Clarke and Saunders (1997) point to the long shadow of traditional notions of HE which often bear no relation to the real contexts in which many tutors and students are working.[1]

The dominant model of teaching and learning as implicit induction, in the past, seems to have been successful both in relation to the teaching and learning of specific disciplinary knowledge and of academic literacy practices, not least because of the restriction of HE to small numbers of students from privileged backgrounds. However, the relevance of such a model to an HE system which has grown in size and social diversity, and, importantly, without the corresponding increase in resources that would facilitate the regular and close student/tutor contact characteristic of an earlier time, has been questioned in recent years.

Indeed, in the specific context of literacy practices in HE, questions about the usefulness of a pedagogy construed as implicit induction have been discussed for some time. In the mid-1980s, during the early period of the recent shift towards a mass higher education system, Hounsell (1984, 1987) signalled a significant gap between students' and tutors' understandings about academic literacy and knowledge-making practices. Working from within a psychology-of-learning perspective, Hounsell suggested that the distance between student-writers' and tutors' expectations of essay writing was the result of different frames of reference (1984). Exploring students' perceptions of what constitutes an essay, he argued that there was a range of perspectives, which differed both across and within discipline areas. For example, in history, some students conceived essay writing as a matter of 'argument', others as an 'arrangement of facts and ideas'; in psychology, some students focused on 'cogency', others on 'relevance'. Hounsell also pointed to students' perspectives on the value of personal opinion; this was usually seen as 'value added' rather than integral to the writing.

In general, he argued, it was difficult, if not impossible, for students to find out from their tutors what they were expected to do in their essays. The cause, in Hounsell's view, was what he referred to as 'the broken cycle of communication' between tutor and student: 'where students' conceptions of essay-writing are qualitatively different from those of their tutors, communication cannot readily take place because the premises underlying the two disparate conceptions are not shared or mutually understood' (1987: 114).

He gives an example of a student's understanding of 'argument', quoting the student as saying, 'Well, from the comments on the essay, I gathered the tutor wanted me to argue about something, but I mean, by presenting the material as the research had demonstrated, it was a mild form of argument. I wasn't going to get aggressive, in an essay' (1987: 115).

Other researchers have, in recent times, loudly echoed Hounsell's emphasis on the distance between tutors' and students' understandings of academic writing conventions. In particular, the criticism has repeatedly been made that the conventions students are expected to write within are difficult to learn because they remain implicit in pedagogic practice, rather than being explicitly taught.[2] Whilst such criticism often points to the limitations in current pedagogy with regard to students in general terms, some writers signal the dangers inherent in such a pedagogy for students from social groups historically excluded from higher education. Gee, for example, has argued that, on the whole, the language and literacy practices which are valued in schools are not taught to those who do not already know them, with the result that formal institutions continue to privilege those who are already privileged within society (see Gee 1990, 1996). Flower (1994: 122–47) has critiqued so-called 'immersion' approaches to the teaching of writing, which support 'insiders' most. In a similar vein, Delpit (1988) has criticised progressive educators for failing to teach Black students how to manage dominant conventions successfully.

Problematising the current response: writing skills

A key pedagogical response in the UK to the increasingly acknowledged gap between institutional demands and students' understandings of these demands, alongside the changed material circumstances of HE, has been to frame writing as a 'skill', as discussed in Chapter 1. In contrast to the notion of teaching/learning as implicit induction, a specific focus on the teaching of writing skills, in the form of additional provision, is increasingly on the agenda in HE institutions. The most publicly visible manifestation of this is in official policies on 'core' 'transferable' skills and the current growing institutional practice of providing students with advice on academic writing, as part of a study skills approach (see Chapter 1 for discussion; for published examples of 'study skills', see Gibbs and Habeshaw 1989; Race and Brown 1993; Brown and Knight 1994; Drew and Bingham 1997). In these approaches, the distance between tutors' expectations and student-writers' understanding of such expectations is problematised as a mismatch which can be resolved if tutors state clearly to student-writers, in written or spoken words, what is required. This approach can be illustrated by considering the following example of advice on how to approach the 'essay' question. I include this not only because I think it is typical of advice given in study skills manuals but also because it illustrates the assumptions underlying much of the pedagogy surrounding student writing in the university:

> Step 1 of 7 steps towards essay planning is presented as follows:
>
> 1 Interpret the question. This step overwhelmingly determines what follows; it is also likely to be the greatest source of difficulty. *Assuming that the question itself is clear, and reflects the instructor's intentions,* the student needs to be satisfied as to *the meaning of the question and any unclear words checked out.*
>
> (Biggs 1988: 194; my emphasis)

Such advice works with a conduit view of communication and a transparency notion of language, as discussed in Chapter 1, and is particularly evident in the wordings that I've put in italics. Moreover, the advice in the extract indicates not only that meaning resides in the wording of the question, but that, should any difficulty arise, students will be able to consult with their tutors in order to make sense of the demands of the question. This advice on essay writing thus presupposes the following: a) that conventions can be taught in a straightforward way – by tutors telling students what they are; b) that tutors themselves are able to articulate the nature of such conventions;

make clear the link between claim and supporting evidence (a)	avoid such vague wordings as 'etc.', 'lots of . . . ' (b)	check that it is clear what 'this', 'these' refer back/forward to (c)
make clear why a particular section was included (d)		say why particular examples used (e)
	'BE EXPLICIT'	
make links between sections (f)		say why particular punctuation used (g)
show that you understand key terms (h)	show how you are using contested terms (i)	link content with essay question (j)

Figure 3.1 Exploring *be explicit* with one student-writer, Amira

and c) that there are opportunities for students to consult with tutors should any difficulties arise. All three assumptions are questionable, as is evident in the student-writers' experiences outlined in the rest of this chapter.

Consider, for example, one directive (spoken and written) that tutors often use to advise students in their writing, and which student-writers often find problematic: 'be explicit'. In Figure 3.1, I point to specific instances of my attempts to clarify the directive to 'be explicit' in my talk with one student, Amira, over the writing of three texts. The figure challenges any presumed straightforward notion of 'explicitness', pointing instead to a number of specific meanings within the context of student academic writing.

It is clear from the figure that explicitness is not a unitary text phenomenon (see Nystrand and Wiemelt 1991; see also Gee 1990: 60). Each one of the attempted clarifications of the directive 'be explicit' raises further questions and demands further clarification. For example, (a) raises the questions of what is a claim and what is supporting evidence. These questions, in turn, raise further questions about what can count as claim and evidence in this context. The clarifications (h) and (i) raise questions about what are the key/contested terms in this context. The extent to which each one of the attempted clarifications raises more questions for the student-writer, hence demanding further clarification, depends on the extent of the individual student's familiarity with essayist conventions.

Moreover, even if further 'clarifications' are given by the tutor, there is no guarantee that what the tutor says s/he requires in an essay is what s/he actually wants or, importantly from the student-writer's perspective, what s/he will use to guide her assessment of the final draft of the text. In their research on tutors' assessment practices, Clanchy and others decided that the only way in which they could discover the criteria which were significant in tutors' actual practices, was 'to ignore what they [tutors] *claimed* they wanted and, by collecting and classifying what comments they actually made on hundreds of first year essays, gradually distil the key criteria on which they graded' (1985: 3).

Attempting to make sense of the tutor exhortation to 'be explicit' was only one, albeit perhaps one of the most complex, of many difficulties faced by the student-writers. Table 3.1, below, lists the most obvious[3] questions about essayist conventions that were raised by the student-writers during their first year of study.

The enactment of the institutional practice of mystery

Mary [angry]: Some of these rules are made up for no reason what-
soever [laughs]. That's why it's difficult to learn, you see,
because sometimes there's no reason why.

Consider for a moment Table 3.1. In organising the student-writers' questions in a way which is meaningful for the reader, I am aware that I have super-imposed a framework of coherence constructed out of my insider's knowledge about writing in HE. Such a framework is useful to the extent that it enables those of us who are familiar with essayist conventions to see quickly areas that are unfamiliar to the student-writers. But it is a distorted representation of the student-writers' actual experience. Their questions might be more validly presented as a series of repetitive, unconnected and unbounded questions in order to indicate the sense of confusion they experience, as signalled by Mary in her comment above.

I want to look in more detail, now, at the confusion experienced by the student-writers in their attempts to make sense of subject tutors' demands and the conventions therein, by focusing on one important and opaque aspect, the meaning and demands of the 'essay' question. The inverted commas around 'essay' are for two interrelated reasons: firstly, they signal that the term 'essay' is commonly used, by tutors and in guidelines, to describe the texts that students are asked to write, even though the exact nature of these texts may vary considerably. This supports Swales' general comment on the labelling of institutional communicative events; that is, that the labelling of such events (he refers to 'lectures' and 'tutorials') is driven by institutional tradition rather than by any presumed straightforward linguistic-descriptive interest (Swales 1990: 55). Secondly, the inverted commas serve as a reminder that, whilst the writing the students are asked to do falls into one broadly recognisable category to those of us who are already familiar with essayist literacy, the conventions governing this practice often remain a mystery to the student-writers themselves. It is not surprising that students who are

Table 3.1 What do they want? Trying to work out essayist writing conventions

---

The essay/assignment question

What does it mean?
What do they really want?*
What does a particular wording mean – for example, 'advise', 'argue', 'critical', 'discuss'?
What's the difference between a report and an essay?

Content and the use of sources

Does this answer the question?
What is relevant/irrelevant?
What is counted as evidence?
When do I cite authorities (and when not)?
What type of evidence is acceptable?
What is plagiarism?
How much literature do I bring in?
How do I bring in examples from my own research?
How do I support my own opinion?
Which bits of my own experience/understanding/research are relevant?
How do I reference?
Why are references important?
How do I use direct quotes?
When does personal experience count as evidence?
Does personal experience count at all?

Presentation

Can subheadings be used?
Can lists be used?

Global structure

How much do I write on each section?
What should be in an introduction?
What should be in a conclusion?
Where do I put description, analysis?
How do I organise content into argument?
How long can my text be?

Punctuation

What is standard punctuation?
When do I use a full stop, comma, semi-colon?

Language and wordings

Which words/ings can(not) be used?
What is Standard English?

Clarifying voices in the text

How do I separate voices?
How do I make my own voice clear?

Being explicit in academic writing

What does being explicit mean?
How do I make sections of my text obviously relevant?

Being assessed

What are the assessment criteria?
How do I get a distinction?
Are marks lost for grammar mistakes?
Is this of degree standard?
Are long words necessary for high marks?

Note *Apart from being a question explicitly raised, I think that the question 'What do they really want?' was a driving force behind their decision to meet with me as tutor-assessor-researcher.

unfamiliar with an institution should be unsure about its practices. However, what is at issue here is the extent to which current pedagogy facilitates their understanding and learning of such practices, in particular, of essayist literacy.

Bridget:[4] 'It turned out she liked it'

With all ten student-writers, much of our talk centred on the meaning of the 'essay' question and the possible responses expected from the tutor. For Bridget, a first-year social work student, her confusion about what a successful response to an essay question might look like was a continuation of her experience of study at Access level (see Appendix 2). In our first meeting, I asked Bridget to bring along an essay from her Access course that she had considered to be successful, as a first step towards clarifying what she might want us to talk about. When I asked her why she considered it successful, she said she had got a better mark for it than for her other essays. However, she had little sense of what made it better:

> It was better in terms of marks. It was one of those essays I wrote and I didn't really know whether I was writing *what she wanted*. So I just sort of did it to the best of my ability. And *it turned out she liked it.*
>
> (my emphasis)

Bridget seems to suggest it was mostly a matter of the individual tutor's taste (indicated in italics) that the essay was successful, and she has little sense of the specific ways she has fulfilled criteria, and hence how she might do so in future. The mystery surrounding what 'they' really want is still with her in her first year at university, where she focuses predominantly on the wording of the essay questions in her attempts to work out *what they're really asking.* Relying mainly on the wording of the essay question, however, is not illuminating for her:

> The more I read the question, the less sure I am.

Nadia:[5] 'She didn't like it one bit'

The perception that success and failure depend greatly on individual tutors' quirks can be further illustrated by Nadia's experience, where her misfortune contrasts with Bridget's unaccountable success. Nadia was frustrated by the tutor's dismissal of a part of the content of her essay. In her second year of HE, but her first year of the particular course she was studying, Education Studies, she writes on the following essay question: 'Working-class children are underachieving in schools. How much of this may be attributed to perceived language deficiencies?'[6]

When working on a draft for this essay, Nadia talked of focusing on monolingual working-class children but also thought she would focus on the experience of bilingual children. She was pleased that she would be able to draw on what she had learned from a previous course, Language Studies. However, the response from her tutor was not what she expected.

Opening section of Nadia's final draft	Tutor's written comment
Throughout this essay I will be focusing on the types of underachievers.	Your beginning section moves away from essay title.
Firstly, the working class bilinguals and the misleading intelligence tests, of which bilingual children are expected to do.	Need to organise your thoughts more carefully and adhere to the essay title more clearly.
Secondly, the working class monolinguals which are underachieving.	
Thirdly, I will seek information on how much of this may be attributed to perceived language deficiencies.	

Nadia sought oral feedback in a seminar in order to clarify why the tutor felt she hadn't focused on the essay title:

> She [tutor] didn't like it *one bit.* . . . She said not all bilingual kids are working class. And I turned round and said not all bilingual kids are middle class. She said the question wasn't about bilingual kids.

61

Nadia

Nadia is 22 years old and from a Yemeni background. She speaks Arabic and English. She has lived in England all her life.

Nadia was brought up in an Arabic-speaking environment, both at home and in the wider community. She attended a monolingual English primary school where she struggled – mainly, she felt, because of managing neither Standard English nor Standard Arabic well:

> Because I remember when I were at school and at home, we used to be at home learning Arabic, the alphabet, and I used to be at school and they used to teach English grammar, and I kind of got them mixed up. And I think from that, that's how I think my English and Arabic has come to so bad a level.

On leaving school Nadia went to college to study for a BTEC[7] in First Aid, Health and Social Work, but had a serious road accident six months into the course and did not complete it. However, she returned to college and did a BTEC in Social Work, which she really enjoyed. Towards the end of this period, she had an arranged marriage. This ended in violence after several weeks and she spent four years sorting out a divorce.

Nadia decided to start a higher education course whilst working as a bilingual support teacher in a primary school. Although she had never thought of herself as capable of going to university during her school and college years, she began to change her mind during the brief period of her marriage:

> After I got married, I knew that I didn't want to be studying for the next thirty years and not getting anywhere. I thought, I don't want to go through every job. —— And I thought I've got to do it for myself and for the kids, so they can think, 'Mum's done this', so it gives them a bit of encouragement.

Nadia was worried in general about her ability to study in HE and particularly concerned about the language she would be expected to use for higher education.

> *N:* I think it's totally different.
> *T:* In what way?
> *N:* The words. My English and that degree English is totally different.
> *T:* What do you mean about words?
> *N:* Actual words, meaning. Like one big word may sound, may mean something similar to something else . . . I think my English has got to be a thousand times better than what it is now to be at university.
> *T:* Does it worry you?
> *N:* Yeah, I think it's a big problem actually. I think I'm going to have to change the way I put words together to form a sentence . . . definitely. I've been thinking about that, about how am I going to do that? Go to the lessons, do my best, go for extra help in English.

Nadia sees this as an individual quirk of the tutor, rather than a dimension to meaning making within the context of culture of HE where particular meanings are privileged. In this case, there is an expectation that she will take monolingual as the norm and focus on monolingual, rather than monolingual and bilingual, working-class children. Nadia sees the tutor's comments simply as personal opinion, albeit with institutional power, as is indicated in her comment below:

She's nice, but what she wants, she gets. You can't argue with her.

Connections . . .

Spoken tutor feedback after my first essay in an HE course, in Spanish literature. Both the essay and the tutor's comments were written in Spanish. The feedback was given in a tutorial with three other students.

Tutor: Este ensayo no esta mal, Theresa, pero es bastante ingenuo. [Transl.: This essay's not bad, Theresa, but it's quite *ingenuo*.]

I knew he couldn't mean 'ingenious' but what did 'ingenuo' mean? I asked a bilingual fellow student from Panama. He told me it meant 'naive'. I was confused. Was the tutor describing my essay or me? I didn't know what to do with such a comment. I certainly had no intention of asking him.

Tara: 'Who do I "advise"?'

In some instances, as in Bridget's case, the student-writer attempts to discover the expectations of the tutor in the wording of the question. On other occasions, the student-writer identifies a particular word as the source of her problems in trying to understand what is required. For example, Tara, a first-year law student focused on the word 'advise', which was used in two essay questions. Trying to work out what this wording seemed to demand became the main focus of our talk about the writing of these texts. Below are the two 'advise' questions we discussed in full.

Question 1

Justine Snook runs a small catering service from her home, providing hot lunches for the management of three firms in Sheffield. She has two employees – a driver and an assistant cook.
　　She would like to bid for catering contracts at more firms and possibly expand into catering for private dinner parties, but could

Tara

Tara is a 30-year-old, white working-class woman, originally from a mining village in Wales. She lives with her partner and has a 12-year-old son.

Being successful in formal education was not something that was expected of her or her brothers by her parents:

> I mean, even exams . . . I wasn't expected to take any exams even. At home, none of my brothers passed their exams and it wasn't expected of me. I was never pushed or encouraged to do it. I thought, well, all right, I can just do the same as everybody else. And get a job.

After leaving school, Tara worked in a local factory and shortly after got married. She had a son and continued to work, but, along with some girlfriends from the factory who were bored with the routine work, decided to sign up for GCE evening classes. Tara began studying for three GCSEs: English Language, Computer Studies and Law. However, she did not complete these courses, a main reason being her separation from her husband, which left her as a full-time carer for her child. She could not afford a baby-sitter and had no means of transport to the college. She returned to her studies some time later when her new partner, who was studying at university, encouraged her to start a Step Forward course. Spurred on by positive comments from tutors on this course, Tara began an Access to Higher Education course.

Throughout the Access course she was trying to work out whether she had the ability to study at university:

> When I started the Access course, I *wanted* to study at university, but I wanted to see how well I was doing at first. It wasn't until I was half way through that I thought I could do it.

She was now in a position to pick up her longstanding interest in law, which she was deeply enthusiastic about, although she had no formal links with it.

> It's a *really* interesting subject. I could read about law all the time, like. Everything we do is linked to law. If I read the papers, the most interesting bits are to do with law. I can link a lot of what we do to law.

English is Tara's first language, although her father often spoke Irish Gaelic to her and her brothers until they reached school age; she also learnt Welsh as a separate subject at school. However, she says she would not describe herself as a competent speaker of English:

> I don't know how to phrase it. Mine is working-class English. I speak like a working-class person would, not like a middle- or an upper-class person. I speak lower down the spectrum rather than the top. And I can tell.

not do all this from her home; and she is worried about how she would manage the operation. One of her worries is that she has no experience beyond institutional catering.

a)   Advise Ms Snook about alternative forms of business organisation available to her, explaining the legal implications and the advantages and disadvantages as they apply to her situation.

b)   Ms Snook's anticipated expansion will necessitate considerable amounts of funding. Advise on possible sources of finance and examine whether particular forms of business organisations will act as a constraint on finance availability. Which form of business would you advise her to accept?

2,000 words

Question 2

Shortly after 3 a.m. PC Williams is on foot patrol in a part of town where there are many pubs and clubs frequented by young people as part of Steelville's city council's policy of creating a '24 hour city for the 21st century'. He notices a young man, Jean-Claude, leave one such club. As he leaves Jean-Claude tosses a cigarette box into the street. PC Williams calls out the [as in original] Jean-Claude to stop and pick up the litter. Jean-Claude makes a rude gesture to the officer and continues to walk away. Williams shouts to Jean-Claude again, telling him to stop and demanding his name and information about where he lives. Without stopping, Jean-Claude gives his name but says he is a temporary visitor from France with no local address.

Williams catches up with Jean-Claude, takes hold of his arm, and tells him he is under arrest. Jean-Claude immediately struggles, and in an attempt to free himself, begins to strike at Williams. A passer-by, 'Big Frank' attempts to assist Williams. He aims a punch at Jean-Claude. He misses, and instead, his fist lands on William's [as in original] nose. Williams loses his grip on Jean-Claude, who runs away. Williams takes 'Big Frank' to the police station, where he is charged with wilful obstruction. Jean-Claude, meanwhile has been gently recaptured and is gently taken to the police station.

At the station Jean-Claude's pockets, and his bag, are searched and a substantial quantity of prohibited drugs are found. The custody officer, Howard, tells him that he is to be detained for questioning on suspicion that he is a dealer in such drugs and that he will be able to provide information as regards his suppliers. He is told that in the circumstances it is not appropriate to allow him to communicate with a lawyer; nor that his mum should be informed of the fact of his detention.

Jean-Claude is questioned at length. On the following day, exhausted, he admits numerous offences in connection with prohibited drugs.

Advise Jean-Claude and 'Big Frank'.

No specific guidelines were given in relation to these essay questions. They were not, for example, presented as part of an explicit role-simulation within professional practice but were located only within the academic context of the course (for discussion of the impact of such role-simulation on writing, see Freedman, Adam and Smart 1994).

The main obstacle Tara faced in trying to frame her essay was to decide who her writing was meant to address: the 'advise' directive seemed to suggest that her writing should be directed at the fictitious client, yet Tara knew that the real addressee was the tutor. For the writing of her second essay, she pursued this with her tutor, seeking explicit guidance. Here she recounts her attempts to clarify how she is to interpret 'advise':

> I've asked loads of questions but they said, 'you advise him' [Jean-Claude] and I said, 'yeah, but do I speak to *him* so I'm giving *him* the advice, or . . . ?' He said, 'Well, if you do that then you won't get all the Acts done.' So . . . he just couldn't be bothered I assume.

Tara knew she had to show as much legal knowledge as she could for the benefit of the tutor-assessor, yet the directive to 'advise' the client still worried her. This was particularly true of the second essay where she was concerned that the knowledge she knew she had to show the tutor would not, in a real-life situation, be shared with the client, Jean-Claude. In our discussion, she pointed to the dilemma she faced in attempting to follow the tutor's direction to 'advise' Jean-Claude:

> If I was directing this to him personally, it'd be pointless me saying this and this and this . . . 'cause he wouldn't understand it. So I have to maybe, in the . . . is it the third person maybe? Not to him directly, not advising him directly but pointing out *how* I would advise him. Not advising him personally. Should I put that maybe in the introduction?

In her introductions to both her essays Tara tried to accommodate this double readership by trying to direct her comments to the two presumed addressees: the tutor as actual addressee and Ms Snook/Jean Claude as the fictitious addressees.

In the introduction to both essays Tara stays close to the real context of writing for a tutor-assessor whose aim will be to assess her knowledge of relevant legal statutes. She does this, in the first introduction, by repeating

Introduction to essay 1	*Introduction to essay 2*
In order to advise Ms Snook about expanding her small catering service, this essay will discuss what are the alternative forms of business available to her. It will also show what are the legal implications and the advantages and the disadvantages that expansion may incur. Furthermore this essay will examine what sources of finance are available to Ms Snook and whether these alternative forms of business organisation, could act as a constraint financially. Lastly, after looking at all the alternatives and financial information given, I will advise Ms Snook on what form of business organisation would best suit her needs at this present time.	In order to advise Jean Claude in relation to his arrest, search and detention and Big Frank's charge of wilful obstruction, certain relevant statutory powers related to the Police and Criminal Evidence Act 1984 (P.A.C.E.) and subsequent case law. Lastly, I will attempt to substantiate whether their arrests were lawful and what will be the possible outcome for both parties involved.

much of the wording of the set question, and in the second text by referring to a relevant Act. If the addressees were the fictitious clients, she might be expected to do neither of these. She also refers to the clients in the third person rather than the second; thus, there are references to 'Ms Snook', 'her', 'Jean Claude', 'Big Frank', 'their', whereas if she were addressing them, she might be expected to use 'you'.

But Tara also works at addressing the fictitious clients, particularly in the first text. For whilst in both introductions she indicates that she is advising the clients, Ms Snook and Jean Claude, in the first, she refers to Ms Snook three times, and ends by saying 'I will advise Ms Snook'. By the time she comes to write the second introduction, she seems to be abandoning the idea of addressing anybody other than the tutor-assessor. This is particularly apparent within the main body of the text, where her principal aim seems to be to demonstrate relevant knowledge:

> If it appears later that PC Williams had originally suspected Jean Claude of carrying prohibited drugs but arrested him for other reasons, which did not have a power of arrest, then the decision based on Christie v Leachinsky (21947) AC 573 would apply 'where if a reason for arrest was given that was inadequate in law (e.g. because the offence mentioned does not carry a power of arrest), the fact that the arrester had other suspicions which would have justified him in detaining the suspect does not validate the arrest' (John Sprack; 1995, p. 380).

67

In attempting to make sense of the essay questions and how she is expected to respond to them Tara draws together both spoken and written comments made by the tutor. In the first essay, for instance, as well as trying to make sense of the written directive 'advise', Tara was also trying to understand the spoken instructions of the tutor who had called for 'not too many facts and to argue it'. Tara states

> I'm only there to advise her anyway. I'm not there to say anything else. I mean, there's a lot of information I could put down, but, like I said, when I look at it, I can't really *argue* it in any way.

There are significant problems surrounding the words 'advise' and 'argue' which, in Tara's mind, conflict. She knows she has to display all the relevant knowledge for the benefit of the tutor-addressee. But in trying to accommodate the client-addressee, Tara assumes she has to provide a range of perspectives, in order to 'advise', rather than give one preferred option, which is what 'argue' suggests to her. This is further complicated by the presumed need for Tara, as writer, to be absent from her text, as indicated in the written guidelines on writing for her course:

> Write in the impersonal third person. There are few things so irritating as the constant intrusion of the author *via* the (unnecessary) first person 'I think . . . '.

The function of the adjective 'unnecessary' is ambiguous here – does it refer to all uses of 'I' or is it signalling that some uses are in fact justified? Tara, based on spoken comments by tutors in seminars, understands it to mean that all uses of 'I' are prohibited. Yet such a prohibition seems to contradict the tutor's statement in the feedback comments on the final draft of Tara's second 'advise' essay:

> Some good discussion of some of the issues involved. However, some evidence of what *you* thought the likely outcome would have been, would have been useful.
>
> (emphasis in original text)

This seems to contradict Tara's understanding of the directive not to use the first person, which she understands as meaning not to include her own opinion. Overall, the combination of directives to advise–argue–write in the impersonal third person, and the directive, after completing the essay, that 'what you thought would have been useful' are confusing, to say the least, and make it difficult for Tara to respond in a coherent way to the essay question.

Diane

Diane is a Black[8] working-class woman, 32 years of age, living with her three children aged 2, 5 and 13. She describes herself as bilingual in English and Jamaican Creole, although until recently she thought of the language she spoke at home as *broken English*, which is what she was told by both parents and her schoolteachers.

Although Diane remembers enjoying primary school, things were very different at secondary school where she felt a gulf grow between her and the teachers:

> I can remember writing stories and I'd think oh that's really good that. But they [teachers] never thought it was good. I never really understood what was wrong with it. But I was bad at school anyway. I never paid attention. I was just rebellious for some reason.

She, along with a small group of girlfriends, missed many lessons; when they did attend, they spent time gambling at the back of classrooms. Diane left school without any qualifications.

On leaving school she did a YTS (Youth Training Scheme) in catering, followed by PATH (Positive Action Training Scheme aimed at young people from minority ethnic groups). An experience in this last scheme re-awakened her interest in learning. While on placement in a central information service, one of her tasks was to bring information on local interest groups up to date:

> I thought to myself, Gosh, I really don't know a lot! There's lots of things I don't know, even in updating their system. I mean, I never recognised it before, but I do now. —— I had to phone round different places and find out information. I never knew those places existed. I thought, when have all these things been happening? —— I thought, 'God, I didn't know these things were about.' I thought, 'I'm not living.'

Diane left the PATH scheme because she was pregnant. She wanted to look after her child full-time, but was also determined to continue studying. She went to adult education classes to study for GCSE English. She failed this at the first attempt but a year later passed GCSE English Language, as well as Psychology, Sociology, Home Economics and Law. This success led her to study a higher education level 1 course in Language Studies, which appealed because of her interest in language.

In her second year in higher education, Diane still feels an outsider. She thus appreciates lecturers who attempt to bridge the gap between her and the institution by acknowledging cultural and ethnic diversity – particularly when they do so in ways which are specific to her identity, for example as a Rastafarian woman. This helps her to feel more at ease as a Black woman in HE and more able to accept what she sees as being on offer: the opportunity to learn.

Diane: 'Trick questions'

Trying to establish what tutors expected in answer to the 'essay question' was a central concern in discussions with all student-writers. In the second of the two essays Diane and I talked about, she moved beyond the wording of the essay question and focused on the teaching context; that is, she waited for the relevant lecture related to the essay question, in order to help her make sense of the question. Yet this caused greater confusion, as her comments below indicate.

2,000-word essay for Communication Studies Diane's comments after lecture

'It is not enough to show that stereotypes exist in the media; we need also to show their causes and effects.' Discuss with reference to media portrayal of ONE of the following; industrial relations, women, black people, deviance.	D: Since we've had the lecture, he's just totally put me off. T: Why? D: Because they, like, give you these questions and they're like bloody trick questions. T: So what's trick about this one? D: He doesn't want . . . first of all *he doesn't want to know that really stereotypes in the media exist. They already know that. What they want to know is the causes and effects.* (my emphasis)

Although it seems that all the lecturer has done is to repeat the wording of the written question, his oral gloss actually changes the focus of the question. In the written question, the directive 'discuss', placed as it is outside the inverted commas, makes both of the preceding clauses its object, thus suggesting to Diane that she should discuss both. She had thus begun by discussing the first clause, by attempting to briefly define what is meant by 'stereotype' and to provide examples from the media. However, when she heard the lecturer's comment, reported in the table above (see italics), she became confused. In his oral gloss on the question, the lecturer tells the students that he only wants the second clause/proposition – 'we need also to show their causes and effects' – to be discussed; the first – 'it is not enough to show that stereotypes exist' – is not to be discussed, but taken as given.

Diane points to the confusion she feels in the essay question and makes clear to the seminar tutor her new interpretation of what the question requires, based on the sense she has made of it after hearing the lecturer's comment:

> I even said to the woman in the seminar, and I said, you know when you give these questions out, it's like you're trying to trick students,

like, that doesn't look how, it doesn't say, I don't mean talk about
what stereotype is, just talk about the causes and effects.

There is no further clarification from the seminar tutor so, throughout her
writing of the essay, Diane continues to try to make sense of both the essay
question as written, and the lecturer's spoken comments. In attempting to
do so, she returns time and time again to the written text, but with the words
spoken by the lecturer always in mind:

[reads] 'We need also to show their causes.' It's this what gets me.
Causes and effects.

In this context of a set essay question, the 'we need' functions as an indirect
command to the student to tell her what to write. Here, then, if Diane focuses
only on this clause and reads it as a command, her lecturer's comment to
write about causes and effects is coherent. However, this understanding of
the task continues to contradict what the written question indicates; that the
student-writer should discuss both propositions within the question. So Diane
is left with an overriding concern that whatever she does she cannot meet the
expectations of the lecturer. In this instance, she decides to try to respond to
the essay question, as glossed by the lecturer, and to focus on the causes and
effects, without considering in any detail notions of stereotypes and their
existence in the media. At this point, it should be noted, Diane assumes that
it is this same lecturer who will be assessing her essay.

However, it is the seminar tutor who reads and marks her essay. From
the written feedback on the essay, Diane discovers that she might have been
more successful, in terms of marks, had she worked with her original
understanding.

Essay question	Tutor comment on final draft of essay (made by seminar tutor)
'It is not enough to show that stereotypes exist in the media; we need also to show their causes and effects.' Discuss with reference to media portrayal of ONE of the following: industrial relations, women, black people, deviance.	What I'd like you to consider further is the notion of stereotype. Can it (stereotype) adequately illustrate how and why unequal power relations are reproduced or does it merely demonstrate they exist? You need to address and critically evaluate the concept itself in order to fully answer the question.

There are several points to make here. Firstly, the two tutors involved in
the teaching and assessing of the course – the lecturer and the seminar tutor
– seem to have different views about the nature of the task or, at least, have

significantly different ways of communicating their views as to the nature of the task. Whatever the nature of their difference, it is the student-writer who is left guessing. Diane felt that the lecturer had specifically emphasised that he did not want a discussion about whether stereotypes exist and had specifically requested that the students not spend time in defining stereotypes; the second teacher, the seminar tutor, who in this case is the tutor-marker, disagrees.[9]

Secondly, it is only from the second tutor's feedback on the completed essay that a key, but implicit, demand of the essay question becomes clear: 'Can it (stereotype) adequately illustrate how and why unequal power relations are reproduced or does it merely demonstrate they exist?' These references to power relations and social reproduction are absent from the original question.

Diane receives a mark in the low 50s (out of 100). What does Diane take away from this experience? Although she had been awarded a distinction (above 70) for a previous essay, which was also a 'discuss' essay question, she feels that this experience demonstrates that she does not know how to write such essays:

> And I'm not doing anything that says 'discuss'. I'm going to do things that say 'describe' next time.

Here Diane moves away from the necessary practice she was beginning to develop, that of making links between wordings, meanings and expectations in this socio-discursive context and fixes her attention on the wording of the question, the assumption being that the wording/meaning will remain constant. But, of course, those of us who are familiar with essayist practice in higher education know that this is not the case. An obvious example is that, even when the wording in an essay question at HE level directs the student-writer to 'describe', the expectation is that she will engage in some type of analysis rather than in description alone.

Student-writers' desire for dialogue

That the student-writers in this project want dialogue with their tutors is clear: this is reflected in their decision to spend time with me, as tutor-researcher, to talk about their writing, as well as in the many comments they make about wanting more time with tutors. Their desire for dialogue contrasts with the frustration and disappointment they often feel about the type of relationship they have with tutors. An extreme example of the distance between students and tutor is Tara's account of the abuse a lecturer had hurled at a lecture hall full of 100 students. She recounted how this lecturer had shouted at the students because, he said, one student had dared to leave an anonymous note under his door seeking clarification on the structure of the assignment.

After berating the students for being cowards for not speaking to him directly about their questions (although, according to Tara, some had done so) the lecturer, Tara said, gave them these guidelines:

> He goes on the board then and said . . . 'erm, This is how you do it, introduction, main body, conclusion, that's it. Go off and do it now.' So we all said to ourselves 'Thanks very much, like, you're a bloody big help.'

This is an extreme example of two themes running through the student-writers' accounts: a) the assumption that the essay is an unproblematic form, that is, that the conventions surrounding student writing are 'common sense'; and b) the lack of opportunity for dialogue between students and tutors.

More common examples of the monologic space that exists between tutors and students are those already discussed throughout this chapter, where student-writers not only found it difficult to make sense of the demands but were frustrated by the little opportunity to explore such difficulties with the tutors. The encounter between Nadia and her tutor, reported by Nadia in talk with me, illustrates the type of talking–learning relationship the student-writers feel they have with tutors, in contrast to what they would like (in italics):

> N: I'm not really taking them [the spoken and written comments made by the tutor] into account.
> T: Ignoring her? Why?
> N: Ignoring her basically. *If I could go and talk to her about it* then maybe I'd take them into consideration, but I'm glad I actually changed from her to somebody else.
>
> (my emphasis)

In this instance, Nadia, having been given the essay question, attempts to make sense of it without ever re-negotiating her understanding with the tutor. She writes the essay and receives feedback, but sees such feedback as idiosyncratic rather than as helping her to learn more about the nature of the task in which she has engaged. So, although one obvious way for student-writers to make sense of what they are trying to do is to ask their tutors, the experience of the student-writers discussed in this book suggests that this is often neither possible nor, if it does happen, useful. In general, they felt extremely frustrated by the type of talking space they encountered. This was even the case in an area of study where dominant academic practices are often critiqued. So that Kate, even though she felt generally positive about the course she was studying, Women's Studies, did not dare to ask for clarification of expectations or assessment criteria. The limited opportunities for dialogue with tutors was the major reason she gave for deciding she could not study in such an environment and, although passing her course work with marks in the 60s, decided to leave at the end of her first year.[10] I explore, in Chapter 6, the kinds of dialogue that student-writers seem to desire with their tutors.

Addressivity and meaning making within higher education

The confusion that all the student-writers described about the expectations surrounding essay writing, as exemplified in the specific instances discussed in the previous sections, was central to their experience of writing in HE. Moreover, such confusion was not confined to particular tutors, departments, institutions or areas of study. I would therefore argue that it is important to view such confusion not as an individual student phenomenon but as indicative of a dominant practice in HE, which I am calling here the 'institutional practice of mystery'.

As can be seen from the examples discussed in the previous section, this practice is enacted in different ways. In the first two examples, Bridget and Nadia do not understand why their essays are successful/unsuccessful and, in both instances, they perceive success and failure as the consequence of individual tutors' quirks. Thus, through such experiences, Bridget is no clearer as to the criteria for a successful essay and Nadia is no closer to understanding the conventions underlying such criteria; she does not know, when writing the essay or after tutor feedback, that within the context of culture of HE, she is not expected to bring 'minority' issues to the centre of her response to an essay question unless explicitly told to do so (even then, student-writers feel constrained; see discussion in Chapter 4). In the third example, that of Tara, it is a series of directives as if these were transparently meaningful and mutually coherent that causes the student-writer difficulties. In particular, the use of the wording 'advise', emerging from the hybrid context of law-as-profession and law-as-academic discipline, creates substantial confusion. In the fourth example, that of Diane, problems are most obviously caused by one tutor's reading and interpretation of the underlying intention of the question being at odds with the interpretation of a second tutor.

A central dimension to these different and specific experiences of the student-writers in the examples above is the dominant type of addressivity within which their meaning making takes place. I find it useful to draw on Bakhtin's notion of addressivity here (Bakhtin 1986; see discussion in Chapter 2), rather than talking of student–tutor relationship or writer–reader relationship, for two, related, reasons. Firstly, addressivity signals the need to view the impact of such a relationship as being not only important (as in, for example, Flower 1994) but central to an individual's meaning making. Secondly, addressivity signals that language(s), or voices, are powerfully bound up with such relationships. Within this framing, the real or potential addressee contributes to what can be meant as much as does the addressor. Addressivity is central to Bakhtin's understanding of language and meaning making, linking with his notion of the living utterance as one in which meaning comes into being between participants, rather than being trans- mitted from one to another; thus in any instance of meaning making, addressor and addressee are involved in a chain of speech communication (see discussion in Chapter 2). The socio-discursive space which is inhabited by student-writers and tutors, as illustrated in this chapter, is fundamentally monologic, in that it is the tutor's voice that predominates, determining what the task is and how it should be done, without negotiating the nature of the expectations surrounding this task through dialogue with the student-writer. Within this monologic relationship, there is denial of real participants, that is, actual tutors and student-writers with their particular understandings and interests, the elaboration and exploration of which might have done two things: a) enabled the student writers to negotiate greater understanding of what was being demanded; and b) enabled a range of other meanings to be made.

In relation to academic writing, it is important to emphasise that such monologism, where there is a denial of actual speaking participants, is not separate from academic writing but is closely bound up with the practice of essayist literacy. In Chapter 4 I explore further the nature of this monolo- gism in the student–tutor relationship and the implications for meaning making. Here, I wish to stress the way in which this dominant addressivity contrasts with the student-writers' desire for dialogue, as well as ignoring the demonstrated positive benefits of the acknowledgement of real participants surrounding the production of written texts (for a study pointing to the importance of reciprocity see Nystrand 1990; see also Clark and Ivanic's emphasis on 'reading for real', 1997: 238).

Conclusion

Whilst the view prevails that essays/student academic texts are unproblematic forms, the construction of which should be part of students' 'common sense' knowledge, experience from this and other studies indicates that student academic texts are expected to be constructed in and through conventions which are often invisible to both tutors and students. That the student-writers should struggle with the conventions of an institution which is strange to them is not surprising. However, this strangeness is compounded by the fact that such conventions are treated as if they are 'common sense' and are communicated through wordings as if these are transparently meaningful. Tutors may know essayist conventions implicitly, having been socialised into them through years of formal schooling, and in many cases through socio-discursive practices in their homes and communities. But students, particularly those from so-called 'non-traditional' backgrounds, may not, as is reflected in the recurring questions listed in this chapter. What is at stake is the students' participation in higher education.

I have signalled that current pedagogy, whether driven by a model of teaching and learning as implicit induction and/or whether informed by current skills approaches to communication, is inadequtae to the task of facilitating the student-writers' learning of academic writing conventions. The material conditions that have historically facilitated learning as implicit induction, a marker of the traditional elitist HE system in the UK, often do not exist, and there are fundamental limitations to the current emphasis on a skills approach to writing, evident in official discourse and much pedagogy.

The confusion the student-writers experience is so all-pervasive a dimension of their experience in HE that it is useful to name this the 'institutional practice of mystery'. This practice is ideologically inscribed in that it works against those least familiar with the conventions surrounding academic writing – that is, students from social groups historically excluded from higher education. Such a practice works against their participation in HE in the following interrelated ways.

Firstly, exclusion occurs because what is assumed to be 'common sense' is in fact only one privileged literacy practice; student outsiders cannot know the conventions embedded in such a practice unless these are taught. I return to the question of how these can be taught in Chapter 6. Secondly, the dominant monologic addressivity within HE does not facilitate access to the privileged/privileging resources of essayist literacy. The writing and reading of students' written texts is consonant with the fictionalisation of participants in essayist literacy. However, whilst student-writers need to become familiar with this aspect of the practice – the denial of actual students and tutors with specific histories and interests – it unnecessarily complicates the students' learning of essayist literacy. Writing for someone who, they feel, is working with them at meaning making, is likely to be of more use at this stage of their participation in higher education. (See Chapter 6 for examples of more collaborative approaches to meaning making in writing; see Chapter 5 for a discussion of student desires for other kinds of writer–reader relations.)

The effect in the short term is as follows: student-writers spend inordinate amounts of time attempting to sort out the nature of their tutors' expectations, which could be more usefully spent on other activities; they may achieve unnecessarily low marks; some may even decide to leave the institution. This was the case with two students, Kate and Sara (see p. 114 for patterns of participation in HE). In practical terms, what is required is more contact between student-writers and 'knowledgeable insiders' in order to negotiate and re-negotiate the nature of specific writing tasks, including, for example, the expectations surrounding particular essay questions and the conventions that the student-writers are expected to write within. Although this may be considered difficult, if not impossible, to organise within the constraints of current resources, it is a price that has to be paid if our aim is to widen access to higher education.

Notes

1 Whilst I think the points made here about elitism and pedagogy are valid for the purposes of this chapter, I am also aware of the danger of oversimplifying the history of HE in the UK. For discussion around, for example, the impact of Newman's views, see Bell 1973.

2 For examples, see discussions in Ivanic and Roach 1990; Norton 1990; Andrews 1995; Lea 1995; Scott 1996. These echo discussions from a number of different geographical contexts, for example Australia – Ballard and Clanchy 1988; Prosser and Webb 1994 – the US – Delpit 1988; Rose 1989 – and South Africa – Angelil-Carter (ed.) 1998.

3 By 'obvious' I mean concerns that were phrased as an explicit question, rather than the many comments which signalled further questions and concerns.

4 See page 7 for introduction to Bridget.

5 See page 62 for introduction to Nadia.

6 Wordings in extracts from written texts – both of student-writers and the tutors – are as in the original.

7 See Appendix 2 for descriptions of UK exam qualifications and courses.

8 'Black' is the term used by both students in the project from Afro-Caribbean/British backgrounds to describe their social and ethnic status/position. They also use the term 'Afro-Caribbean'.

9 It is common practice in UK HE institutions for different teachers to be involved in different teaching contexts of a course; this involves, as in this instance, one teacher being responsible for lectures (lecturer) and at least on other teacher (tutor) being responsible for smaller group sessions, seminars.

10 Whilst foregrounding here the student-writer's experience, it is important to note that the material constraints acting on individual tutors, schools and disciplines obviously plays a major part in determining the opportunities for student–tutor communication: in this instance, Women's Studies as an academic field was being squeezed out of this particular university at the time.

4

THE REGULATION OF
AUTHORING

Introduction

In the previous chapter I argued that there is a dominant pedagogic practice within HE which works against student-writers' learning of essayist literacy conventions. This dominant practice of mystery works towards excluding them from the project of higher education as currently configured. Exclusion at another level also occurs: that of excluding certain ways of meaning. For although the conventions of essayist literacy surrounding student academic writing remain implicit, they are in operation, and work towards regulating meaning making in specific ways.

The specific features of this culturally available representational resource, and the ways in which it privileges particular meanings and relationships between writers, readers and texts, has been explicated by writers in a range of related disciplinary fields: linguistics, critical discourse, rhetoric and composition. There has been less emphasis on exploring the ways in which producers of texts experience writing within the constraints of this practice-resource.

My aim in this chapter is as follows: firstly, to give an overview of the ways in which researchers have explicated the particular meanings privileged in essayist literacy; secondly, and drawing on the heuristic discussed in Chapter 2, to illustrate how actual instances of individual student meaning making in writing are regulated, by focusing on specific instances of student-writers' texts and their talk about these texts; and, thirdly, to present fragments of stories around meaning making which foreground the tensions students experience in their writing in academia, in particular, tensions between the kinds of social identity that essayist literacy privileges and the student-writers' sense of identity(ies).

How essayist literacy conventions regulate

The features of essayist literacy and the ways in which it constitutes particular ways of meaning have been explicated in various ways. Gee, as discussed in

Chapter 2, points to the following as key features of essayist prose style: a particular kind of unity, where the emphasis is on one main point or theme; a particular kind of relationship between writer, text and reader, where the text is expected to stand alone; a particular kind of language, that is, the standard version of a language. Gee emphasises the ways in which this discursive practice privileges particular ways of meaning, and being, and hence works towards the inclusion of particular social groups in institutional practices, whilst excluding others (see Chapter 2 for further details).

Other writers have focused on the common linguistic features of essayist literacy and the ways in which these constitute particular ways of meaning.[1] Ivanic draws on a number of writers, including Corson (1985) and Halliday (1988, 1989, 1993b) to provide an overview of these features:

> high lexical density, a preponderance of relational and mental process clauses, very few material process clauses, a highly nominal style, the use of carrier nouns and graeco-latin vocabulary, the lack of expressive metaphor, scare quotes and/or attribution to other writers.
>
> (for discussion, see Ivanic 1993: 220)[2]

That these are not to be viewed as formal features, separate from the meanings being made, is emphasised in social approaches to grammars, most powerfully in Halliday's functional grammar (1994).

A basic premise of writers drawing on Halliday, but working within the tradition of critical linguistics is, in Kress's terms, the 'motivated nature of the sign' (1995), and hence the ideological nature of all features of discourse. One widely cited example from Hodge and Kress is the way in which the discourse feature of nominalisation obscures human agency: broadly speaking, nominalisation is when what could be expressed as a verb is expressed as a noun. An example from Hodge and Kress is the shift from 'picket' to 'picketing' in the following clauses: 'the strikers picket a factory', 'picketing curtails coal deliveries' (1993: 20–3). In the first clause, the agents of the action are visible, in the second they are not. By foregrounding the recurrence of particular textual features, in this case nominalisations, they argue that such features contribute not only to the construction of specific types of texts, but to specific ways of meaning within society.

When an individual writer makes use of the discursive features associated with a particular practice, in this case essayist literacy, she is enacting a particular way of meaning. As Ivanic states: 'A single instance of language use draws on conventions which are determined by particular values, beliefs and practices in the context of culture' (1993: 43).

This notion, that individual meaning making is regulated by existing representational resources, is informed by Foucault's more abstract discussions of the ways in which dominant social discourses, of medicine, criminality and sexuality, regulate what we as social beings come to know and to be (see for example Foucault 1972, 1973; Sheridan 1980; see also Weedon 1987, Fraser 1991; Griffiths 1995). As discussed in Chapter 2, Fairclough appropriates some of Foucault's framing notions in order to theorise the relations between specific instances of language, texts and social practices. My primary interest in this book is in the relationship between orders of discourse in relation to individual meaning making; more specifically, the relationship between a particular element of the order of discourse, essayist literacy, of a particular institution, higher education, and the meaning making of individual student-writers.

Key questions posed by those interested in student academic writing in relation to essayist conventions can be summarised as follows. To what extent are existing dominant conventions intrinsic to intellectual inquiry (as is suggested for example in Halliday's comments on early science 1993b)? To what extent do such conventions function ideologically, in relation to both the objects (what can be known) and the subjects (who can know it) of knowledge (see discussion in Chapter 2)?

These questions have been salient in North American debates, where questions relating to 'non-traditional' students' writing and meaning-making practices within HE have been the focus of attention for some time. As with Gee's critique of essayist conventions, researchers have discussed the ways in which the continued use of dominant discourse features works towards including privileged groups and ways of meaning in society and marginalising others. Some have engaged predominantly in discussions at the broader level of discourse, with little attention to specific textual features (see for example Berlin 1988; Bizzell 1990, 1991, 1992). Others have focused on links between specific social groups and specific rhetorical features. One example is the work of Villanueva (1993), who traces dominant Western ways of making meaning in academia to Plato and the privileging of plain, precise ways of Latin, as compared with Cicero, who was accused of being 'Asiatic' because of his use of specific features of discourse, for example, amplification. Villanueva identifies this particular feature with the English and Spanish used currently by Puerto Ricans: an example he gives of amplification in current written Spanish, and one not appreciated in the academy, is the use of increasingly more ornate sentences in constructing an argument (1993: 85).

Feminist critiques of dominant ways of meaning within academia focus on the prominence of logocentrism at the expense of personal connection and affective accounts of experience (Flynn 1988; Nye 1990; Campbell 1992). Further criticisms include the dominant discursive practice of what Frey calls 'the adversary method' (Frey 1990). By this she means the practice of attacking and criticising other scholars' work in order to advance the author's own position. She foregrounds this as the dominant practice within the journal of the Modern Language Association, based on an analysis of articles published between 1977 and 1985. This echoes Stanley and Wise's criticism of the 'uncharitable academic three-step' prevalent in academic journals (1990: 46; see also discussions in Elbow 1991). A further and more fundamental critique of essayist literacy as a particular practice-resource is that it works within a binary framework central to Western rationality, privileging one subsystem of binaries over the 'others': logic over emotion; academic truth (published theory and research) over personal experience; linearity over circularity; explicitness (a form of) over evocation; closing down of possible meanings rather than open-endedness; certainty over uncertainty; formality over informality; competitiveness over collaboration (for further discussion of binary and modernism within the context of literacy, see Davies 1997). I return to discuss this binary frame of essayist literacy in Chapter 5.

Texts and their producers

The emphasis in many of the works mentioned above is on elucidating the nature of essayist literacy as a representational resource, through linguistic and discourse-focused analysis. Whilst important for signalling connections between discourse features and possibilities for meaning making, this approach is problematic to the extent that it privileges the analyst's position over and above that of the producer of the text; that is, the analyst as expert decides which features of text are particularly significant or worth highlighting, without necessarily concerning him/herself with the perspective of individual producers of texts at specific moments in time.

This expert stance is mitigated in some studies where there is an attempt to draw closely on the perspective of the producer, when problematising features of the text. Lu (1987) has explored both her own experience as a Chinese-American woman in moving through different discourses, signalling the importance of particular wordings[3] in specific acts of meaning making in the home and at school. In her practice as a writing teacher, she has drawn attention to the importance of exploring producers' perspectives on the use of particular wordings in writing academic texts (1994). A similar approach is adopted in the work of Ivanic, who, through discourse-based discussions with student-writers, has been able to foreground their feelings and perspectives of particular lexicogrammatical features (words and grammar) in relation to both their desires in writing and the constraints they experience. Thus, for example, Ivanic and Simpson (1992), have explored the different types of authorial presence (see Chapter 2) in texts by analysing a number of linguistic features, such as personal pronouns (for example, 'my', 'your') and the length of sentences. Clark has also foregrounded student-writers' perspectives on their use of specific discourse features. In her teaching, she has problematised the use of certain dominant features – for example, nominalisations, hedging,[4] use of the first-person pronoun ('I') – in order to make visible dominant ways of meaning and to encourage student-writers to explore possible alternatives (see Clark and others 1990).

In my research with student-writers, my aim has been to explore those conventions of essayist literacy practice which were identified as significant, in large part, by the student-writers. A key theme across talk about their meaning making was the tension between what the student-writers felt they wanted to say and what they felt they were allowed to say in their academic writing. The rest of this chapter focuses on this tension, drawing on the heuristic introduced in Chapter 2, where the questions of what you can(not) say, how you can(not) say it and who you can(not) be are located within the contexts of situation and culture, as mediated by tutor–student addressivity.

In the following section, I map specific instances of regulation, drawn from student-writers' texts and extracts from transcribed discussions around their texts, against this heuristic, in order to illustrate the nature of regulation. In the subsequent section, I present fragments of stories about individual students' meaning making in writing, which foreground the tensions between the kind of social identity that essayist literacy privileges, and the student-writers' sense of identities.

The regulation of student authoring

By analysing extracts from student-writers' texts and their talk about their texts, we can glimpse the ways in which essayist literacy, as enacted in the institution of HE, works in relation to individual meaning making.

What you are (not) allowed to say

Extracts from texts	*Talk about texts*
1 There has been a large increase in couples living together without being married. In 1989, one in ten couples were cohabiting (General Household Survey 1989). There are many reasons for this. Some cannot marry because one partner is not divorced, some do not want the financial responsibilities which come with marriage and others live together as a sort of 'trial' marriage.	1 Bridget, in talking about this draft, comments on what she thinks tutors are looking for: B: They just want to know that we understand what they're trying to teach us. They're not interested in what we think about it [laughs] . . . they want to know that we've understood.
2 I can actually say that I did slip through the system and am unable to identify any support system which has been successfully supporting the bilingualism of minority language speakers, such as myself, during those years.	2 This section disappeared in the final draft. *T* asks Nadia why. N: X [tutor] says you shouldn't say that T: Why not? N: He says you don't want to offend anybody.

T: So who are you likely to offend?
N: The education officers or the education . . .
T: Who's going to read this?
N: Just you and X and the moderator.
T: So who are you going to offend?
N: The education system.

3 I am not a monolingual because I speak two distinctive codes (English and Creole) and I'm not recognised as bilingual by certain linguists, psycholinguists, and educationalists.

3 *M:* I feel there are things you can say and things that you cannot . . .
T: Like?
M: [Laughs] like those white people, what I'd like to say would be out of context.

Mary said she had found writing about Creole, particularly reading about white views on Creole, really hard going. I asked whether she couldn't include some of her anger in the essay.

M: It's too big. When that feeling comes to you, it's like, you really want to, you know [lowers voice], bring it out. But the way you bring it out probably is not nice. Not swearing, I wouldn't swear. ——— It's just that when I read certain things ——— I thought what the heck with these people. And I thought, I'm only caught up in it, following the rubbish. That's what I started to think. I think that even now. What am I going there for? I just don't want the employment centre to be harassing me for a job. I'm not going to work for £45 a week. I'd rather go and do this.

In the first of the above extracts, Bridget, writing for a Social Work course, expresses the view that the institutional expectation of her meaning making is knowledge telling. It is not surprising, therefore, that in her texts she works at repeating what she feels her tutors want to hear and excludes her own views and thoughts (see also the gendered dimension of *running to everyone's demands* in Chapter 5).

However, even when it seems that student-writers are being encouraged to go beyond a transmission model of learning and to claim authorship in their writing, certain views may be being excluded. Examples 2 and 3 are from a Language Studies course where, in written guidelines around the writing of these essays, several of which focus on bilingualism and education, students were encouraged to draw on their personal and educational experience, as students and workers, as well as on published theory and research. Yet it is clear from their accounts that they feel severely constrained about what they can say about their perspectives on their experience of bilingualism, schooling and racism. How their voices are regulated clearly varies in the examples. Example 2 shows direct tutor control at the level of context of situation. Nadia had planned to include a comment on her personal experience, which had emerged during a talk-aloud session.[5] But she edited this out on direction from a tutor.

Such explicit and direct control is probably more unusual than indirect forms of control and highlights not only the power relationship between tutor-reader/assessor and student-writer, but points to the significance of different tutors' status within the institution. In example 2, it is a Black tutor who advises against what he perceives to be 'rocking the boat', reflecting perhaps his own sense of vulnerability within a white institution.

Example 3 is more representative of the way in which what can be said in the institution is regulated. Example 3 arose out of me asking how Mary felt about what she had written. Whilst her written text does not reflect her frustration and anger around experts' views on Creole, her spoken comments indicate that not being allowed to say what she wants to raises serious questions for her, about whether she should be involved in a course in an academic institution. Her comments also illustrate the material risks involved in saying what she wants to say and potentially annoying those in power: given that her current life choices are between unemployment and higher education, taking the risk of losing her preferred option is too great.

How you are (not) allowed to say it

Extracts from texts	*Extracts from taped discussions on students' texts*
4 The media reflects what society thinks as a whole, or just reflects the hierarchy ideas. Women are portrayed in the media as being total airheads.	4 *T* reads, emphasising 'airheads'. *R:* [laughs] Can you not use that? *T:* Well, what do you think? *R:* No you can't. *T:* Why not? *R:* Because it's slang. *T:* It was good to see it in a way, but in terms of an academic essay, it probably wouldn't be looked on too well. *R:* I know. *T:* So, can you think of another word, or words instead of that?

R: Er, in a derogatory way. But I don't like using these words 'cause it sounds . . .

T: It sounds what?

R: It sounds as if it's been copied off somewhere . . . It doesn't sound like my work.

5 Although there are various definitions of bilingualism which focus on four areas of linguistic ability, I *can't* really find one that describes the situation for me as a Creole/English speaker – *I'm* not recognised as bilingual.

(my emphasis)

5 *T* asks about use of contracted forms: 'there's', 'can't', 'I'm'. Mary says she supposes it's not acceptable to use them.

M: It makes me sick . . . I don't think it's important at all [laughs]. But you have to do it? It's like I'm imprisoned, honest to God [laughs]. That's how I feel. And that's why a lot of people are not interested —— *I am not*. What am I saying? I know what I'm saying, but it's like, what for? Everybody knows what 'I'm not' means. It's like trying to segregate, you know, you've got like a boundary that sets, you know, you apart from other people. Why? What difference does it make as long as you get your message across . . . ? You're separating yourself from the reader or audience, whoever you're talking to, whoever. You're separating yourself . . . why? Why is that? Why do you have to do that in language?

6 When Skinner is trying to identify, that by the gradual bilingual up to on operant behaviour, by reinforcing successive approximation on animals which sustained the response.

6 Nadia, talking of the essay in general.

N: I've tried to do it to their standard, yeah.

T: Whose standard?

N: Well, you know to get a good grade to pass. I've tried to do it, yeah, but I still feel that the assignment isn't good enough. I've tried to change the whole form of writing, like . . .

T: Actually changing the words that you use?

N: Yes I've tried changing your everyday like, the way I talk to friends.

The examples above focus on the relationship between authorial presence and wordings in students' texts. Example 4, where I suggest that 'airhead' might not generally be accepted in academic texts, raises several important issues. The first relates to my role as tutor-researcher attempting to act both as 'knowledgeable insider' (Harris 1992: see Chapter 3), trying to inform students of the implicit and explicit expectations surrounding the production of student academic writing, whilst at the same time attempting to provide a space for them to reflect on what they might want to do. I will return to this in Chapter 6. In example 4, I am clearly telling Reba that an alternative wording would be preferred. Other tutors may have different views, highlighting the differences in tutor practices that students have to face, already mentioned in Chapter 3. The important point to note here is that the student-writer clearly has a readily available alternative wording, *in a derogatory way*, which could be considered appropriate in formal texts and therefore she does not 'lack vocabulary', as might be and indeed is often assumed in such instances. Reba clearly knows what vocabulary is preferred in this context. However, by listening to Reba we find out that she doesn't feel comfortable with this wording: it's not part of her existing, and currently preferred, routine ways of wording/meaning, or habitus (see Chapter 2). Her comments that such wording makes her feel as if she's copying brings a dimension to plagiarism that is not usually raised in university regulations. Of central importance to the student-writer here, and so should also be to tutors in HE, is the reason why her wording is, according to dominant conventions, inappropriate. Why can't she use 'airhead'? I return to a discussion of Reba's choice of wordings below (I discuss one instance of 'plagiarism' in Chapter 5; for discussions on plagiarism see Scollon 1995; Ashworth, Bannister, Thorne and others 1997).

Example 5 highlights another wording issue, where Mary questions the widely held view that contracted forms cannot be used in student academic writing. Her comments point to the potential force of what might be considered to be insignificant and minor conventions to separate and exclude people from academic texts and, indeed, from formal education. As somebody who feels herself to be an outsider to the world of higher education and who thus has mixed feelings about taking part, she is keenly aware of attempts to distance.

Example 6 is an example of numerous sections of text in Nadia's final draft of her first essay. Her feeling that she could not use *her* words for writing an academic essay was a central theme in our first discussions around her writing. She felt strongly that she could not use her words, which were *common* and *not good enough,* yet at the same time she was worried that if she used other words her written texts would not make sense. The section of the text shown justifies her concern, where although she has clearly attempted to draw on and use wordings relevant to the subject area, she has failed to construct a sentence which is meaningful either for the writer (she could not understand what it meant) or reader. I return to a discussion about Nadia and her words below.

Who you're (not) allowed to be

Extracts from texts	Talk about texts
7 This is because I am expressing myself in a totally different context, which is in the dimension of education.	7 *T* asks *M* how she feels about using 'I' in her writing. *M:* I think it's great. I think everybody should be allowed to say 'me' 'my'. It feels so . . . what can I say? When you're writing you should feel at one with yourself, you know all together. But you're sort of like told to come apart. I think it's very false. Do you get what I mean? I think I produce much better writing as well.
8 I myself do codeswitch and all members of my family are involved in codeswitching.	8 *A* says it is important to use 'I', 'we', 'our' and bring personal information to her writing although she feels she can only do it towards the end of an essay. *T* asks why it is important. *A:* Some people don't care, but some people might be able to write better if they could include themselves in everything. Because you're more confident in what you're writing. If you're writing something you believe in, it helps you. If you're writing to please somebody else, then a lot of things are stopped. So you might not put a lot of your ideas into your assignment.
9 This leaves women either having to take on masculine ideals and deny their femininity or it results in them feeling alienated in an unfriendly atmosphere where assumptions, agendas and issues are all male orientated.	9 I tend to write from a personal point of view [in writing outside academia]. I never see academic writing as personal. It's cold.
10 Sara's writing in general.	10 After discussing her final draft of her second essay, *S* asks *T* if she has

87

noticed anything specific to bilingual writers, commenting as follows:

> *S:* See, when I say I think of myself as English [when she writes academic essays] what I mean is that I'm trying to imagine how an English person would be writing, thinking in that sense – trying to programme myself, to make myself think as if I'm an English person writing this out. It just helps me sort of concentrate a bit more, you know, leave my Urdu aside —— if they're [tutors] asking specifically for my experiences and what I feel, then that's fine. But if not, then you have to think, you have to put yourself away from that, you know, basically write what they want you to write.

All the students with whom I was tutor-assessor as well as tutor-researcher were surprised when I told them that they could use the first person, 'I', in their writing. Mary in extract 7 was initially unconvinced that I, as tutor, had sufficient institutional power to encourage her to claim authority over her text in this way. Her concerns signal the importance of addressivity in meaning making, at the level of context of culture as well as at the level of context of situation, to which I return below. When Mary decided to use the first person, 'I' and 'me', particularly in sections of her text which were about her personal experience, she found it to be a positive experience, as shown in her comments above (see example 7). Telling students to use 'I', when as in this case they have been told and/or have learned that 'I' is inappropriate in formal writing, is the most obvious way of telling them they have a right to exist in their writing and in the academic institution, as I think Amira is saying in example 8, and is particularly important for those who feel they are outsiders. This is not to suggest that such an 'I' will be static or unitary. After the discussions above, Mary has talked about the different 'I's that she is aware of in her writing: the 'I' close to her sense of individual self, and the 'I' which signifies her self as a member of the wider Afro-Caribbean community.

Example 9 links with the view expressed by most of the student-writers who said that they would like to feel personally connected to their texts, but felt that the conventions of academic discourse do not generally allow this. The extract from Kate's text, alongside her comments, in example 9, indicate that although she is able to write successfully in an impersonal way, she would prefer to write differently: her text about women is written in the third person, 'they', 'them', and there is no visible connection between 'them' and Kate's experience as a woman (for further discussion, see Chapter 5).

Example 10 points explicitly to the importance of socio-ethnic identity in student academic writing. In the context of the institution of HE, Sara feels that there is no space for her sense of self as a Pakistani, Urdu-speaking woman. In 'inventing the university' (Bartholomae 1985; see also Chapter 2), Sara finds little space for being who she is: in informal discussions with other students and myself, she felt that in her writing she would, and could, give 'them' what they wanted. However, as I discuss below, this is not as straightforward as students sometimes may imagine.

It is important to stress, at this point, how difficult it is to get at the ways in which conventions regulate individual student meaning making in writing. Much of the 'editing' is invisible, either because it is done in drafts which tutors/researchers may not see or because meanings are edited out before they even become drafts. So, for instance, in example 2 I only knew that editing had taken place because I had copies of several of Nadia's drafts (but not necessarily all the drafts that she had written). In example 3, Mary had been talking about how difficult she was finding it to write her essay on bilingualism with specific reference to Creole. Her frustration seemed to centre for a good part of our discussion on the difficulty of dealing with so many books. It was only after about forty minutes talking that she made the comments in example 3, where she indicates a more fundamental concern about being a Black Creole speaker having to read racist accounts of Creole language in a white institution of learning. Likewise, Sara's comments on the significance of being a Pakistani-English woman writing in HE, made in example 10, were offered by her after a year of us meeting to talk about her writing.

The examples provide us with glimpses of the meaning making of individual student-writers. However, they also point to the ways in which seemingly 'neutral' prototypical conventions are ideologically motivated. The specific instances above signal regulation relating to specific social areas of experience and identity: race/ethnicity is most obviously marked by student-writers (examples 2, 3, 10); social class is often marked in an oblique way (4, 5, 6). Other dimensions emphasised are personal experience, connection and involvement with knowledge making (1, 7, 8 and 9) and power relations between reader and writer (2).

The examples discussed above allow us to begin to explore the complex ways in which regulation works and point to the significance of the notion of addressivity for exploring such regulation. Some of the instances seem to point to regulation at the level of context of situation, through the monologic type of tutor/student addressivity. An obvious instance is example 2, where the tutor explicitly directs the student-writer to edit out what he (the tutor) deems to be inappropriate content. Other instances point to regulation at the level of context of culture through the workings of a more abstract addressivity. For example, in extract 10, Sara is drawing on her voices, as language and experience, in order to respond to/invent the university, in her meaning making (see Chapter 2 for discussion of voices and addressivity).

In the rest of this chapter, I continue to explore the tensions surrounding student-writers' participation in essayist literacy, focusing in particular on the tensions between language, regulation and identity. The following fragments of stories from four student-writers – Nadia, Mary, Reba and Sara – illustrate what's at stake for student-writers as they sit down to their writing in academia.

Regulation, language, identity

Nadia: 'New words bring a little tingle in my ear'

As stated above, Nadia's overriding concern throughout our discussions was that her own words were *common* and *not good enough* for using in her academic writing. She thus attempted to avoid *her words* with the result that she often produced confused written text, as illustrated in example 6 and as further exemplified below.

Text	Talk about text
Once this had been repeated several times, the child will instantly know what he or she has done *in order that the adult has said no.* (my emphasis)	*T* asks *N* what the 'in order that . . . ' means.
	N: I'm quite shocked! I don't know what I've wrote.
	T re-reads aloud complete sentence.
	N: That means that the adult has said no, so the child, 'cause it's repeated 'no' several times before, the child instantly knows 'no' and knows it's not supposed to do it.
	T reads aloud section 'in order to . . . '
	N: Because the adult said 'no'. So the child knows that [hesitant]
	T: Yeah, go on.
	N: So the child knows that it's done wrong because the adult has said so.
	T: Does that make sense now?
	N: Yeah it . . . I'm quite shocked actually [laughs].
	T asks where 'in order to' came from.
	N: Because I think I saw it so many times, when it's first written it sounds brilliant! [laughs]

Nadia works at imagining the type of words which will be to *their standard*, 'their' referring here to a non-specific dominant culture of HE as addressee. However, in attempting to use what she imagines to be appropriate language rather than drawing on what she views as her own language, Nadia is often worried that her text will not make sense. In the example above, Nadia's talk illustrates how she has avoided using the more obvious (common?) wording, 'because', in her attempt to sound more academic and, in so doing, produces confusing text.

Although I have emphasised the way in which Nadia feels obliged to avoid her own words and use 'new' words, her relationship with new wordings is not (always) negative. On one occasion, talking of 'new' words, she states: *They sound good. I don't know* [laughs], *they bring a little tingle in my ear, yeah. Some words sound really, really nice and I like them.* Nadia here points to a physical enjoyment of new words. She feels excited about using these words as is indicated by her re-telling here of an event from the previous night.

N: I [laughs] used a word on Reba last night.
T: What word was that? It wasn't subtract*
N: [No. We were talking about where to meet. I says I'll probably be in Boots. And she says well don't be late because I've got to be at 4 o'clock with Theresa. I says 'I'll take it into consideration' [laughs]. She says, 'Nadia, the way you talk', and she starts laughing.
T: So is that a new word, then, consideration?
N: I just made that one up. I just make things up. I don't know, I just pick things and I just use it, words that I like, I'll use them yeah. Reba's noticed it in the lessons as well.
T: What does she say?
N: She says you try and use words in the lessons. I says, 'Do they sound daft?' 'No', she says, 'It's as if you're aware of these words, so that's why you're using them.' So I just think, oh all right.

   * subtractive – a word that Nadia had been trying out in a class discussion on bilingualism

This episode illustrates two points about using language: firstly, that 'wordings' is closer to what student-writers mean when, like Nadia here, they talk about *words* or the *big words* you're expected to use in academic writing. That is, they are not necessarily referring to single words, but to phrases, clauses and sentences; secondly, that they want opportunities to try out wordings on a real and trustworthy addressee, usually absent in essayist literacy practice, and, in so doing, to try out not just saying, but being somebody else.

Following on from her comments above, I later asked Nadia why she might feel daft about using *take into consideration*:

N: 'Cause I just thought I needed somebody else, don't know. I can hear what I'm saying but I can't get the other person's point of view. I asked Reba, yeah, someone close to me, someone I know, who's not going to laugh or say 'ha ha' or take the mick . . .

T: Do you think by using those words it sort of changes you?

N: Yeah.

T: How?

N: [laughs] I think it puts me up a bit.

T: In what way up a bit?

N: You know, like you've got job prospects, I mean I know I'm only an UMES [Unified Multicultural Education Service] staff but I think it puts me the same level as a teacher, a degree level, you know, got a degree and *entitled to use* those words.

(my emphasis)

Nadia's physical enjoyment and excitement in using new words is bound up with the opportunity they seem to offer for a change in her social status, as is indicated in her wording *entitled to use those words*. In a more instrumental mode in example 6 (p. 85) she suggests that she needs new words to get better marks in her essays. These combined potential benefits resulting from her use of new words stand in contrast to the negative status of her own words, which she attempts to avoid. Whilst she clearly enjoys and desires new words, I would suggest that her subtractive stance towards the use of her own wordings denies her the possibility of authorial presence and works against Nadia producing meaningful text on many occasions.[6] This adversely affects her chances of success in her courses of study which, in turn, may prevent her from attaining the social status she desires.

Mary: 'I don't want no fancy nonsense. But I do want words'

Mary expresses the view that she wants new words for her meaning making, but

I don't want no fancy nonsense. But I do want words, I do want to improve. Course I do. I *need* it to say what I want to say. 'Cause what I've got to say needs to be expressed *better*. And I think at the moment, with the vocabulary that I've got, it's not *that bad*. But it doesn't, I miss out a lot of things 'cause sometimes when you find a better word you can say more things in that one word, whereas when you *go down lower the vocabulary*, it means very few sometimes. You know what I mean?

(my emphasis)

Like Nadia, Mary wants new words. But there are significant differences between the two student-writers. Nadia tends to focus on the higher social

Mary

Mary is a 23-year-old Black working-class student. During the first year of our talking about her writing, she was studying a Language Studies course and also working as a part-time support teacher in a primary school.

Mary was brought up in a household where predominantly Creole was spoken – by mother, grandparents, uncles and aunts. She feels very positive about this experience and continues to read and write poetry in Creole. Her mother also taught her to read in English at home. Mary remembers feeling very bored for the first two years at school:

> I think school slowed me down. Because they weren't pushing me. The level of . . . look, what I knew before I went into school, it wasn't developed or advanced. It was, like, they kept me at a certain pace with some other kids who didn't know how to read or write.

She remembers enjoying school between the ages of 7 and 11, when she felt she gained confidence and was successful. At secondary school things changed:

> I remember being quite good at English at school, in the junior school, but as I got to secondary, that's when things went right to rock bottom. I were put in the low set for everything —— so I thought, forget it.

She left school with two GCSE A–C passes, in English language and Art. She went to a further education college to re-sit her exams but did little: she was unable to settle to studying, more concerned with finding paid work in order to contribute financially at home. The following year she began two A level courses – English Language and Psychology. During this period, Mary began to think about the possibility of going to university. A key influence was her mum's decision to do an Access course.

> It [university] could be a place for me. I used, I always thought I was really stupid. I thought I can't do this, I can't do that, I can't, can't, can't. But then I thought well my mum can do it.

Mary was anxious about having to use standard English: although Creole *keeps her alive* she had a feeling that her standard English might have been better if she had not been brought up using two 'non-standard' languages, Creole and Yorkshire English. Moreover, the English A level tutor's obscure criticisms of her writing were strong in her mind and had left her with a general concern about her grammar, although she did not know what exactly this meant.

She had a general sense of not being able to express herself in her writing, and said she had *deep concerns* about writing at university: *I can write pretty reasonable, but I have to really, really think. It's like something that's, disembodied. It's not even me, it's like a totally different dimension altogether* [laughs].

status she feels the use of new words gives her and takes a subtractive approach towards her own words. Mary too shares Nadia's perspective, that particular wordings have a lower status, as is indicated by the wordings in italics in the extract. But, in general, Mary takes what seems to be an additive approach to choices about wordings. That is, she says she will use new words as well as her words, if she feels they enable her meaning making.

But this meaning making does not take place in a vacuum. Mary's decisions about using particular words are powerfully influenced by how close or distant she feels particular wordings are to her sense of social identity; that is, what she wants to say and how she wants to say (it) are bound up with who she wants to be in HE. The extract below shows an instance of Mary deciding to use a new word – *reinterpreted* – which had emerged during our discussion of a section of her text.

Extract from text	Talk about text
Writing about Black children being sent to schools for the 'educationally subnormal'.	*T* asks *M* to explain how she's using Cummins' ideas.
Here the interpretation of Cummins' two concepts (CALP) and (BICS) are anticipated in the opposite direction.	*M:* Well Cummins' concept of surface fluency could be sort of applied to Creolised speech by West Indian children. When any person in education hears them, it gives them the impression, because of the nature of the language and its structure, it'll give the impression that this child's incapable of academic work. But sometimes people who speak Creole can read English and understand it quite well.
	T: I think you've got to say something like Cummins' concept of surface fluency has got to be reinterpreted
	M: I never knew that such a word existed, 'reinterpreted'.
	T: What other word would you put?
	M: I don't know. I don't think there's anything wrong with it. I think it's all right. I think it saves a lot of time. Yeah, 'cause I didn't know what word to use. I was thinking I've got this idea and I can't say it.

Mary uses *reinterpreted* in her final draft. Her decision to use this new word contrasts strongly with her rejection of another word she had briefly considered using in another section of her text: *prerequisite*. She sees this word as *fancy*, as not enabling her meaning making:

94

Because prerequisite can be described in a lot of other ways, you see. You don't need it, it's just fancy, it's just an extra word. Reinterpreted, now, which means er being interpreted again in a different way, I can't see any other word for saying that, without having a long string of words and make it unclear.

And she clearly associates *prerequisite* with a social group which has nothing to do with her own:

> M: A sort of stereotype I would have would be people who would use words like that are real academics and people sit down and talk about 'prerequisite' [speaking in an exaggerated RP , 'posh',[7] accent: laughs] over coffee and tea [laughs]. And I just don't experience those kinds of things so why should I . . . I could be left out from my own community, why am I talking like that for?
>
> T: And you don't want to be part of that community?
>
> M: No, 'cause I don't fit in 'cause I'm Black. How can I fit in there? No way, no matter how qualified, how much qualifications, they'll still see me as black and that's it. And I don't relate to those people anyway, no, no.

Mary says she feels like that about a lot of words. She has particular concerns about how others around her who have not studied after leaving school will see her:

> They'll see me differently and I don't want them to, at all. At all. [laughs] —— Oh they'll probably say something like erm, what's she using that word to me for? They probably *do* know what it means but they think there's no need for that. It's unnecessary. It's like putting on airs and graces in a way.

She also has concerns about how she will feel about herself writing in academia:

> M: I mean, if I write like that, if I use certain words that are just unnecessary, I'm just going to feel out of it.
>
> T: Out of what? [they laugh]
>
> M: Sort of like I'm not me, you know? It's too much of a big stride.

In working at meaning making in her academic writing in HE, Mary wants words which she feels are part of her routine ways of meaning, habitus (see Chapter 2), as well as 'new words' emerging from the context of academia. A prominent criterion Mary works with, in deciding which of the new words she will use, is their potential usefulness. However, this 'usefulness' is bound up with Mary's sense of who she is and wants to be, both in relation to her community and the academic institution. Her comments in the extracts above point to a continuum of closeness and distance between particular wordings and Mary's sense of personal/social self. But, as with all the student-writers, she must also work at responding to the context of culture of HE. Thus, although Mary is perhaps the student-writer who most confidently asserts her desire to make decisions about drawing on existing and new habits of meaning, she has also to concern herself with what the abstract addressee of HE will accept. In constructing this addressee, it is important to point to the ways in which the student-writers listen out for wordings in a very real sense associated, through individuals, with particular social groups. So Mary says she often looks at sections of her texts and asks herself: 'Does that sound right? Have I heard it before? If I have heard it before, who though? Like if my uncle said it, Oh God! [laughs], but if John Major [British Prime Minister] said it last night on TV, it's okay.'

In listening out for words that fit, Mary as a Black student-writer listens specifically for white words, words spoken by powerful white people. And where she can't actually hear such voices, she has to imagine them.

> M: Sometimes when I'm writing I think how would they say it? [laughs] And I'd like be going through a few sentences before I put it down.
> T: When you say they
> M: [the whites innit?
> T: Do you think of all whites speaking the same?
> M: Similar.
> T: You don't think there's a difference in social class?
> M: Oh there is, there is. But I mean, a *particular* class, *obviously*, how would they say this?
> T: So you had to imagine that then?
> M: Yeah. *Course* I do, I have to imagine it all the time.
> T: Are you still doing that now then [towards the middle of her second year in HE]?
> M: Yeah, because it's not me is it?

Thus, whilst Mary feels strongly that she wants to take decisions about how her authorial presence – how she says things – connects with the type of authority – who she can be – in her academic texts, her decisions are powerfully influenced by the nature of her imagining of the dominant context of culture.

Connections . . .

Wordings, addressivity

Extract from an earlier draft of this chapter	*Comment by one reader on my use of the wording 'imbricated'*
This involves viewing student academic writing as a social act, imbricated in the social context in which it takes place rather than an act of autonomous and individual meaning making	*Reader:* Why are you using this word, imbricated? *Me:* I don't know. I like it . . . *Reader:* Aren't you just falling into the trap of using the sort of language that your students complain about? You know, unnecessarily complex words?

I liked this word and it felt intuitively right to use in the way I was using it. But where had I actually got this word from? It clearly wasn't a word I'd normally use. And shouldn't I work out where I'd got it from in any case, in order to decide whether I wanted to consciously use it, to own it, or not?

I thumbed through numerous articles and books to see if I could find this word but couldn't. Then one day I suddenly remembered . . . Berlin, it's from Berlin.

> Our consciousness is in large part a product of our material conditions. But our material conditions are also in part the products of our consciousness. Both consciousness and the material conditions influence each other, and they are both imbricated in social relations defined and worked out through language.
>
> (Berlin 1988: 489)

Okay. So I think that's where I got it from and I seem to have taken it up because I like what Berlin is saying here, and the way he says it. But: *Who am I writing to? And how does using this word 'imbricated' help me to talk/write to who I'm talking/writing to about what I want to say?*

Is this just about me sticking with what is accepted practice in academic writing? As to Berlin. . . . He, like other writers (most I think) who argue that dominant academic practices serve to exclude significant numbers of people from powerful knowledge-making sites, such as the university, makes no comment on his participation in maintaining such practices through his use of language. Elbow has stressed this – he gives as an example Berlin's use of the word 'epistemic':

> Berlin uses a special term, 'epistemic' – One might call it a technical term that is necessary to the content (you can't talk about penicillin without the word 'penicillin'). But (and colleagues argue with me about this) I don't think 'epistemic' really permits him to say anything he couldn't say just as well without it – using 'knowledge' and other such words. Admittedly it is the mildest of jargon these days and its use can be validly translated as follows: 'A bunch of us have been reading Foucault and talking to each other and we simply want to continue to use a word that has become central in our conversation.' But through my experience of teaching this essay [Berlin 1982] to classroom teachers (the very audience that Berlin says he wants to reach), I have seen another valid translation: 'I'm not interested in talking to people who are not already part of the conversation.'
>
> (Elbow 1991: 145)

I got rid of 'imbricated'. But of course, I've used lots of other 'academic' words . . .

Reba: 'Not being who you are really'

As with Mary, Reba's feelings about wordings and her decisions to use them or not, cannot be put into any straightforward category of, for example, formal versus informal wordings. For although in example 4 (p. 85) she chose not to use *in a derogatory way* because it didn't sound like her words, in the same text she writes the extract shown below.

Extract from text	Talk about text
Language is a powerful human tool and we must begin to ask what role it plays in maintaining existing social structures. What contribution it makes to our hierarchically ordered classist, racist and sexist societies.	Reba had just expressed her views about the use of *airhead*. T: Are these your words, 'hierarchically ordered'? R: That's okay because I couldn't find another word for it. Not what I can't think of. T: But you think 'derogatory' is not your word. What about these [hierarchically ordered]? Would you use these, say, when you're talking? R: There's no other words for hierarchy, you could say the 'ruling classes' or something but . . .

Reba

Reba is 20 years of age and from a Bangladeshi family. She is bilingual in Sylheti-Bengali and English. She describes Sylheti-Bengali as her first language: she speaks it at home most of the time, although from an early age she has spoken *bits and bobs* of English with her older brothers and sisters. She has lived in England all her life and has been through the English school system. She would like to be as competent in Bengali as she is in English, but feels she has an English accent when she speaks Bengali. She sees it as *no big thing* to be bilingual.

When Reba started school she attended a nursery where most children were speakers of Sylheti-Bengali. She can't remember much about infant school. She does remember however being called names, such as 'Paki' at junior school, insults she says she still hears at work in a multilingual primary school.

The first language she learned to read in was Arabic, in order to read the Qur'an, which she can read but cannot translate. She can't remember learning to read and write in English but knows she learned to do this at school. She also learned to read Bengali at Bengali community school. At the community school she thought of herself as a good reader but a poor writer.

She feels she did *average* at school, gaining five GCSEs. She started to study for A levels in Psychology, Sociology and English, but had to leave because of family circumstances.

In her first year of study in HE, Reba had to balance study, work – she worked in an office – and home responsibilities. At home, it was difficult to find both time and physical space for studying. Another important reason she gave for not putting in what she considered to be enough time to work on her studies was the uncertainty of her future:

> *T:* Is there anything that you can think of that would have made you put more time into writing the essays for the course?
> *R:* If I knew I was going somewhere with it. I don't know.
> *T:* You mean, like, at the end of the course?
> *R:* Yeah. Heading to something else. Like a degree or something.
> *T:* And that wasn't part of your plan?
> *R:* It was [sighs] . . . at the beginning.

Like Mary, she suggests that she uses words which are 'necessary', words which help her to say what she wants to say, rather than because they are 'better' in any way. But, like Nadia, she is conscious that particular wordings have a greater value in the context of HE and decides she may use them if it helps her to get more marks.

In later discussions, where we again consider her feelings about the wordings for the first essay, Reba comments on her feelings about *big words*:

> You know the essay that I just did, I didn't really think about it. But I've always realised that I don't use big words . . . But then I thought,

you know, what if you lose more marks, by using stuff like that
[airhead] rather than more formal words.

Unlike other student-writers who feel they have to seek out new words from
the dictionary or thesaurus, Reba expresses the view that she has always
known big words but has consciously avoided using them: 'I've always realised
that I, er, avoid words. Even if I come across a little word like "dysfunction"
or something I sort of, er, break it up into smaller words . . . Just so I don't
have to write that word.'

Using the example of *derogatory*, I asked Reba what she actually does, when
a big word like that comes into her head:

> R: No, forget that word. [Tells herself not to use it.]
> T: Why?
> R: Why? I don't know.
> T: Why not stick it down? What's the problem with it?
> R: 'Cause it's not something that I use in my language, the way I speak.
> T: So you feel uncomfortable with it?
> R: Yeah.
> T: If you use words like that, what does it say about you then?
> R: I don't know . . .
> T: Does it mean you're somebody different from who you are?
> R: [laughs] Yeah. Not being who you are *really*.
> T: [laughs] And who are you really then?
> R: I don't know. [They both laugh.] It's because it's not me really.
> T: What do you mean, not you?
> R: 'Cause I don't speak like that. But I can write like that.

Reba highlights the view expressed by other student-writers: that the use of
certain wordings signifies belonging to a particular social group. Like Mary,
she takes the view that she will use big words as a last resort; when her smaller,
more informal words won't help her say what she wants, then she will use
them. This is part of a wider concern about pretence in writing in academia,
of not being who you are really. Using the minimum number of new words
seems to offer the possibility of staying close to who you are, and who you want
to be.

Reba's final comment above also indicates that, whilst it is possible to
disguise yourself in your writing, it is not in talk. This is a theme that emerges
strongly from Sara's comments, as I discuss below.

Sara: 'I disguise myself in my writing'

Pretence is a strong theme in Sara's talk, as illustrated by example 10 (p. 88),
where she points out that there is no space in academic writing for her

Sara

Sara is a 25-year-old Pakistani woman born and brought up in England. She is married and lives with her husband and three children. She is a fluent Urdu and English speaker and uses both languages on a daily basis. She feels positive about being able to speak two languages.

Before she went to school, both parents taught her and her younger sister to read the English and Urdu alphabets. Her mother was *the storyteller* at home, telling stories in Urdu regularly, and her father read Urdu stories from books. When Sara started nursery school, she knew only a little English and felt that the teachers thought of her as stupid rather than a learner of English. She remembers feeling unhappy about explicit prohibitions of Urdu:

> I do remember a teacher saying 'Excuse me, can you speak in English please?' Why can't I speak my own language? It was playtime. I felt that the teachers felt maybe we were talking about them and saying bad things about them.

However, Sara did well at school, achieving six O levels. She was particularly successful in the sciences and was encouraged both by the science teachers and her parents, both of whom had degrees from Pakistan, to continue towards A levels and university. But she left school and went on a YTS (Youth Training Scheme) in hairdressing.

Although university had been presented to Sara – both by teachers and parents as a real possibility – it still seemed distant:

> S: I think I thought, yeah I can do that, and others thought, yeah she can do that. But the thought of going to university, I thought, am I capable of going there? Do I deserve going there even?
> T: Why wouldn't you deserve to go there?
> S: I don't know . . . I just think because I'm . . . because I'm not English I suppose, because I'm a foreigner, you know. I feel as if I'm not on the same level as an English person.

While on the YTS course, Sara realised she had more qualifications than anybody else and that she could do *better than this*. She did a BTEC diploma in business and finance, achieving a distinction. At this point she felt she had to make a choice between marrying her fiancé who lived in Pakistan, and having a career. She chose to get married and moved to Pakistan for two years where she had two children. When they returned to England she did voluntary work in playgroups, working with young bilingual children. During this period, she decided she wanted a career. She began working full-time as a bilingual support teacher in a primary school and decided to study a level 1 higher education course, Language Studies, as a first step towards becoming a qualified teacher.

sense of self as Pakistani. Such a lack of space demands that she disguise herself as English (only). She feels this to be necessary, even in a specific context of situation where there was encouragement by tutors for her to include her perspective as a Black bilingual woman, even though she states that she will include her experiences if asked to do so. Yet Sara's meaning making in writing seems to be more powerfully shaped by the dominant context of culture in Britain, and to which she must respond. In this context of culture, where what is valued is being white and English, she decides she has to put away her Pakistani self and *give them what they want*. Here we are talking in general terms about her second essay on childhood bilingualism:

T: So is this your English point of view?

S: No it's not, but it's like, I don't know, it's like thinking, it's not an English point of view but I'm thinking well, I'm pretending that. It's difficult to explain, I can't explain it.

T: It's hugely difficult.

S: But it's two different identities. I'm writing something that they might want to hear, might be curious about. If I was this person writing this out, then what kind of questions would come into my mind, if I was this English person and if I was a Pakistani person, what kind of questions would that type of person be asking. So it's like two different views really.

[Interruption]

T: There's a limit to how much you can say what you really think.

S: That's it, without it affecting your life. Obviously if they didn't agree with it, they'd say 'I'm not going to let her have that, she's going to get marked down for that.' People have their own views, don't they, obviously.

T: But is that specifically to do with, I mean talking about these two people, are you specifically worried about the Pakistani side of you

S: [coming out, yeah

T: Coming out?

S: Yeah, the strong views that you have of being a Muslim or whether it's about your language or your cultures and how you feel about how people treat you. I mean that can come out in your writing and you have to be really careful about that.

T: So you feel you've got to keep that out of it?

S: Yeah. And if you don't, you can get into trouble.

However, students may not guess accurately what specific tutors and departments want. Consider the extract from Sara's text below which, through our talk, I discovered she had considered editing out.

The teachers only understood the importance of bilingualism when their monolingualism failed, after which they had to revert to asking a child for help in translation.

I said I liked how Sara had expressed this idea. Sara made no immediate comment but returned to consider this extract some time later in our discussion:

S: I was a bit worried about putting that in actually.
T: Which bit?
S: You know, the teachers' bit, about them failing.
T: Why?
S: I thought it might be a bit too strong, a bit too pushy, you know, I thought 'oh God, I hope I don't get marked down for that'. I was a bit . . . but I thought, oh I'll put it in anyway. Because I knew you were going to have a look at it before I hand it in.

Here Sara is drawing on personal experience inside and outside formal learning institutions, as both pupil and worker, to make decisions about what she should include in her essay. It becomes clear from other discussions that she feels she must not upset 'them', that is, the powers that be and, where necessary, in order to get her degree in the future, will say what 'they' want her to say rather than what she wants to say. In this instance, it is reasonable to suggest that in faculties of education and language, her statement would not be seen as a threat or too *pushy*. However, she, as do all students, draws on her experience to construct her addressee and, perhaps by linking it to her current role as bilingual teacher in a school, where she knows that such a statement would be extremely controversial if made in the class or staff-room, assumes that this is also the case in the context of HE.

The decision that Sara took in including the extract above involved risk taking on two levels: firstly, the more obvious risk in relation to tutor assessment; secondly, the more profound personal risk of letting 'them' know who she really is and consequently of how they might construct her (as a pushy Pakistani woman? See Chapter 6 for considerations of gender).

Sara, echoing comments made by Reba above, also expresses the view that it is more difficult to disguise herself in talk than in writing. In the last section of the extract above, and at other points in our talk, she expresses concern about tutorials and seminars:

I disguise myself in my writing but when I'm speaking, I might put my foot in it [laughs] and say something that they might disagree with. And later on when they see me, or marking papers, then *anything* can happen.

She is afraid that in face-to-face situations her views will slip out, whereas it's easier to control potentially unwanted views in writing. This didn't mean, in Sara's view, that by playing the game in order to succeed, she was compromising her beliefs and identity:

> But they're not changing me, are they? 'Cause I've got my own views.

Sara's comments here point to the importance of disguise for being able to participate within HE: it allows her to preserve her own views and sense of identity, echoing Mary's comments on 'imagining', whilst still participating in HE. This view connects with the significance attached to masks/disguise by many Black writers (see for discussion, Anzaldua 1990).

> Hemos tenido que cambiar caras como el cambio de color en el cameleon- cuando los peligros son muchos y las opciones pocas.
> (We have had to change our faces, like the chameleon changes colour, when the dangers are many and the options are few.)
> (Rosario Castellanos in Anzaldua 1990: xv)

If disguise in writing is possible, it may mean that student-writers can survive and succeed in the dominant culture of HE without having to lose their own sense of selves. But there are two, at least, important questions to raise. Firstly, to what extent is disguise possible, given the difficulties both writers and readers face in controlling the voices they draw on? Secondly, what is at stake for both the individual and institution with such practices of disguise? The individual has to struggle to edit out her views and self; the institution loses potentially new meanings and new identities.

In terms of Sara's individual struggle, it seems that the need to disguise may have been too heavy a burden; although she was successful in her first year of study, she decided to leave HE because she felt there was little space for her and her interests.

Conclusion

The conventions of essayist literacy practice-resource regulate student-writers' meaning making in a complex way. Although direct control of content is an aspect of individual students' experience (the tutor tells student what s/he can (not) say), indirect regulation is more common, manifesting itself in the examples discussed in two ways. The most obvious form of indirect regulation over content occurs at the level of context of situation, through tutor comments on what might be considered to be relatively unproblematic conventions surrounding acceptable features in academic writing, for example contractions such as 'I'm', 'it's'. If we listen to student-writers, we learn how such apparently insignificant and seemingly 'neutral' prototypical conventions may marginalise writers and readers, and ensure that only a particular type of writer–reader relationship is maintained in academia.

Specific instances of regulation discussed in this book signal their ideological nature: student-writers indicate the ways in which particular kinds of identity, notably relating to 'race'/ethnicity and social class, are excluded. Other dimensions emphasised are personal experience, connection and involvement with knowledge making and power relations between reader and writer. I return to the potentially gendered nature of these dimensions in Chapter 5.

The second form of indirect regulation of student writing relates more broadly to the context of culture of higher education, through the more abstract workings of addressivity (see Chapter 2). Given the denial of real participants in writing pedagogy and essayist literacy, signalled in both this and the previous chapter, 'invention' rather than negotiation is central to meaning making in student writing and is necessarily a complex activity. In 'inventing' the institutional voices, the student-writers draw on the voices they bring as language and experience from the many socio-cultural domains of their lives. An example discussed in this chapter is that the student-writers, in inventing the university, draw on their previous and current personal and professional experience in education in order to establish what author-ities within the institution want to hear. The more abstract addressee student-writers work with is sometimes named as 'the university' but on many occasions the student-writers work with a notion of 'they', which seems to refer not only to the dominant context of culture of HE, but to British society more generally.

All the student-writers point to problems in drawing on their habits of meaning within the institutional context of HE, in relation to wordings, content and the nature of the task. Nadia, Reba, Mary and Sara in particular point to the problematic relationship between their habits of meaning, their sense of self and the institutional context. Nadia feels that by using more formal wordings she acquires a new social status. Yet a problem she faces, in attempting to use wordings which are not her own, is that she produces meaningless text which reinforces the tutor-reader's view that her work is not of an appropriate standard and thus, as one tutor told Nadia, she should not be at university. Whilst Mary likes and wants some new words, both she and Sara point to the enforced need to imagine themselves and their words as white in order to disguise their selves, their Black, bilingual selves, in their academic writing. Both feel that the risk of presenting their selves in their writing is too great, both in terms of tutor marks and of how they will be viewed. Reba, too, is concerned about having to pretend to be somebody she isn't in her academic writing, although she doesn't say how or why.

Feelings about regulation vary according to individual student-writers and specific moments in time. Mary and Sara express strong feelings of anger, whereas Bridget never does. Bridget's comments seem to indicate an acceptance of education as transmission: that is, learning is learning what someone tells you counts as acceptable knowledge. This parallels Nadia's concern to use institutionally appropriate words rather than her *common words*, a view with which many tutors might agree. Mary expresses anger at the type of writer she is supposed to be and expresses a strong desire for a different type of relationship between writer and reader. In her talk about her texts, Mary challenges the notion that, for example, wordings marked as informal make what is being said any less significant. She points instead to the way in which conventions of formality contribute to particular types of relationships between the writer and her text, and the writer and potential readers. Sara expresses the desire for a different talking relationship between student-writer and tutor-reader around meaning making in writing and learning more generally. I continue the discussion of student-writers' desires in writing in HE in the next chapter.

Notes

1 Whilst I acknowledge the significant differences across disciplinary discourse practices, my emphasis here is on essayist literacy as an overarching literacy practice in academia. See discussion in Chapter 2.

2 See Ivanic 1993 for full discussion and examples of these features. For those readers unfamiliar with these categories, they can be defined, broadly, as follows: high lexical density = large number of vocabulary items per clause; relational clause = clause with verb of being – for example, be, seem; mental clause = clause with verb of thinking, believing; material process clause = clause with verb of action; nominal style = clause led with nouns rather than verbs, for example, 'the scientific treatment of music', rather than 'the Greeks treated music scientifically'; carrier nouns = noun as subject in relational verb clauses, for example, 'the argument is complex'.

3 I use 'wordings' to refer to single words, as well as phrases and sentences.

4 An example of hedging is, 'This *may be* important', instead of 'This *is* important'.

5 Whilst none of the students wanted to engage in talk/think-aloud sessions as part of the research project, several decided that they wanted to talk aloud to themselves during their composing. This was the case with Nadia who, in this instance, taped herself talking aloud while writing a draft and gave me the tape to listen to.

6 I'm using the notions of subtractive/additive from writings on bilingualism. See Lambert 1977 for use of these terms.

7 This exaggerated form of Received Pronunciation (RP) – that is, a pronunciation closer to that of the aristocracy than to current BBC pronunciation – is referred to as 'marked RP' by Honey 1997.

5

ESSAYIST LITERACY, GENDER AND DESIRE

Introduction

Historically, higher education has been the domain of a privileged, predominantly white, male elite, both in terms of participation and the construction and privileging of its representational resources. In terms of participation, it was only at the middle of the nineteenth century that women were allowed entry to higher education, and more recently still that men and women from working-class and Black groups have begun to gain access (see discussions in Stiver Lie and O'Leary 1990; Brooks 1997: Weiner 1998). Just as particular social groups have been privileged in their historic access to higher education, particular ways of meaning have been privileged through the continued validation of particular representational resources. This was discussed in the previous chapter, where dominant meanings, and relationships around meanings, in essayist literacy texts were explored.

My aim in this chapter is to focus on the ways in which students from groups historically excluded negotiate their desires around access to higher education and their use of its representational resources. Foregrounding in particular the significance of gender, I draw on student-writers' accounts to signal the ways in which individual desires are contingent upon socially structured local contexts and resources: that is, what people want to do, to be and to mean is closely bound up with the possibilities and opportunities on offer in the different contexts of their daily lives.

In the first section, I illustrate the ways in which changes in local contexts facilitate shifting individual desires, including the desire to participate in formal schooling and higher education. Secondly, I explore connections between feminist critiques of essayist literacy and the student-writers' desires for meaning making. In particular, I point to the ways in which the student-writers problematise the fundamental binary framing of essayist literacy.

Desires for participation in HE

The question 'Who am I?' cannot be understood apart from the question, 'What am I allowed to do?' And the question 'What am I allowed to do?' cannot be understood apart from material conditions that structure opportunities for the realization of desires.

(Norton 2000: 8)

Gaining access

Connections . . .

Teacher: [uninterested] And what do you want to do then when you leave school?

Me: [nervous] Er, I thought about studying Spanish and French at university

Teacher: University? Are you sure?

Me: Well I've got seven O levels.

Teacher: Have you [surprised]? Let's have a look. Hmmm yes, I see [unconvinced]. Okay. So have you thought about which university?

Me: Er, Leeds.

Teacher: Why Leeds?

Me: Er, I support Leeds United [popular football team in the north of England].

Teacher: [perplexed] Why? Have you got relatives there or something?

Me: [perplexed] No. I just support Leeds United.

Making football, rather than academic study, the main reason for going to university, allowed me to convince myself that I had a right to go there. After all, I was going for the football, wasn't I? Going to football matches was also a way of maintaining some kind of connection with roots, a way of establishing allegiances with working-class students (then, not now) through talk about football and, probably more importantly, by providing a safe place to go on a Saturday afternoon. Safe from the middle-class world of academia.

Whilst no formal prohibition exists in the UK against the participation of particular social groups in higher education, access to this privileged institution continues to be severely restricted. How such a restriction operates is a complex question but it is powerfully linked to structural inequalities enacted at a number of interrelated social sites. These are, not least, the family, local community and institutions of formal schooling, which are marked in terms of gender, race and social class as illustrated in the women's accounts that follow.

Bridget, a 45-year-old student, points out that, during a time when working-class children had little expectation of going on to higher education, girls had even less so. In her words, *girls just weren't pushed to go to university.* Neither she nor her family ever had any expectation of her going into HE.

From a different cultural background and a different moment in time, Reba, a 21-year-old student, experienced similar constraints. She left school before completing A levels (see Appendix 2) because of the demands placed on her by her family to support them.

As well as pointing to a lack of expectation from immediate and significant others that they would ever go into higher education, several of the women signal their own desires as reasons why they lost interest in formal schooling. Diane says: *I thought about meeting pop stars and things like that . . . fantasies about meeting Michael Jackson.*

In a similar vein, Amira and Nadia during their teen years were more preoccupied with their future marriages rather than doing well at school. Amira says she was a *nut* at school and that *I wasn't thinking about doing anything. I was thinking about getting married.*

The 'dream of salvation through romance' (Rockhill 1994: 235), evident in the women students' comments was, for some of the young women, like Amira and Nadia, not only tied into Western notions of romantic love but also linked with notions of duty to themselves and their families. For some women, to preoccupy themselves with marriage not only signals a desired participation in romance but a fulfilment of the ideals of Islamic daughterly duty.

Sara, at 15, was happy to accept the future arranged marriage settled by her parents. She was also doing well at school. However, she channelled her energies, not so much into thoughts about romance/marriage but into an associated traditionally defined feminine space: a concern with women and beauty (see discussion in Christian-Smith 1990 of beautification as one of the principal codes of romantic discourse). This, for Sara, stood in marked opposition to Science, at which Sara excelled, but which she felt compelled to reject:

> I just felt, no, I can't [do sciences in the future]. Chemistry is hard. No I can't do that. There were a lot of boys did feel that, as if, if I did science, I wouldn't be able to go all the way. Even though I got the highest mark, B, which is more than all the boys got.

Looking back on her schooling some ten years later, Sara reflects on her teenage decisions:

In the middle [of secondary school] I just lost my mind, if you like. I don't know. I just saw the glamour business, you know, about beauty therapy and all that and I was good with my hands. I liked making things, making people up. But then I actually went into the hairdressing business.

Needless to say, none of Sara's less successful male peer group considered going into beauty therapy or hairdressing.

> *Connections . . .*
>
> I remember, when I was about 13, suddenly it seemed, realising that I was no good at Maths. For the next few years I had constant battles with my Maths teacher who tried to convince me that I was good at Maths, but I wouldn't believe her. I begged to be put into a lower set and she refused. She even organised a meeting with my mum where she told her what she'd been telling me for months. I never believed her.

Just as the women's desires and choices for leaving formal schooling were powerfully gendered, as well as classed, so too were their reasons for returning. Thus whilst Bridget, as a working-class girl, never thought about herself going into HE, as an older woman she decided to return to formal education because her husband became ill and couldn't work. Likewise, Amira returned to education because her husband had no job and she didn't want them to struggle on a low income for the rest of their lives. She states:

I *need* to have a job, I *need* to . . . and my husband, he *wants* me to study. He says there's no point in staying at home and wasting your time. Because he regrets that he dropped out of school.

That the women-students' participation in HE hinged in many ways on the approval/permission/support of their male partners is indicated in Bridget's and Amira's accounts above of their decision to study in HE, and is further illustrated in the interrupted nature of Tara's participation in formal study. Tara lost interest at secondary school but began part-time study as an adult student. However, after separating from her husband she could not continue because she was the main child-carer. Several years later, it is the willingness of a new partner to share in child-care and work responsibilities that facilitates her return to study.

Nadia linked her more recent desire to engage in higher education with her responsibilities as a future mother. Whilst she did not study at school, preoccupied as she was with the future marriage, she explains her wish to return to formal schooling, and HE in particular, as one of duty to any future children: *And I thought, I've got to do this for myself and for the kids, so they can think mum's done this, so it gives them a bit of encouragement.* She is echoing a powerful discourse on women and education across history where education for women is justified in terms of their role as future mothers (see Wilson in Coates 1993: 29; see also the ideology of being a literate mother in Barton and Hamilton 1998: 173).

In these instances, the women describe their return to formal study mainly in terms of meeting the needs of others – to fulfil their responsibilities to partners and family – or as becoming possible because of partners' permission/support. On no occasion was a return to education or participation in HE framed in terms of a right.

Siria, reflecting back on her decision to make major changes in her life, including leaving home, refusing to get married and considering the option of further study, points to the struggle to claim the right to make her own decisions:

> when you've been quiet for so long [laughs], they always say the quiet ones are the worst [Theresa and Siria laugh], from my experience you just get *so* frustrated. 'Right, I've had enough of this. This is *not* me. I'm sure there's another side to me and I *want* to do this, I'm *sure* I can do this but I've never tried.' It gets to a stage where you either speak out or you explode and everyone gets shocked [laughs] 'cause they're not . . . they've not seen you.

'Stealing time' for study

Deciding to apply for, and then gaining access to HE, is not, of course, the end of the tensions surrounding participation in HE. Many 'non-traditional' students, women in particular, have family responsibilities when they study, caring for children and/or other family members, and are also in some form of paid employment. These combined responsibilities mean that finding time and space for study are often key concerns.

In reflecting back over her years as a student in HE, Diane states: *I always felt like I was stealing time,* echoing many comments made by the women-students during our more formal, as well as informal, discussions about their writing and study. Diane talked about getting up at 3 a.m. just to be able to write during the quiet time in her house. Sara's time for writing and studying more generally was after 10 p.m. when the children were asleep. Reba seemed to find it difficult to find any space or time to study, living as she did within an extended family in a small house. The ways in which the women snatched time reflects the material constraints experienced by working-class women throughout this century in their attempts to engage in reading and writing more generally (see Mace 1998).

111

At one level, the women's reasons for studying so late or so early in the day seem simply practical, resulting from the material conditions of their lives. However, the symbolic significance of their studying at times when such study is invisible to the rest of the household, is not to be underestimated. Using 'spare' domestic time is a way of bringing the domain of study/ HE into the domain of home, 'through the back door', in order to avoid tensions in the household. That this is necessary was evident in reactions to the women's attempts to study from male partners, friends – both male and female – and children: responses ranged from ambivalence, irritation and, on occasion, aggression in response to the women's desires for, and engagement in, study.

Diane reflecting on her experience of studying, recounts:

D: I used to get the light turned off on me.
T: Who by?
D: The kids' father when he used to be there. 'Oh no you're not doing that', and lights turned off and it was some right little nasty things like that. Like 'Come on, they're all watching television.' And I'd think, I want to go, I just want to go and study. And they'd all be calling me. 'Cause, I don't know, I suppose they were wasting their time. I suppose it was about spending time together. But every minute you get, you try and study.

Such comments raise questions about who gets to control time and who has a right to decide what counts as a legitimate use of time. Diane's reading and writing-as-studying caused tension and anger at home, and were often seen as an illegitimate use of time, in contrast to her reading of romantic novels, which was accepted. As has been discussed by Rockhill (1987, 1994) and Christian-Smith (1990), literacies which are considered to be functional, meeting basic needs, and romantic, reading heterosexual romance stories, are not seen as transgressing local structural norms. They are not seen as a bid by women to engage in another kind of life.[1]

Stealing time involves taking something from others which is their right, not yours. Therefore guilt is a common theme in the women's talk: guilt about using time on themselves, rather than with families and especially with children. Throughout her first year of study in HE, Sara felt she had little time and emotional energy to give to her children and husband. This was one of the reasons she gave for deciding to leave HE at this point.

Likewise, Diane, reflecting on her study in HE, states:

I know I used to feel guilty. I'd think gosh I should be doing this and that with the kids, I should be looking out for *their* education. I had my chance, now I should be encouraging them.

112

Her concern here, then, is about time in the immediate everyday sense but also in terms of this period of her life as compared with this period in the lives of her children.

Mary was the only woman living alone at the time of studying in HE. She was the only woman who did not complain about restrictions placed on her by other family members, in terms of time and space.

The struggles surrounding the women's participation in higher education are further indicated in the pattern of the students' involvement over a three-year period. Table 5.1 below shows that, just as the women's transition from school to higher education wasn't smooth, neither is their route through higher education. Of the ten, only three sustained continuous participation in higher education over this period; the others completed one or two years, followed by another year or two of breaks for work, childcare or having to move because of a partner's job.

The nature of the women's desires about formal/higher education are obviously not fixed, changing over longer (as in the case of Bridget and Kate) or shorter periods of time (as in the case of Amira and Nadia, for example) depending on a range of local, socially structured, circumstances. The possibility of the women fulfilling their desires to participate in HE is dependent not least on local support from family and partners and on economic circumstances. When these are less favourable, they contribute significantly to the women's decisions not to continue with their courses of study.

Whilst individual desires are bound up with the local historical and structural circumstances of the women's lives, the enactment of such desires, however socially inscribed, enables some of the women to consider making quite radical changes to their lives. Consider Nadia's shifting desires over a period of some six years. As a teenager, Nadia does not imagine herself studying in HE, and focuses her emotional energies and desires on the forthcoming arranged marriage. At this stage, she has no desire for formal learning of any kind. As a wife and future mother, formal schooling and, in particular, higher education, come within her realms of possible desires, linked as they are with Nadia's view of how such education would benefit her children. After a violent brief marriage and a protracted divorce, Nadia's overriding desire is to escape her husband, as well as family/community expectations. In this new context, HE offers up the possibility of a new life rather than a justification for an existing one. 'The dream of salvation through romance' (Rockhill 1994) becomes the dream of salvation through education.

Desires for meaning making

As well as negotiating their desires around participation in higher education, student-writers, once involved in a course of study, also have to negotiate their desires around the kinds of activities in which they are expected to

Table 5.1 Pattern of the student-writers' participation in HE over a three/four-year period

Student	Year 1	Year 2	Years 3/4
Amira	Studies higher education course. (*Language Studies*)	Pregnant. Looks after baby and works as an English instructor in community centre	Returns to higher education. (*Joins year 1 of Combined Studies degree course*)
Bridget	Studies higher education course. (*Social Work*)	Continues into year 2 of same higher education course.	Continues into year 3 of same higher education course.
Diane	Studies higher education course. (*Language Studies*)	Pregnant. Looks after baby and other children full time for two years.	Returns to higher education. (*Joins year 2 of Communication Studies degree*)
Kate	Studies higher education course. (*Women's Studies*)	Decides against continuing degree course. Domestic responsibilities. Begins a GCSE course in Medieval Studies.	Continues with domestic responsibilities. Begins foundation course (part time) in Law.
Mary	Studies higher education course. (*Language Studies*)	Continues higher education. (*Joins Combined Studies degree course*)	Continues higher education with a different course. (*Goes to university in another town in order to study Psychosocial Studies. Joins year 2*)
Nadia	Studies higher education course. (*Language Studies*)	Continues higher education. (*Begins degree in Education Studies*)	Continues higher education. (*Decides to begin another degree course, Social Work*)
Reba	Studies higher education course. (*Language Studies*)	Decides against higher education. Works as bilingual instructor in primary school.	Works as bilingual instructor in primary school.
Sara	Studies higher education course. (*Language Studies*)	Decides against continuing studies in HE. Domestic responsibilities.	Pregnant. Looks after baby and other two children. Begins correspondence course in Islamic Studies.
Siria	Studies higher education course. (*Language Studies*)	Decides against higher education. Works as bilingual instructor full time. Works as part-time youth worker.	Continues work in school and as youth worker.
Tara	Studies higher education course. (*Law*)	Continues into year 2 of Law.	Family moves because of partner's work. Has to leave course.

engage. The aim in this section is to offer a glimpse of such desires around meaning making in essayist literacy and, in particular, to make connections between student-writers' perspectives on the production of texts and existing feminist critiques of essayist literacy.

Feminist critiques of essayist literacy

As outlined in the previous chapter, a fundamental feminist critique of essayist literacy as a particular practice-resource is that it works within a binary framework, central to Western rationality, privileging one subsystem of binaries over the 'others'. Examples of these binaries are as follows: logic over emotion; academic truth (published theory and research) over personal experience; linearity over circularity; explicitness (a form of) over evocation; closing down of possible meanings rather than open-endedness; certainty over uncertainty; formality over informality; competitiveness over collaboration. There are two important points about this binary framing. Firstly, the emphasis is on constructing meaning through a lens of *either/or* – for example logic or emotion – rather than *and*, thus closing down possibilities for playing with a range of conventions in even the smallest of ways. Secondly, the pairs constituting the binary framing are not equally valued. The first in the above list of pairs is the unmarked form, the norm; the second is marked, abnormal. Thus, for example, logic is valued above emotion in essayist literacy, formality over informality, explicitness over evocation. Whilst some of these 'others', or marked forms, in academic writing are associated with social class, for example, particular informal wordings, most of them are culturally marked as feminine/ female, signalling a key way in which essayist literacy can be considered a gendered practice (for marked and unmarked pairs as masculine/feminine, see discussions in Spender 1980; Swann 1992; Lee 1996).[2]

The accounts of the women students below indicate the powerful nature of such binary conventions, as well as the ways in which individual women writers, whilst dissatisfied, work at fulfilling, and thus maintaining, them.

'There's nobody in it'

A key tension for all the student-writers was the institutional rejection – whether at the level of context of situation or culture (see Chapter 2) – of personal experience and involvement in their writing. The writers usually accepted this in constructing their texts but resisted it in their thinking about what their texts are/might be. This gap, between what their texts mean and their desires for meaning, is glimpsed in their talk around their texts.

Diane complains about having to simply *rattrap* what lecturers say, which is all she felt she had done for her essay on language and gender. The essay question was as follows: 'The analysis of interpersonal communication illustrates the pattern of power in society at large. Discuss with reference to

115

either gender or ethnic identity.' Having discussed sections of her final draft with her, I asked Diane what her essay would have been like if she hadn't had to constantly worry about what the tutors wanted.

Extracts from text	Talk about text
Research into gender and power constantly states that men control more power than women, this can be seen in the home in the work force and through language verbal and nonverbal. The speech style that women use is said to stop them from gaining power in society. Lakoff believes that 'women are systematically denied access to power, on the grounds that they are not capable of holding it as demonstrated by their linguistic behaviour along with other aspects of their behaviour' (Cameron 1990 – p223).	*D:* It would have been crap [laughs]. It wouldn't have been, er. Things like, 'I'm not sure if it's true but'. *T:* What, you'd like to be able to ask questions even if you haven't got the evidence? *D:* Or like, talk. I mean, I'm sure I haven't put anything in from my experience, have I? Of life. *T:* Not as you as a woman. *D:* Not my experience from speaking with, and feeling that I'm not heard because I'm a woman. It's just about everybody else. It's, nobody. There's *nobody* in it [laughs]. No[body]. Do you know what I'm saying? *T:* Yeah. *D:* – Like I haven't said, yeah I know men talk to women differently 'cause I'm an only girl in my family, and I've got two brothers and my dad used to talk to me oh more calmer, and he used to talk to the boys rougher and shout at them, and things like that. I haven't put that in. But that's evidence, that's facts. It's about what happened to me. *T:* But you don't think they want that? *D:* No. They probably think, 'What's happened to you?' [laughs]

Diane's comment here on there being *nobody* in her writing echoes the views of more socially privileged women students writing at a very different moment in history. At the beginning of the century, Mary Lee, a woman student-writer at Harvard in 1913 writes on how she must revise her writing in order to conform to expectations:

> I must write it over and make it flat, insipid, take out all individuality, and I can do this. For English A has taught me this one thing: to eliminate interest and to write bad ideas in good grammar, as the section man likes it written.
>
> (quoted in Campbell 1992: 470)

116

Although Diane begins by dismissing as *crap* any essay she might have written without the constraints imposed by the context of academia, she points to the ways in which she would choose to connect her meaning making in writing with her lived experience. Like Karach (1992), she feels that there is no opportunity to include, draw on and connect her lived experience to the formal knowledge-making practices of academia.

This is echoed by other women. In talking with Amira about a section of her essay on the experience of Arabic speakers – of whom she is one – I ask her about the use of 'their' versus 'our'. Just as Amira would prefer (on some occasions) to use 'our' to indicate personal involvement, Mary would prefer (on some occasions) to use informal language, such as contractions ('I'm', 'it's') and particular wordings, in order both to involve herself and her reader. She can't generally do this on her courses, as she knows it will be frowned upon (see discussion in Chapter 4). She can only imagine doing it. Mary talks about how she would like to write using informal language and hand it in to the tutor with a note, saying: *I've used informal language. I hope you don't consider it to be inappropriate. It's just that I really like using it . . .* [laughs].

Extract from text	Talk about text
A strong community has developed within the Yemeni people and there is enough support and encouragement available for Yemenis to maintain *their* language. (my emphasis)	T: Do you think it kind of changes the feeling of it, if you put 'our'? A: Yeah, definitely. T: How? A: It makes you more personal towards it. It would include you more. T: Do you like that idea or not? A: Depends on whether the lecturer penalises it. T: So it's in terms of how it will be viewed that you have to think about it, as somebody writing an essay to be marked. A: Yeah. T: If you had a free choice? A: I'd use 'our'. I think I would have used it in this. But X [tutor] says try not to include yourself so much.

Sara indicates that what she describes as 'guys' (UK, men's) writing' is more in line with institutional demands. Consequently, she consciously works at writing in this male, rather than female way:

117

S: You'd expect guys to be more dynamic, more persuasive, I don't
     know, hypothetically speaking like, and women being more sympa-
     thetic, more emotional in their writing perhaps, er . . .
T: Would you describe *your* writing as emotional?
S: I try not to be.
T: Well that's interesting, why do you try not to be?
S: The reason why I try not to be is because I know it wouldn't help my
     assignments [laughs].

That Sara found it difficult to maintain her engagement with writing, or
indeed study, which excludes personal involvement, is indicated by her
decision to leave higher education at one point. Talking about her reasons
for leaving Sara states: *I've realised that I want to find out about myself, about Islam
. . . courses don't let you do that. You have to learn what other people think. There's
no space to think about what you want.*

Kate, studying Women's Studies, is the only student-writer who feels
encouraged to include herself in her writing and to focus on herself: *That's
what I like about doing Women's Studies. If I thought I couldn't bring myself
into it, it would be an enormous handicap. And it would be very difficult keeping
it out.*

However, whilst Kate desires to include herself in her writing, permission
by her tutors does not enable her to do so, as is illustrated by extracts below

Extracts from texts	*Talk about texts*
One may argue as to the importance of women's interest in conventional politics. (my emphasis)	K: Would it be better to say 'one' may argue? You see I always worry about putting 'I'. But she [tutor] has said 'Put your own personal, you know, state where you stand personally.' So I don't see why I can't do that.
Because women have only achieved equal franchise this century, as relative newcomers to political activity there is a major problem of institutionalised sexism that faces them on entering the world of politics. That is, *they* must participate in an arena designed for and run by men. (my emphasis)	*T* asks why she used 'they', rather than the inclusive 'we': K: It's —— to do with whether you value your own opinion. So perhaps I felt safer saying that [they].
No longer are *they* prepared to be second class citizens and have their needs defined for them by men. (my emphasis)	K: If it said 'no longer are *we*', it's a very assertive statement.

118

Kate

Kate is a 48-year-old white woman from a working-class family. When we met she was about to embark on a BA in Women's Studies, after successfully completing a one-year access to higher education course. She is a mother of three children – all aged between 16 and 22 – and lives with her husband.

She trained and worked as a nurse after leaving school but she left her job after her second child was born. When her third child was born, her father became ill with Parkinson's disease and Kate spent twelve years helping her mother to care for him. Towards the end of her father's illness, Kate, feeling a need of an escape, decided to study a GCSE in music appreciation, which enabled her to share in one of her daughter's main interests. This first taste of learning after many years of caring for those around her was a significant experience:

> After that [music course] I was hooked. I knew these access courses were available. I wanted to carry on somehow. I hadn't a *clue* what I wanted to do. I knew I wanted to study, I knew I wanted to do more. But I hadn't a clue. And I still haven't really, haven't *really* made up my mind.

Kate began an Access course, the most significant aspect of which was a module on Women's Studies. Of Women's Studies, Kate says:

> It's answered an *awful* lot of questions. All my life . . . an *awful* lot of questions it's answered, Women's Studies. It's been really good. I was completely as green as grass, naive. It was like, suddenly having your eyes opened, honestly. Just amazing. And all the guilt I've felt, that's gone. A tremendous amount of guilt of not being happy, you know, of wondering why are you like this. That's all gone. It's wonderful.

Kate pursued her interest in Women's Studies into HE. However, she was unsure about being in an HE institution, feeling that she didn't fit in, mainly because of her age.

Whilst Kate lacked confidence in her ability to study, she felt she was good at writing, preferring writing in general to talking. However, she was concerned about the academic practice of writing impersonally: *I tend to write from a personal point of view. I never see academic writing as personal. It's cold.*

from her texts and her talk about the extracts. These are brief discussions about the use of personal pronouns in her texts.

When we talked about the above extracts and her comments, Kate said that although she was writing within Women's Studies where other kinds of practices were tolerated and/or encouraged, she felt she still had to write her text with the university in general in mind. Here, addressivity at the level of context of culture shapes the kind of authoring she can engage in more powerfully than addressivity at the level of context of situation (for further examples of the workings of addressivity at the level of context of culture, see Chapter 4).

'Running to everyone's demands'

As is indicated in many of the examples above, the student-writers invest considerable energy in producing texts in ways which seek to respond to actual addressees at the levels of context of situation as well as to the more abstract addressees at the level of context of culture of HE.

In talking about attempting to meet these demands, Mary comments on particular tutors on her Combined Studies degree course, indicating the significance student-writers attach to constructing specific audiences/ readers:

> One thing about John, he's a very statistical man, very hard evidence man – I think John don't like to see any creativity in writing, as simple as that. Whereas Pete, I think he's more of a romantic [laughs] – he'll like you to write about certain things. He finds it interesting, even if he don't agree, he appreciates it.

But Mary also says that it's very difficult *running to everyone's demands* and indeed that it's not possible to do so, especially on courses where the students produce a written text for a tutor only once. She feels that she can never get it quite right. Indeed, the student-writers often get it wrong. An example is given in Chapter 4, where I pointed to Sara's mistaken assumptions about how a tutor might view a particular section of her text. In similar vein, Bridget attempts to stay close to what she understands tutors to be looking for, knowledge telling, but in so doing fails to meet their implicit demands (see Chapter 4). Consider a tutor's written final comment on Bridget's essay: 'The issues that you choose to focus on are appropriate, but you *could have dug a little deeper*. There is a tendency to *assume* that there is a current belief in equality for men and women' (emphases in original).

The women writers' attempts to find out, and give, tutors what they want seems a sensible use of energy, given their sense of distance from institutional practices and the belief that what they want to do would be unacceptable. Yet such attempts are often bound to fail because, most obviously, such actions may not help them to meet the tutors' implicit demands. This is indicated in the tutor's feedback on Bridget's text above. But, more fundamentally, such attempts may fail because they represent a challenge to a key premise of essayist literacy: that is, they constitute a challenge to the essayist ideal that the written text should stand alone and, thus, that actual relationships around the text are irrelevant.

120

Thus, whilst students try to work out what tutors want, tutors routinely deny any actual relationship with students in their reading of student-writers' texts. Consider the example below where I, as tutor-assessor at this point in our talk, deny my relationship with Reba and Reba challenges my stance. The talk extract here is taken from talk aimed at getting on with the business as usual of essayist writing. I was asking her why there was no mention of her being bilingual in her essay on bilingualism.

Extracts from text	Talk about text
Many societies have populations which are ethnically diverse. In European countries, post-war economic expansion brought substantial migration of workers from developing countries. In Britain most of these migrants mostly came from former British colonies. Holding on to their language gave them a sense of cultural identity (Jeffcoate: 1982).	R: You *know* that [that she's bilingual], don't you? T: Yeah, but I might know some of this as well. R: But you know who's writing it, though. T: Right, so because I know who's writing it, am I supposed to think, well, she's bilingual, so she knows a bit about what she's talking about, and then she's read these books . . . R: Yeah.

Some of the student-writers refer to this practice as 'pretence', as illustrated by Siria's comment here:

> Right so I've got to pretend – I think what I should have probably done is to pretend. What you're telling me now, that *they* haven't read the other bits. And to introduce, 'this is why', 'cause I've sort of wrote it as if *you'd* understand why. Like, *the reader's* read the first part and *he* knows what's coming in the second part.
>
> (my emphasis)

The wordings in italics signal the difficulty that Siria is having in her attempts to locate 'the reader': she had assumed that I was the reader – hence her comment, *as if you'd understand why*. But being told by me to remind 'the reader' about what's she's saying in her text, she struggles to find this reader, as indicated by her shifting wordings: from *they*, to *you*, to *the reader*, to *he*.

That the student-writers may not know and/or may not want to write as if there were no shared space with the tutor-reader can be further illustrated in the following example. Here Mary and I are talking about a sociology essay she is writing for her sociology lecturer, on the existence of an underclass in Britain (at this stage I was talking with her as tutor-researcher, rather than tutor-assessor). I suggest she should define Marx's position on the nature of an underclass in her text. She disagrees, angrily:

M: Oh come on, Marx, Marx, that's all you hear [angry].
T: But if that's all you hear, maybe that's what they want to see as well.

Mary feels that because Marx is referred to constantly throughout her course she can assume a shared basis of knowledge with the tutor, hence misunderstanding the nature of the dominant type of addressivity in the student-writer/tutor-assessor relationship. This is exemplified in another instance (see below), where Mary dismisses the significance of a tutor's comment on the way she has used source material. Mary knows that she has drawn from the same source text as her tutor and thus assumes a shared knowledge, which, of course, the tutor does not.

Mary's text	Tutor's comment on text	Mary's comment on tutor's comment
The distribution of West Indians, Asians and Whites in the labour market is shown in table 5.2 (see page 7*) —— The distribution of black and white workers in occupation one and two is equal. Only 5% of West Indians are employers, managers or professionals compared to 13% of Asians and 19% whites.	These figures are not in Tables 5.1 or 5.2.	He *knows* what I'm talking about 'cause he [tutor] uses that book for one of our lectures. I know that what I've done is not drastically wrong. All right, I know there's no supervisors in Table 5 but it's the same, same [sighs – angry, frustrated].

Note * Relevant reference given in preceding paragraph of Mary's text.

This extract illustrates not simply an instance of a student-writer not knowing the type of writer–reader relationship privileged in essayist literacy, but rather of her being angry about this practice. She is resisting the practice of writing without actual readers in the same way that several of the student-writers resist the practice of writing as if there were no actual writers.

Writing like a good girl[3]

The way in which the student-writers preoccupy themselves with finding out what tutors want and then trying to produce this in their texts seems to be one of the more visible, although complex, gendered dimensions to student academic writing in two ways: firstly, in respect of accounts of actual women's behaviour; secondly, in respect of tutors/researchers' gendered readings of such behaviour.

The first, whereby women students' attempts to establish the tutor's demands are presented as a preoccupation with 'pleasing readers', has been signalled as a feature of women's behaviour in several research papers on student writing. Bolker for example talks of the 'Griselda syndrome' (1979), which Tedesco later glosses as

> a compulsion on the part of some women students to 'please' their audience to the point of erasing their personal voice. In such cases a paper may be technically superior but will lack the presence of the writer herself, will be devoid of a sense of ownership and exhibit a stubborn refusal to tread on ground that may be controversial or ambiguous.
>
> (Tedesco 1991: 250)

Whilst work such as Bolker's aims to describe actual women writer's behaviour, discussions by other researchers illustrate the ways in which such readings of women's writings may serve to pathologise women writers. For example, Sirc (1989), having analysed narratives by men and women students, came to the conclusion that women's writing is *banal*, as compared with that of men who have a 'grandiose sense of self' as questing hero. In similar vein, Howe points to the passivity and lack of confidence in women's texts (1971).

However, more recent auto-ethnographic work by Dixon (1995) signals the gendered nature of such readings and (mis)understandings of women student-writers' behaviour. Dixon explores her own enactment of dominant gendered literacy and pedagogical practices in academia, by tracing her actions and interactions with a male and a female student-writer. She traces the ways in which she actively worked with a male student at constructing a text which was in line with institutional expectations, in terms of topic, politics, genre and argumentation. In contrast, Dixon discovered that she carried out no such parallel work with the woman student, whose writing she immediately categorised as 'conventional, lifeless'. The woman student-writer was constructed by Dixon, in her words, as the epitome of 'a Good Girl who shrewdly tries to determine her teacher's tastes and write to them: the opposite of one's own man' (Dixon 1995: 265).

It is only much later, through discussions with the woman student-writer, that Dixon learnt about the tensions faced by the student-writer in constructing her text; and the ways in which she, Dixon, had misread such tensions. Dixon signals the way in which the teaching, learning and doing of student academic writing, a key part of the business as usual of academia, is powerfully gendered. This has also been emphasised by Haswell and Haswell (1995), who argue that tutors 'do' gender in complex ways, as they read student-writers' texts. They point, for example, to the ways in which tutors always gender the texts they are reading, referring for example to 'she' says here, 'he' says here, even when texts are anonymous, and they trace the effects of such gendering on tutors' responses. They argue that it is important to bring gender explicitly into any discussion of what counts as 'good' student writing.

That the student-writers may be aware of the kinds of mis/readings of their texts exemplified in the researcher/tutor comments above, whilst not necessarily marking them as gendered, is indicated by Tara's dissatisfaction with her more successful academic writing.

Initially, Tara's predominant concern was to produce the kind of text that the institution required. I have illustrated her confusion about the nature of her position as meaning maker in writing by focusing on the contradictory directives – 'advise', 'argue', 'don't use the first person', 'include what you think' (see Chapter 3). Towards the end of her second year, she was worrying less about such contradictions, and felt more confident that she was beginning to meet the unstated demands in her writing. However, Tara also felt increasingly frustrated with how she was writing. She talked about an essay she had written, which she felt was *boring* because she was too cautious about her ideas.

Extract from text	Talk about text
Essay question, Law: To what extent is the doctrine of undisclosed principal justifiable, given the lack of consensus? Extract from middle of text: It is not only the personality of the principal however, that is a restriction of the doctrine, as the personal nature of the contract itself is important. In *Collins v Associated Greyhound Racehorses Ltd [1928] C631* the plaintiff sought to have his name removed from a register of the members company as the holder of 8,160 shares at 5s each.	I'm not showing them that I know *exactly* what I'm talking about. I'm too afraid to let go on a piece of paper and I think that's what they like. Even if I'm wrong, at least they'd see. I know I have to be more assertive in what I think, put my own thoughts down a lot more, but also still keep to what I'm doing as well, keep it tidy. Keep it well presented. I mean, I'm one of the neatest, but it's boring.

We can map out the features which Tara intuitively recognises as making this text 'academic'. The extract has obvious features of academic discourse. It has two long sentences which are lexically dense whilst of low grammatical intricacy; that is, broadly speaking, there is a simple sentence structure with a relatively large number of vocabulary items (see Halliday 1989: chapter 5). The participants in the first two clauses are abstract – *personality, restriction, nature* – and the verb processes are relational – *is* (Halliday 1994: 119). In the third clause there is a human agent but this is referred to in a lexical item specific to law, *plaintiff*. The extract consists of many such law-specific lexical items. For these reasons, this extract, like much of Tara's essay, 'sounds' more academic than others to date. Yet she is dissatisfied.

Tara feels she has much to risk by *letting go* in her writing, most obviously failure. By playing it safe, she knows her work will pass, but she feels she is limiting what she is doing in her writing. Tara's comments are echoed by Sara in her concerns about being thought of as *too pushy* (Chapter 4).

That these feelings may not be confined to student-writers is signalled in Sara Ruddick's comment about her own experience as an academic which is characterised by what she calls 'timid professionalism': in the context of academic writing, this means authoring in ways which you feel are most likely to be accepted/acceptable (in Belenky and others 1986: 96; see also comments by women academics in Kirsch 1993).

Connections . . .

Of course, this doesn't mean that you/we (always) do this consciously, or that it influences your/our writing in obvious ways.

In an earlier draft of this chapter I'd included many pages on an over-view of research into language and gender. Somehow – not consciously – I felt as if I needed to prove that what I wanted to say was acceptable and the way to do this was to 'knowledge tell'. But it took me too far away from the focus here – essayist literacy – and seemed to indicate to some readers of my drafts that I wasn't clear about what I was trying to do. Written comments included:

Reader 1: *Interesting ideas but inconclusive, written almost apologetically.*
Reader 2: *I like it, but it's too apologetic.*

I hadn't thought that I was being apologetic . . .

A conversation with another reader went like this:

   T: I know there's stuff to say on gender but I'm worried. I feel as if I need to include this overview of research on language and gender in general to show that I know about it . . . to almost be able to claim a right to write about this . . .

   G: Why don't you just say that you're going to emphasize gender because you think it's important? Why do you have to prove that you know all this?

Fulfilling and disrupting the binary framework

One way to construe the women writers' experience of meaning making is that of struggle with an unfamiliar, male-marked resource-practice. Thus, when the women writers complain about nobody being in their writing or of wanting to include personal experiences through the introduction of personal stories, the use of 'I' or the use of informal language, they are simply fulfilling dominant social gendered expectations. From studies within composition, narrative is often presented as a preferred female genre (see for example Kirsch 1993). Studies at compulsory school level in the UK have emphasised girls' preferred reading and writing practices as being linked to the personal and the reflective, as compared with boys' interest in action (Swann 1992). Luke has argued strongly that girls at school learn to gain access to the less powerful genres of society – narrative and affective accounts – rather than the publicly valued genres, such as those associated with law, science and technology (see Luke 1994).

There are two points to make about such analyses in relation to the women's experiences. Firstly, they leave the powerful practices of academia untouched. The women writers and their texts are problematised but dominant academic practices are not. Secondly, if we pay attention to the women writers' accounts in this study, then we see that they are not arguing in favour of replacing the current dominant set of conventions with another. Rather, they are arguing against meaning making which is constructed through a binary lens, where one dimension of the binary is privileged. For whilst a desire for particular kinds of hybridity is generally suppressed and edited out of their texts, in their talk about texts the student-writers provide some examples of what this might involve. Thus, Mary, Amira and Nadia want formal and informal wordings; Amira, Kate, Mary, Sara and Nadia want to be present personally at certain points in their texts; Diane is dissatisfied with *rattrapping* – repeating given knowledge rather than at times bringing in her own experiences; Sara is dissatisfied with having to disguise her ethnic/racial identity so that she can only present her English self, rather than her English and Pakistani-Muslim self.

An example of a student-writer instantiating what constitutes a hybrid practice in academia is Kate's inclusion of poetry alongside argument in her essays. Whilst she struggles to include herself through the use of personal pronouns, as discussed above, she does on occasion make what she views as a personal contribution, by including an extract from a poem or a literary text. The example below is from one of her favourite contributions, which she had written on an Access course.

In later discussions, Kate described this inclusion of poetry as *a little protest against the convention of rational argument*. From her point of view, the poetry is not there for the reader, but for her, the writer. Although she feels that the reader will not see and accept the poetry as supportive evidence for

Poem included in essay	Talk about text

Poem Kate chose to begin her essay entitled 'The function of maternal instinct is to keep women in their place. Discuss.'
 	
THE MOTHER
by Anne Stevenson
 	
Of course I love them, they are my
  children.
That is my daughter and this is my son.
And this is my life I give them to please
  them.
It has never been used. Keep it safe,
  Pass it on.
	I asked her what the poetry contributed to what she wanted to say.
	
	K: It sums up . . . and this poem, to *me* says what happens to women who have families erm, like my mum. Her whole life has been the family. She will argue, but I think she could have done an awful lot with her life. And so, and that poem says 'this is my life that I give to my children to please them'. In other words I do everything for them, and they're precious, 'keep it safe'. In other words you live your life through your children.

her argument, the inclusion of the poetic extract helps her to feel that she is present in her text.

But Kate, whilst critical of the dominant discourse of academia as being male and logic-centred, is also clear about wanting argument in her writings. She expresses her enjoyment at making a successful argument: *because it gives you a sense of control.*

However, the kind of authoring that she would like to do, to include, for example, poetry alongside rational argument, is at odds with the kind of authoring permitted to a student-writer in academia and is therefore difficult for her to adopt and develop.

Desires for learning

Thus far, a principal emphasis in this chapter has been on the tensions surrounding the women's involvement in higher education and their meaning-making practices in essayist literacy. However, it would be wrong to end such a chapter without signalling a powerful driving force behind the students' continued, albeit fragmented, participation in higher education: the sheer pleasure they derive from engaging in learning.

As well as the student-writers pointing to practical reasons for wanting to study in higher education – jobs and financial security, mainly – our talk is peppered with their comments about the pleasure of learning. Bridget's comment *the more you do, the more you want to do*, alongside Kate's admission of being *hooked* on learning, signal the addictive nature of this particular pleasure-inducing drug. Diane indicates the alternative to this pleasured state, in her comments on her state of being before seriously engaging in learning: *I thought, 'God, I didn't know these things* [a whole range of groups/activities] *were about'. I thought, 'I'm not living.'* In contrast, engaging in learning offers up the possibility of living.

The student-writers often talk of *loving* their subjects, their books and ideas. Tara 'loves' law, not necessarily the law course, but anything to do with legal procedures, practices and accounts. She is fascinated by it: *It's a really interesting subject. I could read about law all the time, like. Everything we do is linked to law.*

Mary talks of her specific enjoyment of 'theory'. Her comment was prompted by the prospect of having to write a more practically oriented assignment for a course on social policy: *I like theories more than talking about actual concrete, you know trying to apply theories to today —— but to write theories in general, I like it. I love it, I love theory.*

Sara also talks about *loving* studying and the all-embracing nature of her relationship with learning:

> My mind is like a storm brewing in my head . . . I've got so many ideas just wafting around in my head —— And then I start having dreams about it [her studying] and, like I told you, I was answering the question in my dream [laughs] it was like I was discussing it with another person, you know —— you've still got the adrenaline rush going and you think 'yeah I've got to write this down, I've got to include this as well'. —— This studying, you know, it's *amazing*.

Connections . . .

Getting a grant, spending money on books, reading books, talking about books . . .
I couldn't believe that we got money just to spend on books. (Of course all that's long gone now . . .) It was marvellous. I bought my 'set books', the ones listed as necessary for the courses, but I also spent money on books that had nothing to do with my course – like Hesse. I thought it was fantastic to go to a bookshop, buy books – rows of books by people I'd never heard of, read books and then drink coffee with a friend discussing ideas. I loved it.

Conclusion

It is impossible to talk like, or constitute oneself as a generic woman: the whole woman also has a class, an ethnicity, a cultural position.

(Cameron 1997: 34)

As young, and older, women, the student-writers live the material realities of class and race/ethnicity, alongside the dominant gendered discourses

128

of marriage, romance and caring. Within this tense social space, higher education is/was not seen as a right or as an expected route for any of them during their school and, for some, their adult lives. Their desires for participation in higher education have often been muted.

However, the women's accounts of their lives signal that individual desires are not fixed, but shift as both local – through partners, family, community – and institutional opportunities emerge. Policies of widening access to students previously excluded clearly enable the women to act on a desire to participate in HE. Whilst acting on such desires may constitute, in some ways, an enactment of dominant notions of gender – a good mother should be an educated mother, a working-class woman has a right to study in HE if it is for the benefit of her family – participation in HE may provide a way of challenging rather than fulfilling social gender norms.

In terms of essayist literacy as a gendered practice-resource, the following points can be made. Essayist literacy as a culturally available representational resource provides particular ways of meaning making for student-writers, which are legitimated in daily actions in academia. In line with other writers, I have argued that essayist literacy is constituted by a binary framework, which privileges particular dimensions of meaning making over 'others'. It is no accident that these categorisations of 'other' – for example, emotion, evocation, informality – are precisely those dimensions of meaning that those historically constructed as 'others' should desire. The women writers seem to accept the dominant conventions in constructing their texts, but resist them in their thinking about what their texts are, or might be. Thus, whilst the women write impersonally, they often long for connection. This gap, between what their texts mean and their desires for meaning, is glimpsed in their talk around their texts.

In talking of the women writers' desires it is important to acknowledge diversity whilst signalling common threads. Thus, whilst there is a common thread of desire for connection/involvement, there are also significant differences. For example, Mary's principal interest, during the time of our discussions, was in connection as a means of involving readers from a wider range of social backgrounds than those predominantly associated with academic texts. Kate's main interest is in making connections between her lived experience and the world of academia. Sara (in Chapter 4) suggests she wants to be able to make connections between different dimensions of her identity and her academic writing. She also, as do all the women, wants greater connection with tutor-readers.

The women's preoccupation with establishing what their tutors want echoes the work of some researchers who describe these concerns – without necessarily exploring/explaining them – and still others, who pathologise women writers' behaviour. The women students seem to be caught in a double bind: if they try to work out what is demanded, they may be accused of only ever pandering to their tutors' demands and of having no authority, independence, of their own. If they do some of the things they want to do – use informal language and poetry, include personal experience which involves ethnic-cultural identities as well as white English – they may be criticised for not fulfilling dominant norms.

The student-writers' accounts in this chapter signal the ways in which addressivity is powerfully gendered. Whereas the notions of 'good writing' and the dominant discourse on 'key skills' seek to empty texts of their social subjects, the women writers' accounts throughout this book constantly point to the importance of social identities – in terms of both addressors and addressees – for the construction of meaning. I have already discussed this in relation to 'race'/ethnicity and social class in the previous chapter. The discussion in this chapter foregrounds gender, suggesting that in their attempts to avoid being constructed as 'other', outside of mainstream academic practices, the women students and their texts may be read precisely as that; as women writers who fail to take up authoritative positions according to prevailing norms.

The women writers' accounts warn against any easy reading of their intentions, desires and concerns for meaning making in academic writing from their texts alone: what they mean in their texts is not necessarily what they want to mean. Their meaning making – their desires, intentions, decisions in texts – is powerfully shaped by the context in which they are writing and to which they are responding.

As discussed in Chapter 3, the women writers often indicate a desire for a different kind of relationship around meaning making with the tutor-readers. This relationship would involve re-imagining the student text as a space for trying out ideas and wordings, rather than as a final version from which the tutor reads the student-writer and her meanings. It also involves a re-imagining of the tutor as a reader who is willing to look to student-writers' interests and concerns as they work at meaning making in their texts. Acknowledging that both student-writer and tutor bring gendered as well as class and ethnic identities to their writing and reading of texts is central to this re-imagining of the student-writer/tutor-reader relationship and needs to be brought into our considerations about what is involved and at stake in writing. In the next chapter, I foreground the ways in which the student-writers' desires, for a different kind of relationship around the production of their written texts, can be enacted in student–tutor dialogue.

Notes

1   Of course this doesn't mean that engaging in romantic texts, reading and/or writing them, is always about conforming to dominant narratives of femininity/ masculinity. See, for example, discussion in Moss 1994.

2   Of course, much work within studies on language and gender is framed within a binary – male/female. Early work in socio-linguistics in particular tended to treat gender – male/female – as fixed states; indeed early work uses biological sex

as an organising concept. Whilst later research and theory signals the socially constructed nature of the binary differences between men and women, this binary remained firmly in place. In this later frame, gender, albeit thus socially construed, is understood as building on biological differences: thus, for example, girls and boys on the basis of their biological sex difference learn corresponding masculine/feminine ways of behaving, including ways of using language. For examples of these discussions, see Cameron 1992, 1997; Coates 1993; Johnson and Meinhof 1997. The 'difference' between men's and women's language use and meaning making is theorised in various ways. Some writers emphasise the sexed nature of meaning making – with biology as a fundamental organising principle (for example Irigary 1993), whereas others emphasise the possibility of either males or females taking up either/or/and feminine and masculine subject positions within orders of discourse, as in Kristeva 1986. A further approach is to treat the connection between sex and gender as an 'ideological fiction' (Cameron 1997: 23). An implication of this view is that by signalling differences between two separate groups – men and women – researchers are contributing to the construction of an imaginary binary: we see difference because difference is the starting-point.

3   I first came across this heading in the article by M. Sperling, and S. Warshauer Freedman (1987) 'A good girl writes like a good girl'. Although the title and some parts of the discussion signal the significance of gender, gender is not explicitly explored in the article.

6

DIALOGUES OF PARTICIPATION

Mary: I've never experienced talking to anyone about my essays before, so I find it very interesting and I appreciate —— Nobody's ever sat down and talked to me about my essays. They've just said, oh, 'hard to fathom at times' [laughs].

Siria: It's like going through a narrow corridor, when somebody else looks at it [written text], they probably open a door or window, or turn left, turn right. That's what I think happens [in talk].

Introduction

My aim in this chapter is to engage with the principal criticisms that I have made throughout this book of the pedagogy surrounding student academic writing in HE in the UK. In previous chapters I have signalled how the limited opportunities for tutor–student talk, and the dominant monologic addressivity that constitutes talk when it does take place, works against the student-writers' learning of essayist literacy conventions. Student-writers' desire for greater opportunities for dialogue between tutors and students, as real participants in the construction and interpretation of texts, is repeatedly expressed and seems to hold out for student-writers the promise of learning essayist conventions as a key part of their participation in higher education. At the same time, student-writers signal their desire to work within a transformed addressivity at a more fundamental level, whereby different ways of meaning and relationships around meaning in academia can be enacted; thus, in some ways, enabling them to step out of the norms of essayist literacy practice.

The focus of this chapter is the mediating potential of talk between student-writers and tutor-readers for the teaching and learning of essayist literacy, as well as for facilitating greater individual control over meaning making. I foreground four particular types of dialogue which are necessary to meet these different demands and desires: tutor-directive dialogue aimed at talking the student-writer into essayist literacy practice; collaborative dialogue aimed at 'populating the student-writer's text with her own intentions' (after Bakhtin 1981: 293–4; see Chapter 2); tutor-directive dialogue aimed at making language visible; dialogue which facilitates student 'talkback' as part of 'long conversations' (Maybin 1994).

The examples in this chapter are drawn from talk between student-writers and myself when working not only as researchers but as students and tutor-assessors on a Language Studies course. We were therefore talking within the same institutionally defined roles as the students and tutors referred to in Chapter 3. A key difference is that we had made a conscious decision to make space for talk.

Talking writers into essayist literacy

Mary: To me, essay writing is a bit like implicit knowledge.
Theresa: In what way?
Mary: Not all explicit, is it?
Theresa: What do you mean?
Mary: It's like common sense, not common sense, it's like implicit knowledge. You know it's intuitive in a sense. Like, you *feel* that you should mention his name. The problem is, some people might not feel it.
Theresa: The problem is, how do you get to feel it?
Mary: Yeah. 'Cause I *do* know what you're talking about when you do make your criticisms because I recognise them myself, but I just don't know how to put my finger on it. I wish I could get a bell in my head which says 'Hey, something's wrong here. I don't know what it is but I'm not quite sure but, you know, if I show it to Theresa, she'll point it out and I'll, oh yes.'

Mary's comments indicate that it is difficult to learn the conventions of essayist literacy, but also that a way of learning them is to be with someone who already *feels* what the conventions are; she thus echoes the work of those who foreground the notion of learning as a relationship of apprenticeship between newcomers and experts in a particular community of practice. Heath, for example, argues that 'outsiders' need to be apprenticed to 'insiders' in order to learn culturally specific ways of meaning making (Heath 1983). Lave and Wenger use the notion of 'legitimate peripheral participation' to describe the means by which newcomers come to learn the particular discourse practices of a particular community (1991). They contrast this kind of participation with what they call 'sequestered participation', which is used to describe partial or full denial of access to a community and which, as I have signalled in Chapter 3, figures prominently in the experience of 'non-traditional' students in HE. My aim here is to explore how particular kinds of tutor–student talk can fulfil a basic criterion of legitimate participation, that is, access to the community of practice. This is what the student-writers desire, as illustrated in Mary's comments.[1]

All the student-writers expressed the desire to spend more time talking with tutors in order to learn the rules of the writing game in HE. At the same time, they regularly commented on the usefulness of the talk in which we engaged for learning such rules. In this section, I want to tease out how tutor-directive talk meets this key element of student-writers' desires for talk, by focusing in detail on one episode of talk around the construction of a student-writer's text.

The extracts below are from Sara's first draft of an essay and our talk about the extract. The essay question she was addressing was as follows:

> Discuss the ways in which different linguistic environments affect the development of bilingualism in pre-school (under 5 years) children.

In this extract, my aim as tutor-assessor (see Introduction) is clearly to talk Sara into a specific way of meaning making; in particular, to talk her into constructing the particular kind of textual unity that has come to be privileged within essayist literacy in academia (for more detailed discussion of essayist unity, see Lillis 1998). How does talk achieve this?

In the talk episode below, the institutionally sanctioned roles of teacher and student are prominent. I, as tutor-assessor, control the opening and closing of the sequence. In general, I control the talk by assuming my institutional right to ask questions and make evaluations of the student-writer's comments: there are obvious, although extended, initiation–response–feedback patterns (IRF), for example, at lines 1–7, 26–45, where I act as questioner and evaluator of her work. I engage in what Edwards and Mercer have called, in their analysis of classroom talk, 'cued elicitation'

Text	Talk about text
1 I hope that by the end of this	1 *T:* That doesn't seem to me to be really
2 assignment I may have	2 what you're doing [re-reads section].
3 come to some sort of	3 *S:* What about linguistically capable?
4 conclusion, as to why some	4 *T:* But you're talking about a specific
5 children are proficient in	5 group of children aren't you?
6 some languages and not	6 *S:* Bilingual children.
7 others.	7 *T:* Right, so I think you need to be
	8 specific here as to why some
	9 *S:* [bilingual
	10 children, would that be better?
	11 *T:* Well let's try and follow that through.

12   Some bilingual children are

13 *S:*   [well, yeah.

14   I mean some bilingual children are

15   proficient in some languages and not

16   others.

17 *T:* But if you've already called them

18   bilingual, you've got a problem there.

19 *S:* Yeah, well but the business about

20   what is bilingual though.

21   I mean, who is considered

22   a bilingual, when *are* you

23   bilingual?

24 *T:* Right okay, let's take it like that.

25   [*T* re-reads section]

26 *T:* Have you come to any conclusion

27   about what might be the best

28   environment?

29 *S:* Yes. I mean, there were some things in

30   there [Arnberg 1987] that I thought

31   that's a good idea, I could use that

32   myself.

33 *T:* Well, don't you think then that what

34   you're saying is I may have come to

35   some sort of conclusion as to why

36   certain environments help children to

37   become bilingual more than others.

38   Isn't that what you're doing? . . .

39 *S:* I think that's probably what I'm trying

40   to say but I haven't written it down

41   properly.

42 *T:* It's just that, what you've written here

43   is too vague. [*T* reads extract] The

44   second reason given here should be

45   the key.

46 *S:* Yeah [sounds unsure]. So if I said erm

47   that by the end of the assignment I may

48   have some idea

49 *T:*   [as to why some children . . .

50 *S:* erm . . .

8 what effects different   51 *T:* develop bilingual skills and what

9 environments have on their   52 effect that has on their development.

10 development.   53   I mean that's what you're talking about,

54   aren't you?

55 *S:* *How* they develop bilingual skills.

56 *T:* Yeah.

57 *S:* Can I write that down or I'll forget.

58 *S:* [Writes] As to why, no . . . how some

59   children develop bilingual skills.

60 *T:* I think that's much more what you're

61   saying . . . and then what effects.

62 *S:* Yeah [writes].

at lines 12–14, where I guide the student-writer's contribution by seeking to elicit specific responses; I also engage in cued elicitation as part of modelling written text (see lines 49–52) and joint modelling with the student-writer. I am using 'modelling' here to mean instances in talk where we rehearse sections of written text orally. (For IRF patterns in school-based talk, see for example Sinclair and Coulthard 1975; Mehan 1979. For cued elicitation, see Edwards and Mercer 1987: chapter 7; Mercer 1995: 26–7.)

There is evidence of me attempting to persuade Sara to take up my directives, whilst minimising my directive role through different types of hedging: for example, *that doesn't seem to me to be really what you're doing* (line 1); *don't you think* (line 33); *isn't that* (line 38); *I mean* (line 53). Whilst some of these exchanges take on a particular significance for the teaching and learning of essayist literacy, as I discuss below, they are also politeness strategies; such hedging allows me the possibility of re-directing Sara's construction of text without directly rejecting her current text and views, and thus potentially jeopardising our talking relationship (see Brown and Levinson 1987 for discussion of 'face wants'; see also Baynham 1996 for discussion of significant use of such hedges in adult literacy teaching contexts).

All of my contributions are directed at pushing Sara towards constructing the unifying central focus demanded in essayist literacy. I do this, notably by introducing wordings from the essay question in my talk and then attempting to elicit them in her talk: at lines 4–6 I direct Sara towards the group of people intended to be the focus of the question, *bilingual children*; at lines 26–8 I direct her towards the particular dimension of their experience to be explored, that is, their *environment*. I ignore Sara's comments at line 29–31 on the usefulness of a particular text she has been reading (Arnberg 1987), in order to steer her towards a central focus on the effect of the environment on the development of bilingualism. Having established the focus in terms of the 'who' and 'what' of the essay question, I work with Sara to model written text, at lines 34–50, which she might include in her essay.

Sara actively works with me in the talk, by responding to my direct questions (for example at lines 6 and 29), by offering suggestions (lines 3 and 9), by introducing her own questions about a term (19–23), by introducing her own opinion on a source text (lines 29–32), by echoing my comment that there are problems with the way she is using the word *bilingual* (line 21), and by working with me to model text (lines 34–50).

Repeating wordings from the essay question is a seemingly obvious way of constructing essayist unity within texts, but is not necessarily something the student-writers think of doing. In Figure 6.1 I outline the way in which I cue key wordings from the essay question for Sara to include in her written text. The arrows indicate the introduction and take-up of specific wordings in our talk which, of particular relevance to our interest here, can also be traced to Sara's final draft.

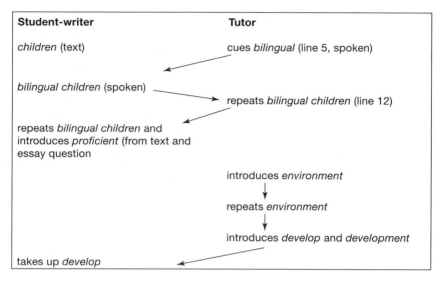

Figure 6.1 Working at constructing essayist textual unity: cueing words in tutor–student talk

The extract from Sara's final draft that follows shows how she reworked the wordings of her first draft by both incorporating wordings close to the essay question – *bilingual, develop, linguistic, environment* – and included other revisions traceable to our talk. Thus, in her final draft, she uses the word *bilingual,* but has shifted it from a description of the child, to a description of skills, and thereby avoids her original problematic use of the term. She also incorporates her suggested use of the word *how,* rather than my proposed *why.* This shows how Sara has not simply transferred suggestions from my talk to her text, but has reworked her text by drawing on our joint collaboration in talk.

> I hope that by the end of the assignment I may have come to some sort of conclusion as to *how children develop bilingual skills* and what effects different environments have on their linguistic development.
>
> (my emphasis)

A significant feature of the talk extract above, and a prominent way in which I talk Sara into the essayist way of constructing unity in her text, is my insistence that I know what she is saying, as compared with what she actually says – either orally or in her written text. This connects closely with what Edwards and Mercer, in their analysis of schoolteacher talk, have called 'reconstructive paraphrasing' (Edwards and Mercer 1985: chapter 7). Such a practice is evident throughout this episode. I open and close this episode by suggesting that I know what Sara is trying to say as compared with what she has written: at line 1, *That doesn't seem to me to be really what you're doing'*; at line 33, *'don't you think then that what you're saying is*; at line 53, *I mean that's what you're talking about, aren't you*; at line 60, *I think that's much more what you're saying.* In closing the episode, I suggest that all of our talk has been about making Sara's intended meanings textually explicit. Sara's comment at line 39, *I think that's probably what I'm trying to say but I haven't written it down properly,* indicates that she is willing to accept my interpretation of what I think she's trying to do, although *probably* indicates her doubts as to whether I, and perhaps she, know her intended meanings. Her comment also suggests that she is willing to go along with my reconstruction of her meanings in order to engage in a practice which is new to her.

It may be the case that, based on my reading of her notes and rough drafts, I understood what Sara was attempting to mean in her written text and was simply offering an alternative wording. However, there is no doubt that whilst I, as tutor, was listening out for the student-writer's intended meanings, I was at the same time working at securing a way of meaning which is acceptable within this specific practice.

Connections . . .

Thinking about the kind of unity I was trying to impose in my talk here with Sara . . . It's been such a struggle to make this particular version of 'unity' visible to myself. It's hard to make visible something that you're working within and have been schooled to work within for so long. In writing this text I'm conscious of how, at every turn, I work at constructing a particular kind of wholeness. Pushing and pulling at wordings, my ideas, the ideas of others, the data-experience . . . Imposing an acceptable unity.

What other kinds of unity might we draw on and work at in making meaning?

Talking to 'populate with intention'

The talk episode above illustrates the features which make tutor-directive talk useful for the purpose of talking someone into a particular discourse practice; student-writers who want to learn to write within the conventions of a particular practice can be talked into doing so, even before they know what the conventions are. However, given the emphasis in such talk on imposing a particular way of meaning, what space can be created through dialogue to support student-writers in their attempts to take control over their meaning making in writing?

An important way of helping the student-writer to populate her texts with intention (Bakhtin 1981: 293; see Chapter 2) is to acknowledge the following:

texts are always meaning in the making, involving struggles around taking control over language which, in turn, are bound up with the writer's sense of authority, authorial presence and authorship (see Chapter 2); tutor/ student dialogue can make visible such struggles and thus facilitate the construction of student-writer-preferred meanings by encouraging her to take greater control over the voices in her text. Dialogue aimed at identifying the diverse voices in the student-writer's text is a step towards establishing which voices the student-writer wishes to own/disown, as I go on to illustrate.

'Education authorities under a great deal of stress'

On reading drafts for Nadia's second essay, I was not convinced, based on listening to her talk about the experience of minority groups in school, that her written text expressed her preferred views. This is indicated by my questions below.

Text	Talk about text
1 The education authorities	1 T: Is that something that you would say,
2 are under a great deal of	2 that *you* think?
3 stress due to the vast	3 N: Well it is true, isn't it?
4 increase of ethnic minority	4 [T re-reads section]
5 children entering British	5 T: Is this what you think?
6 schools.	6 N: Well, it is true. Well, it's not true
	7 but . . . they're not under a lot of stress.
	8 I don't believe in that.
	9 T: So, this sounds as if it's your idea.
	10 N: No.
	11 T: So how do you make sure that it looks
	12 as if it's not your idea?
	13 N: Just say, oh, reference.

Based on what I understood Nadia's feelings to be, from comments on her personal experience as a bilingual learner and a worker in schools, I was surprised at the content of the draft extract above, and for this reason queried whether the text represented her views (line 1). However, Nadia's shift in her response to my query, from *it is true* to *it's not true* (line 6) might indicate that she was simply complying with the obvious dissatisfaction of the more powerful participant (tutor-assessor), rather than coming any nearer to stating her preferred view. At the same time, it is also possible that Nadia's text was conforming to the dominant addressivity at the level of context of culture, in this case dominant perspectives on immigration and schooling in Britain. That is, her text seems to echo the way in which immigration is problematised in terms of numbers, as signalled in the reference to a *vast increase*, and in the emphasis on immigration causing problems for the *host* community, as signalled in the reference to education authorities being under a *great deal of stress* (see Chapter 2 for addressivity; also Sara's concerns, discussed in Chapter 4). The extract illustrates the tensions surrounding any tutor's attempt to support a student-writer in the construction of her preferred meanings. It also signals the need for opportunities for extended talk between student and tutor, if a tutor is to become familiar with the beliefs and interest of the student-writer.

From further discussion about the construction of this text, I discovered, and Nadia realised, that her text was ventriloquating – using words from others' mouths (see Bakhtin 1981: 293) – a Ministry of Education pamphlet dated 1963, rather than presenting Nadia's views. This accounted for the position expressed in Nadia's text, that the *vast increase* of minority ethnic groups was causing local authorities many problems, and the general position in her text that local authorities were providing very good support to second-language learners.

After our talk above, where I question whether the text represents her view, Nadia makes two specific changes to her final draft: a) in relation to the section discussed above where she clearly separates her voice from that of the source text, as follows: *According to the educating authorities in Britain* [in the 1960s], *the authorities were under a lot of stress*, but also, b) in overall content where Nadia shifts the emphasis towards current provision for bilingual learners in state schools, as well as bringing in a brief account of her personal experience as a bilingual learner:

> UMES (Unified Multicultural Education Service) is the body which co-ordinates and promotes minority languages speakers. UMES aims to provide support for black children who are in the education service . . . I work as an ESL support teacher. I am able to clarify what my duties are. I work alongside the classroom teacher to provide extra support for the Arabic children.

From 'lack of participation' to 'exclusion'

In discussing the first draft of Kate's first essay, we spent a lot of time discussing the introduction, which Kate said she felt was weak. She wasn't sure why or how it was weak, but felt dissatisfied. She talked about the introductory section below:

Text	Talk about text
Factors such as cultural attitudes, institutional sexism and power elites will be introduced and discussed in	K: What I want to do is say there are certain things which have led to the exclusion of women in politics and

relation(ship) to the problem of women's lack of participation.	the ones I've picked out are the institutional, sexism, cultural attitudes and the actual power that politics itself has. Does that make any sense to you?

Based on Kate's oral explication of her intended meanings above, I suggest she foreground the notion of *exclusion*, rather than *lack of participation* in her written text:

T: If what you want to say is that there are three factors which still work towards women's exclusion then that's different isn't it? From their lack of participation? Exclusion presumably assumes that something or someone is excluding them. Whereas lack of participation

K: [is not as strong

T: No. And it depends on what you want to say.
[K reads section]

K: I really want to put, that the exclusion is done on purpose, not . . . Do you know what I mean? How do I put that?

T: From what you've said . . . I just wrote down what you said before.

Kate includes the notion/wording of *exclusion* in her final draft:

Women have always been political despite male assertions to the contrary and this essay argues their exclusion has been by design and not by choice or apathy. In discussing the problems, politics will be defined in terms of western democracy and then I will introduce factors in cultural attitudes, institutional sexism and power elites which I feel may have a direct effect on the exclusion.

This example of meaning making in writing is the result of collaboration around attempts to represent the individual's preferred meaning, as expressed orally, in her written text. In this instance, I get closer to the student-writer's preferred meaning through listening to what she says at this particular moment. This stands in contrast to other instances, such as with Nadia above, where my questions about whether the written text constituted the student-writer's preferred meanings were based on what I felt I already knew about the student-writer's views.

'I knew there was something I wanted to say'

Of course, just having the opportunity to be and talk with someone familiar with your disciplinary area, and who is also interested in what you are trying

Text	Talk about text
The general area of study in this project will be social linguistics in which the main focus concerns code-switching. The research centres on two areas of the codeswitching phenomena: 1) pragmatic and discoursal aspects of codeswitching this involves identifying the factors which influence speakers to switch and the underlying meanings.	M: I'll use Halliday if I'm feeling adventurous, to talk about the functions of language. T: With Halliday, it's the business of analysing language in functions and also in terms of M: [in context and situations. Oh thanks, you've just said that, you've just brought something to my mind that I wanted to say. Oh how could I forget that? I was saying that the main thing about my interview is situation and context. That's the core that. Because what I'm trying to say is that the nature of the questions what relate to a particular experience in the life, and within that experience is a situation and a context. So that's what influences the change or switching. And that's what was very important. That's what I wanted to say. I knew there was something I wanted to say.

to say, can powerfully support individual efforts to make meaning. The talk extract above takes place after some ten minutes of Mary expressing dissatisfaction with her text, yet neither of us seemed to be able to make sense of the direction she wanted to go in. Our talk here served to trigger what Mary wanted to say.

The impact of our talk is evident in her final title and draft.

> *Title:* The dependence of codeswitching upon situation and context.

> In relation to the interviewees who are both Creole speakers, the factors which motivate them to code switch could be due to the nature of the questions asked by the interviewer. Since, these questions draw on the interviewees personal experiences which have taken place in a particular situation or context.

Talking to make language visible

In any specific instance of meaning making we draw on available representational resources at the levels of contexts of situation and culture (see discussions in Chapter 2). In order to take greater control over our use of

---

Connections . . .

A conversation about someone else's research.

> *P:* Of course, the emotional dimension to teaching and learning is usually always minimised.
>
> *T:* Yeah.
>
> *P:* Even work which takes a socio-interactive approach seems to end up with an emphasis on the cognitive, backgrounding the significance of the emotional and interactive side.[2]

I knew there was something else I needed to say and that I'd missed out – God, I'd always planned to bring in the importance of particular bits of interaction which, on the face of it, seem to have nothing to do with the 'task in hand', particularly all the laughing that we do . . .

I'll have to bring some of that in at the end of this section . . .

---

specific resources – wordings in this case – these need to be made visible and problematised. Taking control over our use of specific wordings is integral to any attempt to 'populate with intention'.

'Positive'

In the extract below I challenge Sara's written statement that bilingualism is currently viewed as something *positive* in British state schools, on the basis of criticisms she had made earlier in her written text.

Text	Talk about text
1 Bilingualism is being	1 *T:* A lot of your analysis shows that
2 recognised slowly as	2 schools haven't been positive.
3 something positive, but only	3 *S:* In *their* eyes, it is positive though,
4 in certain contexts like	4 isn't it? Maybe that's what I should
5 schools.	5 have written down.
	6 *T:* Right . . .
	7 *S:* They're taking bilingualism as being
	8 something positive. When I say
	9 bilingualism, I'm talking about the
	10 bilingual teachers that they're
	11 employing.
	12 *T:* Right.
	13 *S:* They're realising that they *do* need a
	14 person who's bilingual within school,
	15 not the children, not that sense but

143

```
16      employing bilingual teachers, you
17      know, making that a point to employ a
18      bilingual person, not just a
19      monolingual person. They need
20      bilingual teachers in school.
21  T:  But although they need bilingual
22      teachers, does that mean they see
23      bilingualism as something positive?
24  S:  Not necessarily.
25  T:  No. And what you've said before, you
26      see
27  S:      [But what I was talking about was
28      actually employing bilingual teachers,
29      as that being positive.
30  T:  Okay so that's a positive step.
31  S:  Yeah, a step.
32  T:  Right, I do think you need to explain
33      that then.
```

Sara's oral comment at line 4 indicates that she is coming to see how wordings in the text can mask her intended and more complex meanings, and hence how she needs to attempt to foreground the voices she wishes to own in her text.

In her talk, Sara indicates points of divergence and convergence between her views and official views on bilingualism: divergence – *In their eyes it is positive* (line 3) – indicating that, as in the rest of her essay, she does not feel that bilingualism is viewed positively by policy makers and many teachers in the UK; convergence – *employing bilingual teachers, as that being positive* (lines 28–9) – indicating agreement with initiatives to employ bilingual teachers. However, although she articulates these more complex views in her talk, this complexity is masked in her earlier drafts (as in the extract above) and is only partially realised in her final draft: *Bilingualism is being recognised slowly as something positive, because it is finally creating jobs for bilinguals, but only in certain contexts like schools.*

Whilst in her final draft Sara gives a reason for stating that bilingualism is being viewed as *something positive*, the complexity of her intended meanings which was evident in her talk, is minimised, not least because of the following: a) her use of categorical modality ('is'); and b) her use of the passive and impersonal voice (*bilingualism is being recognised*). Thus, in this instance, talk only went some way towards enabling the student-writer to construct her preferred meanings in the written text. It is important that as tutors we constantly acknowledge this partial, and gradual, impact of tutor/student talk on text construction, as well as the unfinished nature of student-writers' 'final drafts'. The potential value of making explicit to students the linguistic features mentioned above as a means of facilitating greater control is raised in Chapter 7.

Whilst the word *positive* was problematised in a local sense – that is, at the level of a specific instance of meaning making in a specific situation – some wordings can be problematised in relation to more publicly contested discourses at the level of context of culture. This is the case with the wordings *foreign* and *immigrant*, discussed below, which are part of dominant and contested discourses across areas of practice, research and policy within British life.

'Foreign'

In the extract below I query Sara's use of *foreign*. As in the case of *positive* above, in her oral explanation Sara points to the more complex meanings surrounding her use of a particular wording – here *foreign* – and which are buried in her written text. In the written text she ventriloquates, and hence appears to agree with, the dominant discourse on speakers of minority languages as being *foreign*, rather than being British. Yet her talk indicates the following meaning complex; that she is using *foreign* because that is how others refer to British-born Pakistani women (and children); that she agrees that she is *foreign* in the sense that she doesn't feel she belongs and others don't make her feel that she belongs; that she does belong – and hence is not 'foreign' – because she was born in England. However, her use of *foreign*

Text	Talk about text
Children from minority groups can have many distractions towards the second language, in a foreign country.	*T:* Why *foreign* country? *S:* Well, like me, for instance. I'm living here and everything but everybody else considers me as a foreign person because it's not my country, really is it? *T:* Well, you tell me. *S:* Well, I don't feel that it is. Because, I don't get treated, if you don't get treated as if you belong somewhere, you don't *feel* as if you belong. You know. Even though, you probably will because you've been born and bred here and you know, this is the only place you really know but . . . other people don't make you feel as if you belong, I think you still feel like a foreigner, you know. *T:* So this, when you say a foreign country, is that how, like the children view it, or how the people in society view it, or both? *S:* Both.

in the text does not constitute the complexity of meanings that she expresses orally. Given that our talk took place after the final draft stage, it's not possible to see whether Sara would have been able to construct such complexity in a further version of her written text.

'Immigrant'

In the talk episode below, I question Nadia's use of the word *immigrant.*

Text	Talk about text
Repeated use of '*immigrant*' as noun and adjective – 18 instances	T: Is that [immigrant] a word that you would use? N: No, er, minorities.
Examples:	T: I mean, some people might use that word. But is it a word *you* would use when you're talking about the kids you work with?
A huge number of immigrants have entered the UK	N: No. T: But then the problem is you've used this book which uses that word
A few immigrants have little understanding of the English language	N: [a lot T: so it looks as if it's
Immigrant children in our schools	N: [my word T: Your word. Do you see what I mean?
Once the immigrants enter the UK	N: I wouldn't use *immigrant* family. T: Why not?
These immigrants became more regular	N: Because it's kind of offending, isn't it? Being classed as an immigrant. T: When the word tends to be used, the word itself needn't be offensive, it can just mean somebody moving from one place to another. But the way it tends to be used in England N: [it's to offend.

In her final draft Nadia used *immigrant* only twice (as compared with eighteen times in the first draft), one of these being part of a direct quote which was referenced. In contrast she uses *minority/ies* as adjective and noun, as well as *bilingual,* as illustrated in these brief extracts from her final text:

> In Britain there has been no attempt to teach minority children their Mother tongue, let alone establish full bilingual programme.

> ——

> Three of the bilingual children have progressed rapidly.

Nadia therefore makes a significant shift in her final draft from her first draft.

However, given the 'becoming' nature of meaning making (see Chapter 2), Nadia's predominant use of *minority/ies* here is inevitably provisional. Six months after writing this essay, she told me that she felt unhappy with *minority/ies*, feeling that the use of such a term was a way of *segregating everybody from everybody else*. At this point in time she said that, rather than talking as if there were two main social groups – majority (white English) and minority/ies – she felt more comfortable with the idea of using specific group names – for example, Yemeni and Pakistani.

Talking back: a 'long conversation' with Mary

In the world of the southern black community I grew up in, 'back talk' and 'talking back' meant speaking as an equal to an authority figure. It meant daring to disagree and sometimes it just meant having an opinion.

(hooks 1988: 207)

In the Introduction to this book, I discussed attempts to construct a talkback space for, primarily, research purposes. The opening up of the student–tutor talking space enabled the student-writers to describe their experiences of meaning making in writing, foregrounding dimensions usually ignored in the business-as-usual of academia, and which are drawn on in this book. Here I want to focus on the potential of talkback as a pedagogic practice.

As briefly outlined in the Introduction, I constructed talkback sheets after listening to taped conversations between the student-writers and myself: these sheets reflected an attempt to consciously listen to what the student-writers were saying and to bring their concerns and interests to the centre of our subsequent discussions.

In Table 6.1 I provide a further example of a talkback sheet, from talk with Mary, which illustrates the ways in which tutor/researcher-led questioning can open up a space for exploring student-writers' views on dominant conventions whilst still working with/within them. The notes in the talkback sheet below are based on comments made during six taped discussions (see Introduction for talk cycle). The most obvious ways in which the student-writer's concerns and comments are explicitly brought into this talkback space is through direct reference to comments she has previously made. These are marked in bold in Table 6.1.

Whilst points 1, 4, 5, 6 and 8 are more obviously about writing with/within the dominant conventions, that is, getting on with the business-as-usual of academia, points 2, 3, 7, 9, 10, 11 and 12 signal that writing within academia is a social practice, involving, not least, questions about the relationships between language, social identity and institutional practices. A talkback space allows for such interconnections to be explored and thus explicitly brought into debates with student-writers.

147

Table 6.1 Example of talkback sheet (comments drawn from previous discussions with Mary)

Aspects we've previously discussed

1. How to write about somebody else's work/ideas without using their words
You said you'd tried to use your own words a lot more in this second essay and that **you found** this possible to do because the works you were drawing on, i.e. Skutnabb-Kangas, were easier to understand. Where you drew closely on her work you gave a page number. Do you feel clearer about acknowledging the work of others if you draw on their work and about the danger of being accused of plagiarism if you don't? There was also a section which **you said you felt** was important to include although you weren't sure why (see p. 1 essay). How do you work out what's important when you only half understand something? In general do you think this essay was in your words, your structure?

2. Using different/new/alternative words
You gave different reasons for wanting to use new/different words. For example you chose 'primary' for 'elementary' because you wanted to move away from SK [Skutnabb Kangas] text. You used 'beforehand' for 'prerequisite' because **you felt** 'prerequisite' was not a word you felt comfortable with. **You felt** it was a word used by 'real academics' who wouldn't accept you because you were black: your community wouldn't accept you using it either. How do you feel about that word now? You're using quite a lot of different/new words through your study. For example, I suggested the word 'reinterpreted' and you liked it. Why is this different from 'prerequisite'? Are there any dangers/problems/ benefits in using these words . . . and what does using new words say about who you are?

3. Personal voice/separating voices
When we discussed the issue of personal voice and 'I' after your first essay, **you said** you thought it was 'awful but great'. When you were beginning to write your second essay, **you said** it was still a bit of a shock to be asked to use 'I', but **you thought** it was very powerful because it makes you feel part of it, whereas in a lot of your previous writing you felt like an 'outsider'. **You also talked** about the two 'I's: the I personal, and the I as part of a wider community. How do you feel about the 'I's now? Do you think you included them both in your second essay? And how did you feel you linked up these 'I's with the ideas of other writers . . . and do you feel that you managed to separate the voices more successfully than in the Bernstein essay?

4. Sentence structure/syntax
In discussions on your first essay **you said** that you thought your syntax was 'awful'. You were going to underline bits that you thought were awful so that we could discuss them. You didn't because **you seemed to be saying** you didn't want criticism. In discussions on your second essay, at some points **you said** you thought your syntax was awful, especially when writing about your own experience, but at others **said** it wasn't too bad. **One criticism you had** was that it was repetitive. What are you/we going to do about this? I've looked at your sentence structure and it's not awful but there were a few errors in clause

---

boundaries . . . see below and tell me if you think this is what you're worried about.

5. Clause boundaries/syntax
We looked at several examples in drafts and the final draft where the clause boundaries were not marked. 'But this sort of judgement depends largely upon the community in which the bilingualism *exists*. *Since* there are double standards.' In the final draft you wrote it as I suggested. Was that because you agreed with me . . . ? In your final draft there were a couple of similar examples:

> It is evident that language problems are found amongst some African Caribbean *children these findings* were established by the national survey 1980 the ICE.

> Unfortunately a child who has experienced some long term interaction with a linguistic environment *using L2 (which is not learnt proficiently) this can* result in devastating effects such as underdeveloped cognitive skills.

> Whereas an English/Punjabi bilingual child's English surface fluency can be overestimated so the child is expected to have competent academic linguistic skills in *English. But the* experience for Creole speakers has been that their fluency (so to speak) is underestimated and their CALP skills are assumed to be worse than what they actually are.

Can you see the problems with the way these clauses come together? Are these examples of what you mean when you say you have problems with syntax?

6. Grammar
The could of/have came up again in the final draft of your second essay. The other grammatical bit we talked about was prepositions. Examples . . . 'extent *in* which', 'with the aim *to* measure', 'effect *to* bilingualism', 'result *to*'. Do these still seem problematic to you? How can you learn about the use of prepositions in Standard English . . . do you want to?
Pronouns. In both essays we've talked about whether to use s/he or they. It doesn't matter what you use as long as you're consistent. You said you didn't like s/he. What are you going to do in your project?
Conjunctions. In your draft 3, **you wanted** to use however or although in the following point:

> In fact all types of West Indian Creoles should be viewed along a continuum. *However*, there is a large number of Creole speakers, but no one speaker uses a creolised speech to the same extent.
>
> (line 14)

You didn't use a conjunction at all in your final draft. Do you see how using however or although would not be appropriate here because you're not changing direction in ideas?

7. Space to say what you want to say

At the end of your first essay **you said** that **you felt** you hadn't had enough space to say what you wanted to say. When we were discussing a draft of your second essay, **you said** that **you really liked** your argument. What did you like about your argument and do you feel you said more of what you wanted to say in your second essay than in the first?

8. Conclusion

You wrote a good conclusion in the second essay . . . was this because you left yourself more time than in the first essay?

New aspects

9. Style

When we looked at your final draft, we talked about informal language, I'm, can't, not being acceptable in academic writing. **You were angry** about this and **said** you saw it as a way of separating people, that formal language was colder and separated you from your reader. Do you still feel angry about it and what are you going to do in your project?

10. Learning to write/usefulness of our discussions?

When we were looking at one of your drafts, **you said you wanted** to learn how to write and I said our discussions and the feedback I give you was supposed to help you focus on different aspects of your writing. But are these discussions/ feedback helping? How . . . specific example? What would you like us to do differently?

11. What are you allowed to say in an essay?

You raised this when we were discussing your final draft of your first essay. **You said** you wanted 'to slag people off' for saying that Creole was inferior but **you weren't sure** whether you were allowed to do that. You could think of a writer to support your view but not from linguistics and **you wanted** to know whether you could use that. I said you could but I don't know whether you used it in your final draft of essay 2 . . . I don't think you did. Any reason why?

12. Being a Creole/Yorkshire dialect speaker/schooling and university, finding writing hard

When we were discussing your final draft of your first essay, **you said** that **you felt** that you had no standard language and that was a reason why **you found** it so hard to express yourself in writing (in Standard English?). **You said** that it was such hard work that **you wondered** whether it was just not natural for you to study. Yet **you also said** that you knew you'd got the ability to study but just **didn't feel** a part of it all. How do you feel now?

You said several times when you were writing your second essay that **you were finding** it very hard to write although you had your argument and **knew what you wanted to say. You seemed to be questioning** again whether this studying was really for you. What do you feel now?

You said you were fed up with reading about Creole being regarded as inferior and felt the whole area was very political. **You said** it was difficult to focus on language issues when the political issues were so strong. How did you manage to do this in the end?

Moreover, I would argue that allowing space for such areas of concern makes more conventional discussions – such as what is meant by 'grammatical' errors – more meaningful, precisely because questions of grammar are situated within a broader frame of reference. The interconnected nature of the concerns and issues raised by student-writers is illustrated in Figure 6.2, which outlines the key areas of discussion between one student-writer, Mary, and myself over a period of one year.

At specific moments, any one of the above points outlined in Figure 6.2 became the focus of our discussion and thus, temporarily, our principal concern. But the outline above also indicates the way in which specific

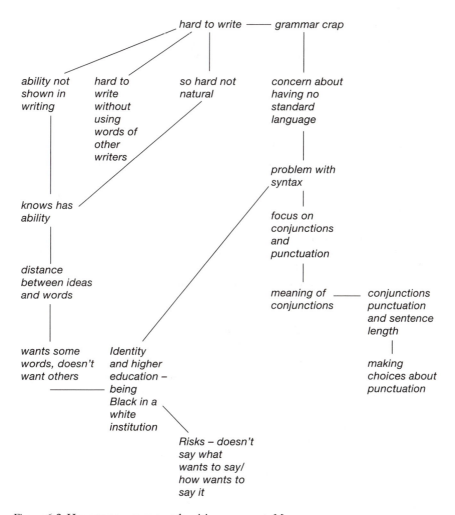

Figure 6.2 How concerns around writing connect: Mary

instances of talk about text are part of an ongoing and interrelated dialogue involving ideas, decisions and concerns about what is involved in student writing in academia. In this case, Mary's experience as a Black student in a predominantly white higher education system is bound up with what she does and means in her writing. Talkback sheets constitute, within this frame, a tool for developing a 'long conversation' (Maybin 1994) which seeks to engage with these interrelated dimensions.

Within this broader framed conversation, it becomes possible for student-writers to do two things, both of which are central to the possibility and nature of their participation in higher education. Firstly, they are provided with opportunities to articulate connections between elements of their experience and understanding which have previously been construed as separate. Secondly, they are provided with a space for contesting dominant meaning-making practices.

I will illustrate both of these dimensions by focusing on specific instances of talk with Mary.

'Crap grammar'

In our first meeting Mary said that her grammar was *crap* and she understood this to be a major problem in her writing. She couldn't give any specific examples of what was wrong with her 'grammar' but assumed that there was something fundamentally wrong with the ways in which she was using language. Through discussion, she began to define her problem as a problem with syntax:

> I must admit, I've got a problem in that I haven't got much confidence in my syntax. I think it is that because sometimes I write my own sentences and I think, does it make sense or does it not make sense? And I have to keep going to my mum all the time and reading it. She says, yes that makes sense.

After reading her texts, the only problems I identified with Mary's syntax were, on occasion, a) her use of some conjunctions as if these were 'empty' of meaning, and b) incorrect punctuation at some clause boundaries. We pursued these problem areas in our talk as I outline on page 153.

The extracts from the talk/talkback sheets illustrate the way in which talk serves the purpose of moving Mary away from an overwhelming sense of having crap grammar, and which was central to her concern about whether she was up to studying in higher education at all, towards naming particular aspects of written standard English that she needed to resolve; that is punctuation and use of conjunctions. However, Mary was still clearly unsure, indicated in the extracts above, about the precise problem with conjunctions. In another discussion, an extract of which is given on page 154, we pursue our focus on the functions of conjunctions.

152

Talk about conjunctions and punctuation

Extracts from texts, talkback sheets, and talk

A Extract from written draft	Whereas an English/Punjabi bilingual child's English surface fluency can be overestimated so the child is expected to have competent academic linguistic skills in English. But the experience for Creole speakers has been that their fluency (so to speak) is underestimated and their CALP skills are assumed to be worse than what they actually are.
B Extract from discussion of final draft	*T:* Whereas, all that, what? *M:* What I'm going to do is to make a comparison between the Punjabi and the Creole speakers, that's all. That's why I put whereas. *T:* That's okay. But if you're going to do that, you need to finish it off. —— Whereas, something is said about a Punjabi-speaking person, something else is said about a Creole speaker. And that's all in the structure. *M:* Ah I understand. *T:* So what do you need to get rid of? *M:* But. *T:* Yes. And the full stop. [*T* re-reads section] *M:* But why shouldn't I put 'but'? *T:* Because it's the same thing. You've already got whereas. If you got rid of whereas, you'd put but in to join them up. *M:* But that's a join, it's just at the beginning. *T:* Absolutely. *M:* And I've put another join in the middle again. *T:* Yes. Can you see that then? *M:* Yeah, now I can.
C Extract from talkback sheet	*T:* Can you see problems with the way these clauses come together? Are these examples of what you mean when you say you have problems with syntax?
D Extract from discussion of point in talkback sheet	*M:* Yeah, I think that's what it is. I don't know. I think it's punctuation, I'm not quite sure when to use it, I don't know.

From the talk episode on page 154, we see how Mary initially viewed 'however' as a linking device, empty of any particular meaning or function. Although we focus on it in one discussion (B), my brief attempt at explanation was of no use; it is not until a later discussion, prompted by my asking why Mary hadn't used it, that Mary seems to make sense of the meaning indicated by 'however' (C). The talk episodes enabled her to do the

Continuing talk about conjunctions

Extracts from texts, talkback sheets, and talk

A Extract from draft	In fact all types of West Indian Creoles should be viewed along a continuum. However, there is a large number of Creole speakers, but no one speaker uses a creolized speech to the same extent.
B Extract from discussion of draft of essay 2	*T:* Why have you used 'however'? *M:* I thought, I'm starting a new sentence. If I like, go straight, say 'there' straight away, to me it doesn't sound right. *T:* So you need something in there? *M:* Yeah. *T:* Well, 'however' introduces a new dimension, whereas you're adding on, continuing. What about 'for'? *M:* I don't like that. *T:* We'll come back to it.
C Extract from discussion based on talkback sheet.	*T:* You took 'however' out in your final draft. Why? *M:* I took it out because I didn't know what the hell was going on. So I thought, forget it. Get it out. I thought 'however' meant another change of thought. *T:* It does, but it means a change of *direction* of thought. *M:* I thought it meant the same direction. Oh, a completely different idea? *T:* It's like, say, I like shopping however I'm not going today. *M:* Whereas I've been saying, I like going shopping however I'm going to buy some [laughs]. *T:* Exactly. ――― *M:* It's serious. And I just used it casually like it was nothing, but it's very serious. ――― *M:* I'm glad you've shown me that anyway.

---

following: a) name the problem with her grammar, and consequently b) begin to take control over a specific linguistic feature in her texts. The talkback episodes above also illustrate the way in which student-writers can be provided with the opportunity to 'participate in the struggle' (Ivanic and Roach 1990: 8) around meaning making in academic writing, and thus claim their right to be writers, students, in academia.

'Why separate people?'

A talkback space also enables student-writers to challenge the ways in which dominant conventions privilege particular meanings, identities and participants in academia. As already discussed in previous chapters, Mary does this in several ways: she challenges the content required in academic writing, the relationships demanded and expected around academic texts, the wordings that writers are expected to use (see Chapters 4 and 5). That these are not discrete dimensions independent of each other is indicated by Mary's comments in response to note (9) of the talkback sheet above on page 150:

M: I do still feel the same about that [note 9]. I do still think 'why separate people?' Why does there have to be a distance, aren't we all bloody humans?

T: But which people are being separated from what, do you think? Everybody?

M: No, the person who's writing the idea is separating himself from what he's actually . . . obviously it's all that stuff about being objective and even if you're writing to somebody official, you never put 'I'. Why? Why? Isn't it you? Isn't it *you* that's writing the letter? Isn't it you you're talking about? Why not be direct and say 'I'?

T: So what's the effect of separating people. Why would the institution want to do that?

M: It's like a standing off, like I'm not interested in the person, I'm just interested in what they've written. Which I think is a bit . . . it's like, I just want your ideas, I don't want to know you.

That the student-writers, like Mary above, challenge dominant conventions in the talkback space has been illustrated throughout the preceding chapters and has been a key dimension to the discussions in this book.

However, what has also been clear from the student-writers' comments is that, in most instances, they are not in a position to enact such challenges in their written texts. Challenges, whilst confidently asserted in the talkback space, are muted in the actual construction of texts. Thus, Mary, the student who most confidently asserts her right to challenge, restricts her oppositional stance to imagining, rather than enacting, her desires for meaning making.

What I'm going to do, I'm going to hand in an assignment, give it in, and put in a little note, a little note at the top, saying I've used a lot of informal language. And I hope you don't consider it to be inappropriate. It's just that I like using it [laughs].

Laughing in dangerous places

Throughout this book, in the many extracts of talk between the student-writers and myself, there have been many references to laughter. This is signalled, but backgrounded, literally, through the use of brackets, as in the last extract. I want briefly to consider the hugely important function that such laughter plays in sustaining students' participation in our talk, and, I would argue, in higher education, by focusing on several extracts from the long conversation with Mary.

Consider the extracts below from Mary's talk where she is expressing some of her concerns about her writing:

> M: When you read my writing it just sounds oh bland – 'er, er, er, er'
> [monotone to indicate rhythm of writing] [laughs].

And

> T: What are you frightened of?
> M: You know, the word order, sometimes 'cause, you know, sometimes
> I'll write 'of' instead of 'have' and I can't see the difference until I
> sit down and really think about it.
> T: So are you saying that a lot of the sentence structure is lifted?
> M: Yeah, the structure yeah [laughs].

And

> M: I knew there was something wrong with that. I was waiting for you to
> point it out [laughs].

Here the laughter can be read both as embarrassment, and as a means of deflecting attention away from the embarrassment that Mary feels about not knowing how to write in academia. As adults, with substantial life experience, and sometimes older than the tutor (me in this instance) students often feel embarrassed, even ashamed, to be told what they feel they should already know. Laughter thus allows the possibility of acknowledging, whilst hedging, the seriousness of the student-writer's concern and thus allows her the possibility of continuing in this often uncomfortable teaching and learning context.[3]

Laughter also serves to dissipate a more fundamental danger: the threat that participation in higher education involves to the student-writer's sense of personal and social identity. This can be illustrated in the two brief extracts below:

> M: I mean, if I write like that if I use certain words that are just
> unnecessary, I'm just going to feel out of it.
> T: Out of what? [they laugh]
> M: Sort of like, I'm not me, you know? It's too much of a big stride.

156

And

> *M:* I feel like that about a lot of words [laughs]. Like sometimes if I'm talking to somebody who's not been to college or anything like that, I'll think, I can't say that word, you know. 'Cause they'll be thinking, 'what the hell's she thinks she's talking to'.

Laughing at these points in talk prevents either of the participants – Mary or I – talking ourselves towards the potentially fatal conclusion, that Mary might be better advised to leave higher education, in order to remain more comfortably part of her community. (I use 'fatal' here in terms of the hopes and aspirations of the student-writers to be successful in higher education.) Likewise, laughter occurs at points in our talk when the content of higher education is too unacceptable and raises questions for Mary about whether she will be able to manage to stay in such an institution.

> *M:* I feel there are things you can say and things that you cannot.
> *T:* Like?
> *M:* [Laughs] Like those white people, what I'd like to say would be out of context.

And

> *M:* I don't know, it's too political. You have to brush past too much political issue before you can really get to the effects of bilingualism. You get drawn into that instead of like, sticking to the question [laughs].
> ———
> *M:* It's too difficult, to tell the truth. I don't think I can cope with this assignment.

The last comment above illustrates the nature of the student-writer's comments when there are no [laughs]. Whereas the laughter in other talk episodes enables us to focus on something uncomfortable yet helps us to move on, this last comment was close to marking an end to our talk about a writing assignment, and, lurking in the background, potentially marking an end to Mary's studying.

The final comment I wish to make here focuses particularly on laughter in relation to Black students' feelings about participating in a white institution, and talking with a white tutor/researcher. Mary signalled her frustration in one of her comments above about what she can't say in a white institution, *like those white people, what I'd like to say would be out of context.* Problematising the racism of a white institution with a white tutor is a potentially dangerous act, hence the need for laughter to deflect tension. This is evident in the comment above and also in Mary's comments here:

M: Sometimes when I'm writing I think, how would they say it [laughs]?
And I'd like be going through a few sentences before I put it down.
T: When you say they
M: [the whites, innit?

Mary does two things here to minimise the risk to the talking relationship with the tutor: she refers to the whites as *they*, rather than *you*; she [laughs] after she has said this. Laughter here helps Mary to raise fundamental concerns she has about being a Black student in higher education, whilst minimising the potential of such comments to disrupt a talking relationship with a white tutor.

Conclusion

In this chapter, I have illustrated four different types of student-writer/tutor talk: tutor-directive dialogue aimed at talking the student-writer into essayist literacy practice; collaborative dialogue aimed at populating the student-writer's text with her own intentions; tutor-directive dialogue aimed at making language visible; dialogue which facilitates student 'talkback' as part of a long conversation. I have argued that together these types of talk serve to mediate student-writers' participation in essayist literacy, principally in two ways: firstly by enabling student-writers to be talked into – and thus to participate in – a practice with which they are unfamiliar; secondly by enacting a more dialogic addressivity between student-writers and tutors, whereby collaboration facilitates participation in meaning making.

The value of talking students into essayist literacy is that such talk-as-apprenticeship, between novice and expert, facilitates rather than denies participation. Such apprenticeship therefore stands in contrast to the model of pedagogy as implicit induction described in Chapter 3, in that it represents an attempt to actively scaffold student-writers into a practice, rather than assume that they will somehow 'pick it up'.

In this way, talk seems to meet the student-writers' desires for learning the rules of the essayist literacy game. Such talk is essential if facilitating access is to be a serious objective of higher education. However, such talk-as-apprenticeship also constitutes what Gee refers to as 'the paradox of literacy' (see Gee 1990: 67); that is, the teaching of essayist literacy may enable students from communities historically excluded to participate in HE, but at the same time it inevitably involves socialisation into dominant practices.

Through the remaining three types of talk illustrated in this chapter, I signal that even whilst working within the confines of the dominant practices within HE, it is possible for tutors to support the student-writer in their contesting of conventions and in their attempts to take control over their meaning making. This can be achieved in the following ways: working with the student-writer to identify the different voices within a text and exploring the voices which the student-writer wants to own; problematising a transparency notion of language by focusing on the relationship between wordings and meanings in texts; working at opening up a talkback space, where student-writers can a) come to name specific areas of difficulty and thus begin to participate in decisions around their own meaning making; and b) contest dominant conventions.

In advocating the usefulness of a number of specific types of tutor/student talk, I do not want to minimise the complex nature of this socio-discursive space. There are obvious tensions, arising, not least, out of the power differential between student-writer and tutor, as signalled in the brief section on the function of laughter. The student-writer will often be under considerable pressure to conform to the tutor's comments and perspectives rather than to negotiate her own position. This is the case even when talk has been ongoing for a considerable time. However, the episodes of student/tutor talk discussed in this chapter indicate the potential value of such talk for meeting the different desires of student-writers for access to and active participation in higher education.

Notes

1   There are many questions to explore about the nature of 'communities of practice' and the ways in which particular participants do or do not gain membership. For example, in the context of student writing in higher education, when and how is full membership achieved? What counts as full membership? If student-writers, as 'students', are by definition always outside the academic 'community', how should their writing be judged? How useful is the notion of apprenticeship to describe current fragmented patterns of participation in higher education and, indeed, students' purposes in engaging in study?
2   The research referred to here is that by Peter Nelmes, whose forthcoming Ph.D. thesis for the Open University is entitled, 'The role of emotions in the discourse of teaching and learning'.
3   Baynham 1996 makes similar points in relation to teaching and learning in an adult numeracy class.

7

RE-THINKING STUDENT WRITING IN HIGHER EDUCATION

Introduction

In this final chapter, instead of taking official discourse as our starting-point for thinking about the 'problem' of student writing in higher education, as I did in Chapter 1, I want to focus on understandings generated from recent work in academic literacies in the UK, including the research project on which this book is based. I will draw on these understandings in order to consider a framework which is more comprehensive in its description of different approaches to student writing and student writing pedagogy than that available in official discourse on communication. As such, this framework can serve as a heuristic, enabling us to consider how we wish to approach the teaching of student academic writing in the future. In many ways, now is a good time for re-thinking institutional and pedagogical practices in HE in the UK; for, whilst the principal argument in this book is that the official discourse on language and communication is, at best, ill conceived, the recent, officially sanctioned, interest in learning and teaching means that there is (some) space for re-imagining pedagogic theories and practices.[1]

This chapter is organised as follows. I begin with an overview of the ways in which the specific research discussed in preceding chapters contributes to the field of academic literacy research in the UK. Secondly, I locate this specific research within a broader conceptual framework emerging from work in academic literacies in order to explore both current and possible future ways of teaching and learning academic writing in HE in the UK. Thirdly, I summarise key points which need to be considered when making decisions about writing pedagogy, as well as raising further issues that we need to explore.

Contributing to Academic Literacies research in higher education

Student writing in HE is a relatively recent focus of enquiry in the UK. This book is a contribution to the growing field of academic literacies in the UK in several ways, whilst providing a point of comparison with work generated in other geographical contexts.

In general, the book provides substantial data-experience about students and their academic writing, in the form of written texts and talk about texts. It thus enhances the current limited availability of case study material for those wishing to pursue further study in this area.

More specifically, the numerous extracts from written texts and talk around the construction of these texts enable us to glimpse the workings of institutional literacy and pedagogical practices in relation to a growing group of students in higher education: that is, 'non-traditional' students. This focus illuminates both the nature of their current participation in HE and the nature of academic practices themselves. Whilst there are currently greater numbers of students from historically excluded social groups gaining access to higher education, I argue that current institutional practices may be limiting their participation. This is particularly evident in Chapter 3, where I illustrated through specific examples the workings of an 'institutional practice of mystery', whereby the institution fails to teach the conventions of the literacy practice it demands. This book thus provides case study support for claims made in other small-scale research studies in the UK (see Karach 1992) and more theoretically driven work, which indicates that higher education continues in its elitist and exclusionary practices (Bourdieu 1994).

In terms of what is involved in meaning making in student academic writing, the book responds in a small way to Ivanic's call for further studies on the ways in which 'specific textual features become imbued with social meanings' (Ivanic 1998: 333) by exploring authoring as a complex negotiation between specific wordings, personal and social senses of identity and institutionally privileged meanings. This is particularly evident in Chapters 4 and 5, where I focused on tensions between individual desire and institutional regulation of meaning making. Specific instances of text and talk around texts illustrate how the meanings student-writers make are regulated by dominant conventions, at the levels of both context of situation and context of culture. At the level of context of situation, direct regulation takes place in some instances, as when, for example, a tutor tells a student-writer what she can(not) say in her text. But indirect regulation is more common; this occurs, for example, when a tutor prohibits specific grammatical forms, such as the personal pronoun 'I' and contracted verb forms, the use (or not) of which contributes to the meanings being made in the text. Regulation at the level of context of culture can also be glimpsed from specific instances of student-writers' construction of texts. As student-writers struggle to construct what they think may count as knowledge within academia, they draw on dominant discourses from their previous and current personal, educational and professional experiences. This involves drawing on wordings which they feel are (or are not) privileged within HE, as well as

161

listening out for the specific wordings from actual speakers who – because of a combination of factors such as occupation, social class, 'race' and gender – occupy more privileged social positions than they do.

Listening to student-writers enables us to learn about the ways in which specific wordings are marked as more or less institutionally appropriate, according to the identities that these invoke. Learning about the perspectives of producers of texts, and their relationships with specific wordings at any one time, should help us to avoid imposing 'expert' readings and thus to avoid reaching dogmatic conclusions about the workings of discourse that Fairclough warns against (Fairclough 1995: 231).

It is difficult to get close to individual desires for meaning making within the context of culture of HE: student-writers' efforts are inevitably channelled into working out what is acceptable within HE, rather than exploring what they might want to mean. However, in the gaps between what student-writers' texts seem to mean and their talk about these texts, we catch glimpses of their individual desires for meaning making, which both converge with and diverge from essayist literacy practice (see Chapters 5 and 6). Convergence is particularly marked by a desire for 'new', academic-related wordings, although the writer's relationship with such wordings is often problematic. Divergence includes desires for greater connection between academic meaning making, personal experience and the individual's senses of personal and social identity. In Chapter 5, in particular, I signalled how individual desires for participation in higher education and use of its representational resources are marked by 'race', class and gender. I foregrounded, in particular, the way in which the student-writers resist the dominant gendered binary framework in essayist literacy.

A further desire, glimpsed in the student-writers' talk about the construction of their texts, is for different relationships around knowledge making, most obviously, for greater opportunities for dialogue with tutors. By focusing on specific instances of student/tutor dialogue around the construction of essayist texts, this book provides an analysis of the relationship between talk and learning, which, to date, has been carried out mainly in contexts of compulsory schooling (students aged 5–16). I indicated, in Chapter 6, the different ways in which specific types of tutor/student talk mediate the student's writing: by talking student-writers into essayist literacy; by facilitating negotiation and control over meaning making; by opening up opportunities for contesting dominant conventions. I stressed the importance of working at constructing a talkback – in contrast to the dominant feedback – space, as part of the development of long conversations between tutors and students. The ways in which talk mediates the construction of texts, moreover, problematises any easy distinctions between spoken and written discourse practices.

My aim in the next section is to locate these understandings within a broader academic literacies framework, in order to discuss their relevance to both current and possible future ways of teaching student writing in higher education.

A framework for exploring pedagogical approaches to student academic writing

Lea and Street (1998) and Ivanic (1999) have offered frameworks for thinking about existing approaches to the teaching/learning of student academic writing in HE in the UK. In Table 7.1, I draw on and make connections between their work, in order to offer a framework which serves as a description of different conceptualisations of student writing pedagogy, and as a heuristic, a means of raising questions about the kinds of practices in which we want/don't want to engage. In so doing, I bring in key notions from Bakhtin (see discussion in Chapter 2) in order to foreground the following: the relative institutional status occupied by different approaches to student writing within academia; the ways in which such approaches are enacted through particular types of addressivity; the kinds of communities of academia implied in actual enactments.

In Table 7.1, I have shaded what I would characterise as the predominant approach experienced by the student-writers in this book, in relation to the other frames identified in academic literacy research above; that is, writing as 'skill'. The reasons for claiming that the student-writers' experiences signal the skills approach are as follows. Firstly, the student-writers were studying in sites of HE where a range of 'skills' initiatives were in place at an institutional and/or department level, albeit in a fragmented way. Thus, the student-writers received written guidelines on academic writing and were provided with sessions on academic writing conventions, as well as, in some instances, study skills modules. Secondly, much of the student-writer accounts and actual instances of tutor written comment on their written texts, indicate the particular kinds of assumptions held about language and literacy, and which, I have argued, characterise the emphasis on communication skills in official discourse; language tends to be viewed as a transparent medium; writing is a matter of conveying ideas into words which are then transcribed; conventions once named are treated as self-evidently meaningful (see Chapter 3 in particular).

However, given the endless jostling across discourse practices, it is not meaningful to separate entirely a skills approach from other culturally available ways of both conceptualising and enacting the teaching of student writing in HE. Rather, I think it's important to signal a complex situation where there is often a coexistence, albeit of an unequal nature, of different approaches within the same pedagogic space. Thus, for example, although the 'non-traditional' student-writers in this book find themselves within a predominantly skills-marked space, as I've outlined above, other approaches can be identified and/or inferred from both tutors' and students' comments.

Table 7.1 Approaches to student academic writing in HE (UK)[2]

Status within HE	Approach to student writing[3]	Model of language	Institutional goal
Dominant	a) Skills – teaching discrete elements of language. *More dominant in 'new' HE sites.*	Emphasis (implicit) on language as transparent system, the elements of which are acquired by individuals.	**Higher education community viewed as homogeneous. Practices oriented to the reproduction of official discourses**
	b) Creative self-expression – teaching as facilitating individual expression.	Emphasis (implicit) on language/meaning as the product of individual mind.	
	c) Socialisation (1) – teaching as implicit induction into established discourse practices. *More dominant in traditional HE sites.*	Emphasis (implicit) on language as discourse practices which learners will/must gradually come to use.	
	d) Socialisation (2) – explicit teaching of features of academic genres.	Emphasis (explicit) on language as genres which are characterised by specific clusters of linguistic features.	
	e) Academic literacies/critical language awareness – teaching as ?: • active apprenticeship • making visible representational resources • problematising dominant conventions.	Emphasis (explicit) on language as socially situated discourse practices.	
Oppositional			**Higher education community viewed as heterogeneous. Practices oriented to making visible/challenging/playing with official and unofficial discourse practices**

As indicated by the lighter grey shading in Table 7.1, pedagogy as implicit induction/socialisation into academic and disciplinary practices may be informing (some) tutors' pedagogy, for some of the time. Indeed, it could be argued that the treating of conventions as if they were transparently meaningful, might, in part, be accounted for by tutors' implicit adoption of a socialisation (1) model of teaching and learning.[4]

What's important for our discussion here is that, as I suggested in Chapter 3, student-writers may suffer because a skills model is not up to the task of facilitating their access to the representational resources of HE, and a socialisation (1) model is neither possible within current material conditions of many HE sites, nor useful in the context of a student population with highly diverse previous educational and life experiences.

A further approach, which is closely bound up with socialisation (1) and evident in both tutor and student comments, is that of writing as creative self-expression (b, in Table 7.1). This approach to student writing, foregrounded as a key approach in Ivanic's framework, has a powerful presence in English teaching in UK schools (see Britton, Burgess and others 1975) and within US composition studies, often referred to as expressionism (see, for example, Berlin's account, 1988). In this framing, the emphasis is on writing as an expression of individual ideas, with a strong tendency to a) conceptualise language as transparent and, relatedly, b) to consider language and experience as unmediated by each other. This stance is evident in some of the routine comments made by tutors and student-writers. Thus, for example, it is not unusual to read a tutor comment which urges the student-writer to 'say what you mean'. Student-writers often conceptualise writing as transferring ideas from the mind to paper. Siria, for example, talks of not really having many concerns about her writing, just the problem of getting her *ideas on to paper*. Even though Mary consistently emphasises the ways in which academic writing practices are socially inscribed (see for example her comments in Chapter 4), she also signals, on occasion, another stance, that of romantic authoring: *Writing's about expressing yourself and how you feel at that time*. On another occasion she says:

> To me an essay's like a mood – it's got a feel to it, hasn't it? Like if
> I read certain essays, like if I read the bilingualism essay and I read
> the project it's got a different mood.

Thus, whilst I have emphasised, justifiably I think, a skills approach to student writing as that experienced by the student-writers in this book, it is also the case that this approach jostles with other approaches and understandings about academic writing. These need to be included in a framework seeking to encompass the range of existing approaches to student writing.

A further approach signalled in Table 7.1, is what I've referred to as 'socialisation' (2): briefly, by this I mean a pedagogy which involves explicitly focusing on the discourse features of written academic texts, usually known as a 'genre' approach. An example would be the identification and teaching of the particular kinds of processes (verbs) and participants (subjects and objects) used in academic discourse more generally, or in a particular academic discourse, for example science. This approach, I would argue, apart from the context of EAP (English for Academic Purposes), is mainly absent from the UK context; it was not in evidence at all in the experience of the student-writers in this book. The importance of teaching such genres and their key elements has been emphasised by writers, particularly in the context of secondary education schooling (see, for example, Martin 1993; Halliday 1993). The potential usefulness of such teaching within the context of writing in HE in the UK needs to be more fully explored.[5]

The categories a–d in Table 7.1 above are descriptive of current approaches to student writing in HE. The last, e, works as an oppositional frame, both in terms of its capacity to make visible the former categories (see Lea and Street 1998) and in terms of potentially offering an alternative frame for re-imagining writing pedagogy. I have linked what Lea and Street have termed an 'academic literacies' model with what Ivanic, amongst others, refers to as 'critical language awareness', because, whilst different in significant ways, they both start from the notion of language as socially situated discourse practices.[6] As a research frame, that is, as a frame which both connects with and illuminates aspects of student-writers' experiences, I hope this book illustrates its usefulness. Less straightforward is how such a frame is/can be enacted in pedagogic practices. Apart from a small amount of work which outlines how a critical language awareness pedagogy can be enacted within specifically defined 'writing support' or language areas of the curriculum, there is little to suggest how we might enact such approaches within disciplinary areas in HE (for some accounts of critical language awareness pedagogy, see Clark, Fairclough and others 1991; Fairclough 1992b; Janks 1999). Moreover, in such work, the emphasis tends to be on problematising dominant conventions; the tensions between pedagogy which seeks to provide students access to the privileged symbolic resources of HE – learning how to write within essayist literacy conventions – whilst at the same time problematising such resources, are often backgrounded (for detailed discussion see Lillis 1998). The experience of the student-writers discussed in this book suggests that we need a pedagogy which attempts to actively work with these tensions. The different types of tutor/student dialogue that I outlined in the previous chapter may contribute to the development of such an academic literacies/ critical language awareness pedagogy.

Principles, choices, questions

In the final column of Table 7.1 – 'institutional goal' – I draw on Bakhtin to signal that any decisions about student writing pedagogy involve questions about the project of higher education itself: What it is for? Who is it for? Which practices are to be valued, and why? The kinds of writing that are demanded, and the ways in which these are taught, cannot be thought of as an adjunct to the 'mainstream' curriculum or pedagogy but rather are integral to our aims in, and for, higher education. If the driving aim is to induct students into already established practices and values, then teaching writing practices will tend to centre on one, or a combination, of the approaches a, b, c, d. However, these approaches may contribute to the continued marginalisation of potentially substantial numbers of students because of a) the limitations of such approaches, which signal that the 'problem' of student writing is principally a 'textual' matter, and/or b) the complex material conditions of current higher education sites.

If higher education is to be reconceived as a site of diversity, with the potential to draw on and enact a range of discourse practices and identities, then our pedagogy will draw on the last frame, e. This last frame problematises the textual bias evident in the other approaches by, not least, emphasising the ideological nature of institutional practices and the ways in which decisions about meaning making in texts are always bound up with socially structured relations of power and of identity. Moreover, an academic literacies/critical language awareness approach involves a recognition of the need for a transformed addressivity, where collaboration and negotiation are central to the teaching of writing. The importance of adopting this frame when working with 'non-traditional' students in particular has been signalled throughout this book.

In this final section, I want to draw on the last frame, academic literacies/critical language awareness, and understandings generated from the experience of the student-writers discussed in this book, in order to foreground key points for consideration when thinking about the teaching of student writing. Each point raises more questions for debate than this book pretends to answer – particularly in relation to the availability and use of material resources in higher education. But the questions can help to set an institutional agenda for discussion about the nature, function and pedagogy of student writing in higher education between policy makers, practitioners, researchers and student-writers.

- **The dominant literacy practice in HE is essayist literacy. Students from social groups historically excluded from HE, in particular, may not know the myriad conventions of this practice and may find them difficult to learn, particularly in the current material conditions of higher education.**

Institutions, departments and tutors need to consider ways in which actively to provide access to the privileged literacy practice in higher education. Essayist literacy, as a historically situated overarching practice, has been foregrounded in this book: diversity across essayist literacy also needs to be acknowledged.

Key questions for exploration in specific contexts are as follows: How is essayist literacy taught to student-writers? Are particular considerations paid to the needs and desires of 'non-traditional' student-writers, and how? What opportunities exist for tutor/student dialogues which serve to talk students into these conventions? How can existing resources be organised in order to facilitate such dialogues?

In this book I have pointed to the distance between tutors' and student-writers' understandings about dominant conventions, and suggested that 'expert' tutors can mediate 'novice' students' participation in essayist literacy by actively talking them into this practice. The extent and ways in which these dialogues could be facilitated through other/additional means needs to be explored – for example, by more expert students scaffolding novices' learning.[7]

There is also a need to define more precisely the ways in which essayist literacy is enacted within different disciplinary practices, and the consequent implications for teaching.

- **The official discourse on communication in HE is implicitly framed by the notion of language as a transparent and autonomous conduit, the limitations of which need to be acknowledged.**

The limitations of a conduit model of communication, both in terms of our pedagogy and our conceptualisations of what is involved in student writing, need to be acknowledged. For example, the increasingly extensive use of written guidelines across institutions has only limited value and should not be seen as the primary means of teaching and learning essayist literacy. Written guidelines tend to become meaningful only when students are already familiar with this practice.

Key questions to be addressed are: How can institutions move away from a reliance on written guidelines and feedback, particularly in the early stages of students' participation in HE? How can opportunities be developed for exploration and negotiation of the meanings of essayist conventions?

In this book I have problematised the transparency model of language implicit in official discourse and illustrated how its routine enactment works towards marginalising 'non-traditional' students. I have signalled the potential importance of expert/novice dialogue for teaching conventions, as well as the need to problematise the presumed transparency of wordings in student-writers' texts. Further exploration is needed in order to establish which kinds of oral and/or written guidelines are useful to student-writers, at which points in their writing. Given the fragmented nature of student participation in higher education, alongside the official commitment to 'lifelong learning', it is particularly important to explore the ways in which students' learning of institutional practices can be facilitated at different moments in time, throughout their involvement in higher education.

- **Current pedagogic practices surrounding the setting and assessing of written assignments work towards confusing rather than illuminating the conventions student-writers are expected to write within.**

We need to become more aware of the many possible points of confusion, some of which are the direct result of our (tutors') own wordings and actions and some of which result from the nature of meaning making within the context of culture of HE.

Key questions are: What is the purpose of 'feedback'? What kinds of metalanguage – ways of naming language and practices – are useful to both tutors and students in explicating conventions? What strategies can be built into pedagogy for exploring students' perspectives on the usefulness of tutors' comments?

I have advocated an approach which builds on practices of 'talkback' rather than feedback. Talkback provides student-writers with the opportunity to respond to, and question, tutor comments, as well as to articulate their criticism of dominant conventions. We need to explore further which kinds of metalanguage are useful to students and tutors in talking about texts. More radically, we need to question the purpose and value of maintaining essayist literacy as the dominant practice in higher education and to explore ways in which alternative literacy practices can be incorporated into higher education culture and pedagogy.

- **Social and personal identity are bound up with ways of meaning making in fundamental ways.**

We need to acknowledge that in making meaning, student-writers are making conscious and unconscious choices about who they are, who they want to be and don't want to be, in their texts.

Key questions are: What kinds of identities are privileged through existing practices? How can traditionally excluded identities be foregrounded and included in teaching, learning and meaning making? What kinds of identities do we want to encourage in higher education, and why?

At various points throughout this book I have signalled that the assumed writer-subject of academic writing is neither universal nor autonomous: the student-writers' accounts constantly point to the significance of the social identities for meaning making, of both addressors and addressees. However, whilst foregrounding the problematic of identity in student writing, the question of how different identities/literacy practices can be included in the project of higher education is one with which I have briefly engaged, but which needs further exploration.

- **Collaborative talk between student-writers and tutors can facilitate greater individual control over meaning making, which in turn may work towards pushing the boundaries of what counts as acceptable meanings within academia.**

There needs to be a shift away from the dominant monologic type of addressivity within HE, where there is a denial of actual participants and where there is emphasis on the student-writer as individual producer. This would involve a significant transformation in the dominant culture of HE, with tutors working with student-writers in the construction of meanings, acknowledging the complex relationship between wordings, intention and identity.

Key questions are: How do we move towards a more dialogic addressivity? How do we come to understand the ways in which wordings signal particular identities and intentions? How do we prioritise our resources in ways which enable tutors to collaborate around meaning making? What are the implications for assessment practices of accepting and valuing such collaboration? What kinds of meanings are acceptable and why?

In this book I have pointed to the limitations of a monologic addressivity and argued that a more dialogic addressivity can contribute to student-writers' participation in essayist literacy and higher education. The ways in which dialogic practices could be built into curriculum programmes need to be explored at specific sites. Sections of this book contribute to understandings about the relationship between wordings and identities as experienced by the student-writers. However, further explorations, over a more extended period of time, need to be carried out.

- **Meaning in written texts is always meaning in the making**

We need to acknowledge the provisional nature of texts. We also need to acknowledge that it is not possible to 'read off' meanings, intentions and understandings from texts alone.

Key questions are: How should we view students' written texts? When is it most useful to view a text as a 'final' draft? How can we organise resources so that negotiation between students and tutors around the meanings in texts can take place? How can assessment practices take account of provisionality?

The provisionality of meaning in students' written texts has been signalled at different points throughout this book, as has the mediating potential of tutor talk on the construction of further drafts of texts. There is clearly a need to build into pedagogic practices opportunities for talk around draft texts. The ways in which this could be resourced in specific contexts needs to be examined at specific sites.

- **Taking greater control over meaning making involves making visible the representational resources that the student-writer is drawing on.**

There is a need to make language – as representational resource – visible in discussions around meaning making in written texts.

Key questions that we need to explore are: What kinds of metalanguage – naming practices – most usefully help to make visible the nature of the resources (wordings, voices, discourses) that students and tutors are using? How can practitioners and students come to share such a metalanguage?

In the research on which this book is based, I did not draw on or impose a particular formal metalanguage in discussions with student-writers about their texts. Instead, particular wordings which became meaningful to both of us over a period of time were used and re-used: for example, some traditional grammatical terms were used such as 'conjunctions', 'pronouns', 'verbs', alongside the more broadly conceived Bakhtinian term 'voices'. The proof of their usefulness is in the extent and ways in which student-writers ventriloquated such terms in their talk with me. Further exploration needs to be carried out over extended periods of time to explore which kinds of metalanguage can be usefully introduced and meaningfully used.

* * *

Sara: You're learning throughout the whole of your life.
Reba: But academic work's different. You should know how to do it in the first place.
Theresa: Why? Who's *born* doing academic work?
Sara: You're always learning. Every single day you *learn* something, don't you? It's just a process. You can't suddenly stop and think, right, I've got to do it myself.
Amira: That's why you're studying here as well.
Sara: That's why you're studying. You're learning.
_____
Reba: But if you can't do it, you shouldn't be here.
Amira: I think nobody can do anything without help.
Theresa: I agree with you there.
Amira: Everybody needs help.[8]

Notes

1   The Dearing Report argues for the need to focus on pedagogy in HE in the UK and has led to the recent establishment of the Institute for Learning and Teaching in Higher Education.

2   The categories in the second column, 'Approaches to student writing', are from Lea and Street (1998), Ivanic (1999) and Clark, Fairclough and others (1991). Lea and Street have offered a three-level model for theorising approaches to student writing in HE, described as 'skills', 'socialization' and 'academic literacies' (1998). These are marked as a, c, and e in my table. Ivanic has provided categories which correspond in some ways to these three frames, as well as introducing others not explicitly included in Lea and Street's model; these are what I have referred to as 'creative self-expression', b (see Ivanic 1999) and 'socialisation' (2), d. Clark, Fairclough and others (1991) have also theorised an oppositional stance in the teaching of academic writing, 'critical language awareness', which I think corresponds in significant ways to Lea and Street's category of 'academic literacies' (see e on table).

3   I have not included a 'process' approach to student academic writing in HE because here I'm signalling different epistemological positions on student writing. A 'process' approach is often linked to creative self-expression, b on the table. However, given that a focus on 'the writing process' usually involves an emphasis on writing activities – planning, drafting, revising – it could be connected with any of the approaches outlined. The specific nature of these activities would differ according to the stance adopted towards language and meaning making.

4   I disagree with Lea and Street, who suggest that in HE practice in the UK, writing-as-socialisation (1) has superseded, chronologically and conceptually, the notion and practice of writing-as-skills (see Lea and Street 1998) for two reasons. Firstly, there is much jostling across specific instances of pedagogy. This needs to be built into any model of academic writing. Secondly, I think many 'new' universities are predominantly skills-marked spaces, which raises important questions about social stratification across HE sites. This difference needs to be foregrounded in any discussion about student writing.

5   Some work with a pedagogic emphasis is in progress in this area. For examples, see Pardoe, Donohue, Wegerif and Coffin. Pardoe is currently building on his research to construct a pedagogical frame which is informed by notions of genre (personal communication). For examples of his research see Pardoe 1993, 1997, 2000. See also ongoing work by Donohue. Wegerif and Coffin's approach (1999) to teaching academic writing in an electronic environment is informed by a 'genre' framing.

6   The most obvious difference is that whilst the academic literacies approach, as discussed by Lea and Street, is presented as one of three models of student writing in HE, 'critical language awareness' is presented as a pedagogic-research tool. However, the writers share a common frame of reference for thinking about student writing in HE.

7   Whilst I think the notion of apprenticeship, whereby students are construed as 'novices' and tutors as 'experts', is useful to the discussion here, there are some fundamental limitations to this frame. I will be exploring these limitations elsewhere.

8   This extract is taken from a spontaneous discussion about who should and should not be studying in higher education, where the tape-recorder had been left running.

APPENDIX 1

Overview of student writers

Writer	First generation at university?	Languages used on regular basis	Age at first meeting	Qualifications on leaving school (see Appendix 2 for details)	Qualifications/courses post-school (see Appendix 2 for details)
Amira	✓	Arabic, English	21	2 GCSEs: Maths, English	BTEC National diploma – social work.
Bridget	✓	English	47	3 O levels: English language, English Literature, Maths	RSA typing and shorthand: Access (1 year) to higher education.
Diane	✓	English, Jamaican Creole	32	——	GCSE English language, Child Psychology, Law, Home economics, sociology
Kate	Father studied at university as mature student.	English	48	6 O levels: Maths, Geography, History, English language, French, Biology	Qualified general nurse (SRN) / sick children nurse (RSCH) 1-year Access (social sciences) to HE
Mary	Mother studied at university as mature student.	English, Jamaican Creole	21	2 GCSEs: English language, Arts	GCSE English literature, A level Psychology, Maths (GCSE)

continued . . .

Name		Languages	Age	Qualifications	Further qualifications/courses
Nadia	✓	Arabic, English	20	—	BTEC First Aid, Health and Social Work
Reba	✓	Sylheti-Bengali, English	20	5 GCSEs: Humanities, Science, Art, English, Bengali	—
Sara	Both parents studied to degree level in Pakistan.	Urdu, English	25	6 O levels: Chemistry, Biology, English language, Maths, Urdu, Art	BTEC National diploma in business and finance
Siria	✓	Sylheti-Bengali, English	24	3 GCSEs: Science, Home economics, Bengali	RSA typing (II) Advanced Play Workers Course SYOCF (3), NVQ 3 Social Care.
Tara	✓	English	36	—	'Step Forward' 3-month Access course, 1-year Access to HE course

APPENDIX 2

Details of UK examinations, qualifications and courses

Throughout the accounts of the student-writers' previous educational experience, I refer to courses and qualifications peculiar to the UK context. Here is a brief guide for those unfamiliar with them.

- *GCE/GCSE* (current) / *O levels* = state examinations taken at the age of 16; the government has in recent years decided that five GCSEs at grades A–C should be the minimum target for every 16-year-old.
- *A levels* = state examinations taken at the age of 18; three good passes (A–C) at A level constitute the traditional route to higher education.
- *BTEC* = vocational courses for students post-16 years of age, often the only option for students from working-class minority ethnic groups, as discussed by Roberts and others 1992 and Sarangi 1996.
- *11 plus* = a state exam taken at the age of 11, the results of which determine whether you go to a *grammar school*, an academically oriented school, or a *secondary modern/comprehensive school*. Currently it is used in only a minority of places in England.
- *Access courses* = courses aimed specifically at preparing for entry to HE those students who do not go into HE by the A-level route (successfully passing three A levels at age 18).
- *UCAS forms* = application forms for university.
- *YTS* Youth Training Scheme = a vocational course whose stated aim was to provide young people with the necessary skills to gain a job.

APPENDIX 3
Data collection and transcription

1 Summary of data collection: talk and written texts

On the next page is a summary of the amount of data collected, in terms of the number of set assignments discussed and the time spent on discussing drafts towards that assignment. The time given in the table refers only to time spent on discussions about texts that students were writing at the time of our meetings. It does not include time spent in discussing texts from previous courses, informal discussions about writing, either face-to-face or by telephone, or literacy history interviews. It does not include time continuing to be spent in subsequent years with with Mary, Nadia and Sara.

Total drafts (including final drafts) collected for analysis	Total taped discussions for analysis	Total time of taped discussions
71	81	approx. 60 hours

I collected copies of all the drafts we discussed, as well as materials provided by tutors and departments in relation to the students' writing, such as essay questions, guidelines on the writing of coursework, background notes relating to the essay content. Some student-writers also gave me copies of essays we did not discuss as well as substantial notes made in preparation for writing their essays. I also kept a diary for some of the time.

2 Spoken and written texts collected during the first two years of the project

	set assignment	Student 1 Amira	Student 2 Reba	Student 3 Sara	Student 4 Siria	Student 5 Mary	Student 6 Nadia
		number of taped discussions around texts					
Phase 1	1	2	2	3	4	3	3
Oct–Jun	2	3	2	3	2	6	2
1994–95	3	4	1	3	3	4	4
Total time in minutes spent in (taped discussion)		327	170	426	263	407	230

	set assignment	Student 5 Mary	Student 6 Nadia	set assignment	Student 7 Bridget	Student 8 Diane	Student 9 Kate	Student 10 Tara
		number of taped discussions			number of taped discussions			
Phase 2	4	3	2	1	2	2	3	2
Sept–Mar	5	4	1	2	1	3	2	2
1995–96				3	1			
Total time in minutes spent in (taped) discussion		555	195		190	257	140	195

☐ students involved in phases 1 and 2 of project.

3 Conventions used for transcribing talk in this book

. , ?	Conventions of punctuation used to indicate in writing my understanding of the sense of the spoken words (see Halliday 1989: 90)
T	initial of person speaking
italics	word stressed
[	overlaps/interruptions
. . .	long pause (longer than 2 seconds)
[sounds unsure]	transcriber's comments for additional description or background information
*	unclear speech
——	gap in data transcribed

APPENDIX 4

Feedback and talkback sheets

Example of assessment feedback sheet

EVALUATING ASSIGNMENTS

STUDENT NAME

ASSIGNMENT TITLE *Language and gender*

INTRODUCTION		TUTOR COMMENTS
1. Interpretation of question and introduction.	Clearly understands question and gives outline of the content of essay.	(10) ✓ Good – although I think your first two paragraphs = introduction. I'd like us to discuss subheadings again.

MAIN PART OF ESSAY

2. Understanding of subject.	Shows clear understanding of subject area.	(20) A good attempt to use project drawn heavily on Spender and Cameron, focusing on the nature of language more than linguistic behaviour although you do explore this more re the second part.
3. Critical approach.	Shows evidence of critical reflection on theory/sources/ personal experience.	(10) A good first attempt. I think you could have focused on whether language can be neutral and considered your experience as pupil and teacher in more detail.
4. Clarity of ideas /logical argument.	Develops a logical argument. Clear links between ideas expressed in the essay.	(10) See notes. Some paragraphing not right. The second section could be lighter
5. Relevant examples/evidence.	Uses relevant examples from sources and/or observation, experience.	(10) Good used examples from texts. More examples from experience would have enhanced your essay.
6. Appropriate use of linguistic terms.	Uses linguistic terms relevant to subject.	(10) Well done. · ✓

CONCLUSION

7. Conclusion.	Draws together the various points made. Highlights key points/conclusions from essay.	(10) I think we need to discuss this. Your conclusion could have more clearly summarised the main points made in the whole essay.

REFERENCES

8. References.	References of all sources used in essay given in appropriate detail.	(10) To discuss. Rd a good first attempt.

9.   OTHER ASPECTS TO BE CONSIDERED   (10)

TUTOR COMMENT

SPELLING-all words correctly spelt.   ✓

GRAMMAR AND SYNTAX-no errors of grammar and syntax.

STYLE-formal style, i.e. no colloquialisms, abbreviations, restricted use of 'I' (writing in first person).   See notes. In some parts you've made 'notes' I think rather than writing in complete sentences.

LENGTH-appropriate length   ✓

LEGIBILITY-very clear and easy to read.   ✓

PRESENTATION-well presented with use of headings, diagrams where appropriate.   Well done with the wpc ✓

Example of talkback notes

POINTS ARISING FROM OUR DISCUSSIONS OF DRAFTS FOR ESSAY FOR MODULE 1

1 **Using new/different/alternative words.** Hierarchy was one word you decided you wanted to use in this essay. In the first draft it looked strange because of the word it was with but in the final draft you used it successfully. You said it was a word you would only use in certain formal situations. Would you use it again and are there any other words like this? In one instance you used a word institution to refer to things which weren't institutions. Do you feel as if you understand this? Are you using any new words for this essay?

2 **Use of inverted commas.** You used them in two ways in your drafts – to quote and to highlight. How will you use them in future?

3 **Writing exactly what you mean to say/talk in your writing.** There were several examples in both drafts 1 and 2 where when you talked about what you wanted to say, you explained yourself clearly but your explanations were not in your writing. Sometimes there were gaps between what you intended to be understood and what was written down. How can you tackle this in the next essay?

4 **Critically reading draft.** You said that one way to help avoid some of the jumps would be to get someone else to re-read your drafts. Are you going to do this this time?

5 **Paragraphing.** In your final draft you split a couple of sections which really would have been better understood if you'd put them in one paragraph. What can you do about this?

6 **Where you position yourself in your writing.** You said that you preferred to write in the third person, they, in order to be neutral about what you were writing. Will you do this in your next essay and where will you fit yourself, your personal experience in?

7 **Sentence structure/complete sentence.** There was one example of a complex sentence which you found difficult to analyse and correct. This may be something to look out for.

8 **Introducing/explaining quotes.** We discussed the need for you to introduce any quotes that you use and also to make it clear to the reader why such a quote might be relevant. Do you think you know how to do this for this essay?

9 **Linking/cohesion.** There were two examples where you used this to refer back to an idea but where it wasn't exactly clear what you were referring to. Perhaps you could check the way you use it in this essay.

10 **Referencing conventions.** We talked about these quite a lot. Do you feel confident about these now?

11 **Grammar.** There was one example of you missing out the subject of a sentence. Do you think this was a slip or do you need to look out for this?

REFERENCES

Ackerman, J. (1993) 'The promise of writing to learn', *Written Communication* 10, 3: 334–70.

Andrews, R. (1995) *Teaching and Learning Argument,* London: Cassell.

Angelil-Carter, S. (ed.) (1998) *Access to Success: Literacy in Academic Contexts,* Cape Town: University of Cape Town Press.

Anzaldua, G. (ed.) (1990) *Making Face, Making Soul,* San Francisco: Aunt Lute Books.

Arnberg, L. (1987) *Raising Children Bilingually: The Pre-school Years,* Clevedon: Multilingual Matters.

Ashworth, P. D., Bannister, P. and Thorne, P. with members of the MA in qualitative research methods (1997) 'Guilty in whose eyes? University students' perceptions of cheating and plagiarism', *Studies in Higher Education* 22: 187–203.

Bakhtin, M. (1981) 'Discourse in the novel', in M. Holquist (ed.) *The Dialogic Imagination. Four Essays by M. Bakhtin,* trans. C. Emerson and M. Holquist, Austin: University of Texas Press.

—— (1984) *Problems of Dostoevsky's Poetics,* trans. C. Emerson, Minnesota: Manchester University Press.

—— (1986) 'The problem of speech genres', trans. V. W. McGee in C. Emerson and M. Holquist (eds) *Speech Genres and Other Late Essays,* Austin, Texas: University of Texas Press.

Ballard, B. and Clanchy, J. (1988) 'Literacy in the university: an anthropological approach', in G. Taylor, B. Ballard, V. Beasley, H. Bock, J. Clanchy and P. Nightingale, *Literacy by Degrees,* Milton Keynes: SRHE/Open University Press.

Barnett, R. (1992) *Improving Higher Education: Total Quality Care,* Milton Keynes: SRHE/Open University Press.

Bartholomae, D. (1985) 'Inventing the university', in M. Rose (ed.) *When a Writer Can't Write,* New York: Guilford Press.

Barton, D. (1994) *Literacy: An Introduction to the Ecology of Written Language,* Oxford: Blackwell.

Barton, D. and Hamilton, M. (1998) *Local Literacies,* London: Routledge.

Barton, D., Hamilton, M. and Ivanic, R. (eds) (2000) *Situated Literacies. Reading and Writing in Context,* London: Routledge.

Barton, D. and Padmore, S. (1991) 'Roles, networks and values in everyday writing', in D. Barton and R. Ivanic (eds) *Writing in the Community,* London: Sage.

Baynham, M. (1995) *Literacy Practices: Investigating Literacy in Social Contexts,* London: Longman.

—— (1996) 'Humour as an interpersonal resource in adult numeracy classes', *Language and Education* 10, 2/3: 187–200.

Bazerman, C. (1981) 'What written knowledge does: three examples of academic discourse', *Philosophy of the Social Sciences* 11: 361–87.

—— (1988) *Shaping Written Knowledge,* Madison: University of Wisconsin Press.

Belenky, M., Clinchy, B., Goldberger, N. and Tarule, J. (1986) *Women's Ways of Knowing,* New York: Basic Books.

Bell, R. E. (1973) 'The growth of the modern university', in R. E. Bell and A. J. Youngsen (eds) *Present and Future Higher Education,* London: Tavistock.

Benson, N., Guerney, S., Harrison, J. and Rimmershaw, R. (1993) 'The place of academic writing in whole life writing: a case study of three university students', *Language and Education* 7, 1: 1–20.

Berkenkotter, C. (1999) 'Making genres and their systems visible: what's in a unit of analysis', paper presented at Conference on College Composition and Communication, Atlanta, Georgia.

Berkenkotter, C. and Huckin, T. N. (1995) *Genre Knowledge in Disciplinary Communication: Cognition/Culture/Power,* Hillsdale, NJ: Lawrence Erlbaum.

Berlin, J. (1982) 'Contemporary composition: the major pedagogical theories', *College English* 44, 8: 766–77.

—— (1988) 'Rhetoric and ideology in the writing class', *College English* 50, 5: 477–96.

Biggs, J. (1988) 'Approaches to learning and essay writing', in R. R. Schmeck (ed.) *Learning Strategies and Learning Styles,* New York: Plenum Press.

Bizzell, P. (1982a) 'Cognition, convention and certainty: what we need to know about writing', *Pre/text* 3: 213–44.

—— (1982b) 'College composition: initiation into the academic discourse community', *Curriculum Inquiry* 12, 1: 191–207.

—— (1990) 'Beyond anti-foundationalism to rhetorical authority: problems defining "cultural literacy"', *College English* 52, 6: 661–75.

—— (1991) 'Professing literacy: a review essay', *British Educational Research Journal,* 21, 2: 219–35.

—— (1992) *Academic Discourse and Critical Consciousness,* Pittsburgh: University of Pittsburgh Press.

—— (1994) 'Are shared discourses desirable? A response to Nancy McKoski', *Journal of Advanced Composition* 14, 1: 271–7.

—— (1997) 'Rhetoric and social change', http://www.hu.mtu.edu /cccc/97/bizzell. html.

Blackburn, R. and Jarman, J. (1993) 'Changing inequalities in access to British universities', *Oxford Review of Education* 19, 2: 197–214.

Bolker, J. (1979) 'Teaching Griselda to write', *College English* 40: 906–8.

Bourdieu, P. (1984) *Distinction,* trans. R. Nice, London: Routledge.

—— (1991) *Language and Symbolic Power,* trans. G. Raymond and M. Adamson, Cambridge, MA: Polity Press.

—— (1994) *Academic Discourse: Linguistic Misunderstanding and Professorial Power,* trans. R. Teese, Cambridge, MA: Polity Press.

Britton, J. L., Burgess, T., Martin, N., McCleod, A. and Rosen, H. (1975) *The Development of Writing Abilities 11–18,* London: Macmillan.

Brooke, R. (1988) 'Modeling a writer's identity: reading and imitation in the writing classroom', *College Composition and Communication* 39, 1: 24–41.

Brooks, A. (1997) *Academic Women*, Buckingham: SRHE/Open University Press.

Brown, P. and Levinson, S. C. (1987) *Politeness: Some Universals in Language Use*, Cambridge: Cambridge University Press.

Brown, S. and Knight, P. (1994) *Assessing Learners in Higher Education*, London: Kogan Page.

Caldas-Coulthard, R. and Coulthard, M. (eds) (1996) *Texts and Practices*, London/New York: Routledge.

Callaghan, J. (1976) 'Towards a national debate (The Ruskin Speech)', *Education* (Journal of the Association of Education Committees) 124, 17: 332–3.

Cameron, D. (1992) (2nd edn) *Feminism and Linguistic Theory*, London: Macmillan.

—— (1997) 'Theoretical debates in feminist linguistics: questions of sex and gender', in R. Wodak (ed.) *Gender and Discourse*, London: Sage.

Campbell, J. (1992) 'Controlling voices: the legacy of English A at Radcliffe College 1893–1917', *College Composition and Communication* 43, 4: 472–85.

Canagarajah, Suresh A. (1997) 'Safe houses in the contact zone: coping strategies of African-American students in the academy', *College Composition and Communication* 48, 2: 173–96.

Cherry, R. (1988) 'Ethos vs. persona: self-representation in written discourse', *Written Communication* 5, 3: 251–76.

Chouliaraki, L. and Fairclough, N. (1999) *Discourse in Late Modernity*, Edinburgh: Edinburgh University Press.

Christian-Smith, L. K. (1990) *Becoming a Woman through Romance*, New York: Routledge.

Clanchy, J. (1985) 'Improving student writing', *HERDSA News*, 3: 3–4.

Clark, R. (1992) 'Principles and practice of CLA in the classroom', in N. Fairclough (ed.) *Critical Language Awareness*, London: Longman.

Clark, R. and Ivanic, R. (1997) *The Politics of Writing*, London: Routledge.

Clark, R. and Ivanic, R. (1991) 'Consciousness-raising about the writing process', in C. James and P. Garrett (eds) *Language Awareness in the Classroom*, London: Longman.

Clark, R. and Lorenzini, M. (1999) 'Focus on writing: an institution-wide approach to the development of students' writing skills', in P. Thompson (ed.) *Academic Writing Development in Higher Education: Perspectives, Explorations and Approaches*, Reading: Centre for Applied Language Studies, University of Reading.

Clark, R., Constantinou, C., Cottey, A. and Yeoh, O. C. (1990) 'Rights and obligations in student writing', in R. Clark, N. Fairclough, R. Ivanic, N. McLeod, J. Thomas and P. Meara (eds) *Language and Power*, London: Centre for Information on Language Teaching for the British Association for Applied Linguistics.

Clark, R., Fairclough, N., Ivanic, R. and Martin-Jones, M. (1991) 'Critical language awareness, Part 11: towards critical alternatives', *Language and Education* 5, 1: 41–54.

Clarke, J. and Saunders, C. (1997) 'Negotiating academic genres in a multi-disciplinary context', *Journal of Further and Higher Education* 21, 3: 297–304.

Coates, J. (1993) (2nd edn) *Women, Men and Language*, London: Longman.

Corson, D. (1985) *The Lexical Bar*, Oxford: Pergamon Press.

Creme, P. and Lea, M. (1999) 'Student writing: challenging the myths', in P. Thompson (ed.) *Academic Writing Development in Higher Education: Perspectives, Explorations and Approaches*, Reading: Centre for Applied Language Studies, University of Reading.

Crowley, S. (1998) *Composition in the University: Historical and Polemical Essays*, Pittsburgh: University of Pittsburgh Press.

Cummins, J. (1984) *Bilingualism and Special Education: Issues in Assessment and Pedagogy*, Clevedon: Multilingual Matters.

CVCP (Committee of Vice-Chancellors and Principals of the Universities of the UK) (1998) *Skills Development in Higher Education*, London: CVCP.

Davies, B. (1997) 'Constructing and deconstructing masculinities through critical literacy', *Gender and Education* 9, 1: 9–30.

Delpit, L. (1988) 'The silenced dialogue: power and pedagogy in educating other people's children', *Harvard Educational Review* 58, 3: 280–98.

DFEE (1998) *Departmental Report*, London: The Stationery Office Ltd.

Dixon, K. (1995) 'Gendering the "personal"', *College Composition and Communication* 46, 2: 255–75.

Donohue, J. (forthcoming PhD thesis) 'An evaluation of explicit genre pedagogy in subject specific academic literacy teaching/learning on a university first year media studies course', Luton University.

Drew, S. (1998) *Key Skills in Higher Education: Background and Rationale*, SEDA Special No. 6, Birmingham: SEDA.

Drew, S. and Bingham, R. (eds) (1997) *Student Skills: Tutor's Handbook*, Aldershot: Gower.

Edwards, D. and Mercer, N. (1987) *Common Knowledge: The Development of Understanding in the Classroom*, London/New York: Methuen.

Elbow, P (1973) *Writing without Teachers*, Oxford/New York: Oxford University Press.

—— (1991) 'Reflections on academic discourse: how it relates to freshmen and colleagues', *College English*, 53, 2: 135–55.

Ellsworth, E. (1994, first published 1989) 'Why doesn't this feel empowering? Working through the repressive myths of critical pedagogy', in L. Stone (ed.) *The Education Feminism Reader*, London: Routledge.

Emig, J. (1971) *The Composing Processes of Twelfth Graders*, NCTE research report no. 13, Urbana, IL: NCTE.

English, F. (1999) 'What do students really say in their essays? Towards a descriptive framework for analysing student writing', in C. Jones, J. Turner and B. Street (eds) *Students Writing in the University: Cultural and Epistemological Issues*, Amsterdam: Benjamins.

Fairclough, N. (1989) *Language and Power*, London: Longman.

—— (1992a) *Discourse and Social Change*, Cambridge: Polity Press.

—— (ed.) (1992b) *Critical Language Awareness*, London: Longman.

—— (1995) *Critical Discourse Analysis*, London: Longman.

—— (1996) Unpublished draft for talk given at AILA (Association internationale de linguistique appliqué) conference.

Fish, S. (1980) *Is There a Text in This Class? The Authority of Interpretive Communities*, Cambridge, MA: Harvard University Press.

Flower, L. (1985) (2nd edn) *Problem-Solving Strategies for Writing*, San Diego: Harcourt.

—— (1994) *The Construction of Negotiated Meaning: A Social Cognitive Theory of Writing*, Carbondale and Edwardsville: Southern Illinois Press.

Flower, L. and Hayes, J. R. (1977) 'Problem-solving strategies and the writing process', *College English* 39: 449–61.

———— (1981) 'A cognitive theory of writing', *College Composition and Communication* 32: 365–87.

Flynn, E. (1988) 'Composing as a woman', *College Composition and Communication* 39: 423–35.

Foucault, M. (1972) *The Archaeology of Knowledge*, trans. A. M. Sheridan Smith, London: Routledge.

—— (1973) *The Order of Things*, New York: Random House.

Fraser, N. (1991) 'The uses and abuses of French discourse theories for feminist politics', in P. Wexler (ed.) *Critical Theory Now,* London: Falmer Press.

Freedman, A., Adam, C. and Smart, G. (1994). 'Wearing suits to classes: simulating genres and simulations in genres', *Written Communication* 11, 2: 193–226.

Freire, P. (1985) *Pedagogy of the Oppressed,* London: Penguin.

—— (1996, first published 1970) *The Politics of Education: Culture, Power and Liberation,* Hadley, MA: Bergin and Garvey.

Frey, O. (1990) 'Beyond literary Darwinism: women's voices and critical discourse', *College English* 52, 5: 507–26.

Gardener, S. (1992, first published 1985) *The Long Word Club: The Development of Written Language Within Adult Fresh Start and Return to Learning Programmes,* Bradford: RaPAL (Research and Practice in Adult Literacy).

Gee, J. P. (1990) *Social Linguistics and Literacies: Ideology in Discourses,* London: Falmer Press.

—— (1996) (2nd edn) *Social Linguistics and Literacies: Ideologies in Discourses,* Basingstoke: Falmer Press.

Geertz, C. (1973) *The Interpretation of Cultures,* New York: Basic Books.

Geisler, C. (1994) *Academic Literacy and the Nature of Expertise: Reading, Writing and Knowing in Academic Philosophy,* Hillsdale, NJ: Lawrence Erlbaum Associates.

Gibbs, G. and Habeshaw, T. (1989) *Preparing to Teach: An Introduction to Effective Teaching in Higher Education,* Bristol: Technical and Educational Services Ltd.

Goodwin, V. (1998) *The Current Provision of Language and Study Support in UK Higher Education,* An audit and discussion prepared for a day conference at the Open University's West Midlands regional office, Birmingham: Open University.

Graff, H. (1987) *The Labyrinths of Literacy: Reflections on Literacy Past and Present,* New York: Falmer Press.

Griffiths, M. (1995) 'Making a difference: feminism, post-modernism and the methodology of educational research', *British Educational Research Journal* 21, 2: 219–35.

Guba, E. and Lincoln, Y. (1981) *Effective Evaluation,* San Francisco: Jossey-Bass.

Halliday, M. A. K. (1978) *Language as Social Semiotic,* London: Edward Arnold.

—— (1988) 'On the language of physical science', in M. Ghadessy (ed.) *Registers of Written English: Situational Factors and Linguistic Features,* London: Frances Pinter.

—— (1989) *Spoken and Written Language.* Oxford: Oxford University Press.

—— (1993) *Writing Science: Literacy and Discursive Power,* Bristol, PA: Falmer Press.

—— (1994) (2nd edn) *An Introduction to Functional Grammar,* London: Edward Arnold.

Halliday, M. A. K. and Hasan, R. (1989) (2nd edn) *Language, Context, and Text: Aspects of Language in a Social-Semiotic Perspective,* Oxford: Oxford University Press.

Halsey, A. H., Lauder, H., Brown, P. and Wells, A. S. (eds) (1997) *Education: Culture, Economy and Society,* Oxford: Oxford University Press.

185

Hamilton, M. (1994) 'Introduction: signposts', in M. Hamilton, D. Barton and R. Ivanic (eds) *Worlds of Literacy*, Clevedon: Multilingual Matters.

Hamilton, M., Barton, D. and Ivanic, R. (eds) (1994) *Worlds of Literacy*, Clevedon: Multilingual Matters.

Harris, M. (1992) 'Collaboration is not collaboration is not collaboration: writing center tutorials vs. peer-response groups', *College Composition and Communication* 43, 3: 369–83.

—— (1995) 'Talking in the middle: why writers need writing tutorials', *College English* 57, 1: 27–42.

Haswell, J. and Haswell, R. E. (1995) 'Gendership and the miswriting of students', *College Composition and Communication* 46, 2: 223–54.

Heath, S. B. (1983) *Ways with Words*, Cambridge: Cambridge University Press.

HEFCE (1999) *Performance Indicators in Higher Education in the UK*, Bristol: HEFCE.

Hodge, R. and Kress, G. (1993) (2nd edn) *Language as Ideology*, London: Routledge.

Holland, C., Frank., F. and Cooke, T. (1998) *Literacy and the New Work Order: An International Literature Review*, Leicester: NIACE.

Honey, J. (1997) 'Sociophonology', in F. Coulmas (ed.) *The Handbook of Sociolinguistics*, Oxford: Blackwell.

hooks, b. (1988) *Talking Back: Thinking Feminist, Thinking Black*, Boston: South End Press.

—— (1994) *Teaching to Transgress: Education as the Practice of Freedom*, London: Routledge.

Horner, B. (1999) 'The "birth" of "basic writing"', in B. Horner and Min-Zhan Lu, *Representing the 'Other': Basic Writers and the Teaching of Basic Writing*, Urbana, IL: NCTE.

Horner, B. and Lu, Min-Zhan (1999) *Representing the 'Other': Basic Writers and the Teaching of Basic Writing*, Urbana, IL: NCTE.

Hounsell, D. (1984) 'Learning and essay writing', in F. Marton, D. Hounsell and N. Entwistle (eds) *The Experience of Learning*, Edinburgh: Scottish Academic Press.

—— (1987) 'Essay writing and the quality of feedback', in J. T. E. Richardson, M. W. Eysenck and D. W. Piper (eds) *Student Learning: Research in Education and Cognitive Psychology*, Milton Keynes: Society for Research in Higher Education and Open University Press.

Howe, F. (1971) 'Identity and expression: a writing course for women', *College English*, 32: 863–71.

Hymes, D. (1977) *Foundations in Sociolinguistics*, London: Tavistock.

Irigary, L. (1993) *Je, Tu, Nous. Toward a Culture of Difference*, trans. A. Martin, London: Routledge.

Ivanic, R. (1993) 'The discoursal construction of writer identity', unpublished Ph.D. thesis, University of Lancaster.

—— (1995) 'Writer identity', *Prospect: The Australian Journal of TESOL* 10, 1: 1–31.

—— (1998) *Writing and Identity: The Discoursal Construction of Identity in Academic Writing*, Amsterdam: Benjamins.

—— (1999) 'A framework for thinking about writing, and learning to write', paper presented at Discourses and Learning conference, Lancaster University, July.

Ivanic, R. and Roach, D. (1990) 'Academic writing, power and disguise', *Language and Power*, London: Centre for Information on Language Teaching for the British Association of Applied Linguistics.

REFERENCES

Ivanic, R. and Simpson, J. (1992) 'Who's who in academic writing?' in N. Fairclough (ed.) *Critical Language Awareness*, London: Longman.

Ivanic, R. Aitchison, M. and Weldon, S. (1996) 'Bringing ourselves into our writing', *RaPAL* 28/29: 2–8.

Janks, H. (1999) 'Critical language awareness journals and student identities', *Language Awareness*, 8, 2: 111–22.

Johnson, S. and Meinhof, U. (eds) (1997) *Language and Masculinity,* Oxford: Blackwell.

Jones, C., Turner, J. and Street, B. (eds) (1999) *Students Writing in the University: Cultural and Epistemological Issues,* Amsterdam: Benjamins.

Karach, A. (1992) 'The politics of dislocation: some mature undergraduate women's experiences of higher education', *Women's Studies International Forum* 15, 2: 309–17.

Karach, A. and Roach, D. (1994) 'Collaborative writing, consciousness raising and practical feminist ethics', in M. Hamilton, D. Barton and R. Ivanic (eds) *Worlds of Literacy,* Clevedon: Multilingual Matters.

Kirsch, G. (1993) *Women Writing the Academy: Audience, Authority and Transformation,* Carbondale and Edwardsville: Southern Illinois Press.

Knowles, J. (2000) *Pity the Poor Students,* University of Lincolnshire and Humberside, Policy Studies Research Centre.

Kress, G. (1995) 'Making signs, making subjects: the English curriculum and social futures', inaugural lecture, London: Institute of Education, University of London.

—— (1996) 'Representational resources and the production of subjectivity: questions for the theoretical development of Critical Discourse Analysis in a multicultural society', in R. Caldras-Coulthard and M. Coulthard (eds) *Texts and Practices,* London/New York: Routledge.

Kristeva, J. (1986) ed. Toril Moi, *The Kristeva Reader,* Oxford, Blackwell.

Lamb, B. C. (1992) *A National Survey of UK Undergraduates' Standards of English,* London: Queen's English Society.

Lambert, W. E. (1977) 'The effects of bilingualism on the individual: cognitive and socio-cultural consequences', in P. Hornby (ed.) *Bilingualism: Psychological, Social and Educational Implications,* New York: Academic Press.

Lather, P. (1986) 'Issues of validity in openly ideological research: between a rock and a soft place, *Interchange,* 17, 4: 63–84.

—— (1991) *Getting Smart: Feminist Research and Pedagogy with/in the Postmodern,* London: Routledge.

—— (1995) 'The validity of angels: interpretive and textual strategies in researching the lives of women with HIV/AIDS, *Qualitative Inquiry,* 1: 41–58.

Lave, J. and Wenger, E. (1991) *Situated Learning: Legitimate Peripheral Participation,* Cambridge: Cambridge University Press.

Layton, D. (ed.) (1968) *University Teaching in Transition,* Edinburgh: Oliver and Boyd.

Lea, M. (1995) 'I thought I could write until I came here', *Language in a Changing Europe,* Clevedon: British Association for Applied Linguistics and Multilingual Matters Ltd.

Lea, M. and Street, B. (1998) 'Student writing in higher education: an academic literacies approach', *Studies in Higher Education* 11, 3: 182–99.

—— (1999) 'Writing as academic literacies: understanding textual practices in higher education', in C. Candlin and K. Hyland (eds) *Writing: Texts, Processes and Practices,* London: Longman.

Lee, A. (1996) *Gender, Literacy, Curriculum: Re-writing School Geography*, London: Taylor and Francis.

Lillis, T. (1997) 'New voices in academia? The regulative nature of academic writing conventions', *Language and Education*, 11, 3: 182–99.

—— (1998) 'Making meaning in academic writing', unpublished Ph.D. thesis, Sheffield Hallam University.

—— (1999) '"Whose common sense?" Essayist literacy and the institutional practice of mystery', in C. Jones, J. Turner and B. Street (eds) *Students Writing in the University: Cultural and Epistemological Issues,* Amsterdam: Benjamins.

Lillis, T. and Ramsey, M. (1997) 'Student status and the question of choice in academic writing', *RaPAL* 32: 15–22.

Lillis, T. and Turner, J. (2001) 'Student writing in higher education: contemporary confusion, traditional concerns', *Teaching in Higher Education* 6, 1: 57–68.

Lu, Min-Zhan (1987) 'From silence to words: writing as struggle', *College English* 49, 4: 437–48.

—— (1990) 'Writing as repositioning', *Journal of Education* 172, 1: 18–21.

—— (1991) 'Redefining the legacy of Mina Shaughnessy: a critique of the politics of linguistic innocence', *Journal of Basic Writing* 10, 1: 26–40.

—— (1994) 'Professing multiculturalism: the politics of style in the contact zone', *College Composition and Communication* 45, 4: 442–58.

Luke, A. (1994) 'On reading and the sexual division of literacy', *Journal of Curriculum Studies* 26, 4: 361–81.

Mace, J. (1992) *Talking about Literacy: Principles and Practice of Adult Literacy Education,* London: Routledge.

—— (1998) *Playing with Time: Mothers and the Meaning of Literacy,* London: UCL Press.

Martin, J. (1993) 'Literacy in science: learning to handle text as technology', in M. A. K. Halliday, *Writing Science: Literacy and Discursive Power*, Bristol, PA: Falmer Press.

Maybin, J. (1994) 'Children's voices: talk, knowledge and identity', in D. Graddol, J. Maybin and B. Stierer (eds.) *Researching Language and Literacy in Social Context,* Clevedon: Multilingual Matters.

Mehan, H. (1979) *Learning Lessons: Social Organization in the Classroom,* Cambridge: Cambridge University Press.

Mercer, N. (1995) *The Guided Construction of Knowledge,* Clevedon: Multilingual Matters.

Michaels, S. (1981) '"Sharing time": children's narrative styles and differential access to literacy', *Language in Society* 10: 36–56.

Moss, G. (1994) *Un/popular Fictions,* London: Virago.

Myers, G. (1985) 'The social construction of two biologists' proposals', *Written Communication* 2, 3: 219–455.

National Committee of Inquiry into Higher Education (Dearing Report) (1997) *Higher Education in the Learning Society: Report of the National Committtee,* London: HMSO.

National Council for Vocational Qualifications (NCVQ) (1995) *GNVQ Briefing. Information on the Form, Development and Implementations of GNVQs,* London: NCVQ.

Newby, H. (1999) *Higher Education in the 21st Century: Some Possible Futures,* CVCP paper VC/99/5, London: Council of Vice-Chancellors and Principals.

Newman, J. H. (1959) *The Idea of the University*, New York: Doubleday (first published 1873).

Norton, B. (2000) *Identity and Language Learning: Gender, Ethnicity and Educational Change*, Harlow: Pearson Educational Limited.

Norton, L. S. (1990) 'Essay writing: what really counts', *Higher Education* 20: 411–42.

Nye, A. (1990) *Words of Power*, New York/London: Routledge.

Nystrand, M. (1990) 'Sharing words: the effects of readers on developing writers', *Written Communication* 7, 1: 3–24.

Nystrand, M. and Wiemelt, J. (1991) 'When is a text explicit? Formalist and dialogical conceptions', *Text* 11, 1: 25–41.

Nystrand, M., Greene, S. and Wiemelt, J. (1993) 'Where did composition come from? An intellectual history', *Written Communication* 10, 3: 267–333.

Olson, D. (1977) 'From utterance to text: the bias of language in speech and writing', *Harvard Educational Review* 47, 3: 257–87.

Pardoe, S. (1993) 'Learning to write in a new educational setting: a focus on the writer's purpose', paper presented at the Symposium on 'Learning to write in new settings', European Association for Research on Learning and Instruction (EARLI), 5th European Conference, Aix-en-Provence, France.

—— (1997) 'Writing professional science: genre, recontextualisation and empiricism in the learning of professional and scientific writing within an M.Sc. course in environmental impact assessment', unpublished Ph.D. thesis, Department of Linguistics and MEL, Lancaster University.

—— (2000) 'A question of attribution: the indeterminacy of "learning from experience"', in M. Lea and B. Stierer (eds) *Student Writing in Higher Education: New Contexts*, Buckingham: SRHE/Open University Press.

Parker, F. and Campbell, K. (1993) 'Linguistics and writing: a reassessment', *College Composition and Communication* 44, 3: 295–314.

Patthey-Chavez, G. G. and Ferris, D. R. (1997) 'Writing conferences and the weaving of multi-voiced texts in college composition', *Research in the Teaching of English* 31, 1: 51–90.

Petraglia, J. (1995) (ed.) *Reconceiving Writing, Rethinking Writing Instruction*, Mahwah, NJ: Lawrence Erlbaum.

Prior, P. (1998) *Writing/Disciplinarity: A Sociohistoric Account of Literate Activity in the Academy*, Mahwah, NJ: Lawrence Erlbaum.

Prosser, M. and Webb, C. (1994) 'Relating the process of undergraduate writing to the finished product', *Studies in Higher Education* 19, 2: 125–38.

Race, P. and Brown, S. (1993) *500 Tips for Tutors*, Kogan Page: London.

Reddy, M. J. (1979) 'The conduit metaphor: a case of frame conflict in our language about language', in A. Ortony (ed.) *Metaphor and Thought*, Cambridge: Cambridge University Press.

Roberts, C., Garnett, C., Kapoor, S. and Sarangi, S. (1992) *Quality in Teaching and Learning: Four Multicultural Classrooms in Further Education*, Sheffield: Training, Enterprise and Education Directorate, Department of Employment.

Robertson, D. (1997) 'Growth without equity? Reflections on the consequences for social cohesion of faltering progress on access to higher education', *Journal of Access Studies* 12: 9–31.

Rockhill, K. (1987) 'Literacy as threat/desire: longing to be somebody', in J. S. Gaskill and A. T. McLaren (eds) *Women and Education: A Canadian Perspective*, Calgary: Deselig.

—— (1994) 'Gender, language and the politics of literacy', in J. Maybin (ed.) *Language and Literacy in Social Practice*, Clevedon: Multilingual Matters/Open University Press.

Rose, M. (1989) *Lives on the Boundary*, New York: Penguin.

Russell, D. (1991) 'Writing across the curriculum in historical perspective: towards a social interpretation', *College English* 52: 52–73.

—— (1997) 'Rethinking genre in school and society: an activity theory analysis', *Written Communication,* 14, 4; 504–54.

Sarangi, S. (1996) 'Vocationally speaking: (further) educational construction of "workplace identities"', *Language and Education* 10, 2 and 3: 201–20.

Scollon, R. (1995) 'Plagiarism and ideology: identity in intercultural discourse', *Language in Society* 24: 1–28.

Scollon, R. and Scollon, S. B. K. (1981) *Narrative, Literacy and Face in Interethnic Communication*, Norwood, NJ: Ablex.

Scott, M. (1999) 'Agency and subjectivity in student writing', in C. Jones, J. Turner and B. Street (eds) *Students Writing in the University: Cultural and Epistemological Issues*, Amsterdam: Benjamins.

Scribner, S. and Cole, M. (1981) *The Psychology of Literacy*, Cambridge, MA: Harvard University Press.

Shaughnessy, M. (1977) *Errors and Expectations: A Guide for the Teacher of Basic Writing*, New York: Oxford University Press.

Sheridan, A. (1980) *Michel Foucault: The Will to Truth*, London/New York: Tavistock.

Sinclair, J. and Coulthard, M. (1975) *Towards an Analysis of Discourse: The English Used by Teachers and Pupils*, Oxford: Oxford University Press.

Sirc, G. (1989) 'Gender and writing formations in first year narratives', *Freshman English News* 18: 4–11.

Skutnabb-Kangas, T. (1981) *Bilingualism or Not: The Education of Minorities*, trans. L. Malmberg and D. Crane, Clevedon: Multilingual Matters.

Spender, D. (1980) *Man Made Language,* London: Routledge and Kegan Paul.

Sperling, M. and Warshauer Freedman, S. (1987) 'A good girl writes like a good girl', *Written Communication* 4, 4: 343–69.

Stanley, L. and Wise, S. (1990) 'Method, methodology and epistemology in feminist research processes', in L. Stanley (ed.) *Feminist Praxis,* London: Routledge.

Stiver Lie, S. and O'Leary, V. (1990) *Storming the Tower: Women in the Academic World*, London: Kogan Page.

Street, Brian (1984) *Literacy in Theory and Practice*, Cambridge: Cambridge University Press.

—— (ed.) (1993) *Cross-cultural Approaches to Literacy*, Cambridge: Cambridge University Press.

—— (1995) *Social Literacies*, London: Longman.

—— (1999) 'Academic literacies', in C. Jones, J. Turner and B. Street (eds) *Students Writing in the University: Cultural and Epistemological Issues*, Amsterdam, Benjamins.

Stubbs, M. (1997) 'Whorf's children: critical comments on Critical Discourse Analysis (CDA)', in *Evolving Models of Language*, Clevedon: British Association for Applied Linguistics and Multilingual Matters.

Swales, J. M. (1990) *Genre Analysis: English in Research Settings,* Cambridge: Cambridge University Press.

Swann, J. (1992) *Girls, Boys and Language,* Oxford: Blackwell.

Tedesco, J. (1991) 'Women's ways of knowing/women's ways of composing', *Rhetoric Review* 9, 3: 246–55.

Tight, M. (1998) 'Education, education, education! The vision of lifelong learning in the Kennedy, Dearing and Fryer reports', *Oxford Review of Education* 24, 4: 473–85.

Training Agency (1990) *The Current Role of TVEI: Focus Statement,* Training Agency.

Turner, J. (1999) 'Academic literacy and the discourse of transparency', in C. Jones, J. Turner and B. Street (eds) *Students Writing in the University: Cultural and Epistemological Issues,* Amsterdam: Benjamins.

Villanueva, V. (1993) *Bootstraps: From an American Academic of Color,* Urbana, IL: NCTE.

Weedon, C. (1987) *Feminist Practice and Poststructuralist Theory,* Oxford: Basil Blackwell.

Wegerif, R. and Coffin, C. (1999) 'Learning online as induction into a discourse community', paper presented at the Conference of Computer Assisted Learning (CAL99), London: Institute of Education.

Weiner, G. (1998) 'Here a little, there a little: equal opportunities policies in higher education in the UK', *Studies in Higher Education* 23, 3: 321–33.

Wells, G. (1985) *Language Development in the Pre-school Years,* Cambridge: Cambridge University Press.

—— (1986) *The Meaning Makers,* Portsmouth, NH: Heinemann.

—— (1994) 'The complementary contributions of Halliday and Vygotsky to a "Language-based theory of learning"', *Linguistics and Education* 6: 41–90.

Wertsch, J. (1991) *Voices of the Mind: A Sociocultural Approach to Mediated Action,* London: Harvester Wheatsheaf.

Widdowson, H. (1995) 'Discourse analysis: a critical view', *Language and Literature* 4, 3: 157–72.

—— (1996) 'Discourse and interpretation: refutations and conjectures (Reply to Fairclough)', *Language and Literature* 5, 1: 57–69.

Winch, C. and Wells, P. (1995) 'The quality of student writing in higher education: a cause for concern?' *British Journal of Educational Studies* 43, 1: 75–87.

Womack, P. (1993) 'What are essays for?', *English in Education* 27, 2: 42–59.

Wyatt, J. (1990) *Commitment to Higher Education: Seven Western Thinkers on the Essence of the University,* Buckingham: SRHE/Open University Press.

INDEX

academic literacies 14, 164, 166, 167; UK research 160–3
access 2, 16–31; gender 109, 110–13; privileged practice 53–77
action: human agency in essayist literacy 79; language as 25
addressivity 43–7, 74–5; academic literacies approach 167; gender 119–20, 130; monologic 170; regulation of student-writers 89–90, 105; tutor–student talk 132–58
adversary method 80–1
agency, conventions of essayist literacy 79
Amira 5, 57, 88, 109–10, 114, 117
amplification 80
appropriateness 24
Athabaskans 38, 48
audiences; skills approach 24–5: *see also* reader
author: absence of 68, 83, 87–9, 100–4, 115–20, 126; addressivity 43; fictionalisation of 38, 76; presence 81, 92
authoritative discourse 48
authority, identity 50
available subject positions 48

Bakhtin, M. 33; addressivity 43–4, 74; becoming 48–9; dialogicality 41–2
Barnett, R. 54
Barton, D. 34
basic writing courses 21–2, 26
Bazerman, C. 29, 33
becoming 48
Berkenkotter, C. 29, 33
Berlin, J. 29, 33
binary framework 81, 115, 126–7

Bizzell, P. 28, 29; discourse communities 30; social practice approach 33
Bolker, J. 123
Bourdieu, P. 31; elitism 161; habitus 34, 48
Bridget 7, 60–1, 82–3, 105–6, 109, 110, 114
Britton, J.L. 26

Callaghan, J. 23
Cameron, D. 128
Campbell, J. 116
Castellanos, Rosario 104
children, addressivity 43–4
Cicero 80
Clanchy, J. 58
Clark, R. 30, 50; producers' perspectives 81; struggle in meaning making 48
class *see* social class
collaborative dialogue 138–42, 158, 170
'common sense', essayist literacy 75–6
communication, skills 23–5
composition classes 21, 26, 165
conduit model of language 24, 168–9; addressivity 43
conferencing 29–30
context: meaning making 28–9; skills approach 24–5; *see also* context of culture; context of situation
context of culture 36; addressivity 44, 45–7; communication 25; gender 120; language as discourse practice 34, 35; regulation of student-writers 89–90, 101–4, 105, 161–2; vocabulary 95–6; wordings 145–7; writing as meaning making 28–9

192

social class 18; access 109; discursive practices 36; regulation of student-writers 89; vocabulary 92–4, 96

social identity 169–70; academic practice 30–1; regulation of student-writers 100–4; vocabulary 94–6

social practice 33–51

socialisation 30; approach to student writing 164, 165–6

speech communities 30

Stanley, L. 80–1

Street, B. 28, 30, 163; academic literacies 166; literacy 37

student-writers: addressivity 44–7; desires 2, 14, 107–30, 127–8, 162; essayist literacy 40–1; fictionalisation of 76; identity 49–50; implicit induction 54–6; perspective of 81–2; regulation of 78–106, 161–2; relationship with tutors 72–5, 120–2; research 4–12; text research 27; tutor–student collaboration 170; tutor–student talk 132–58, 162; understanding essay questions 58–72; writing to please the reader 122–5, 129–30

students: age 17; conferencing 29–30; ethnic minorities 17; non-traditional 16; statistics 17; women 17

study skills courses 22

subjectivity 18, 49–50

Swales, J.M. 58

Swann, J. 126

talk around texts 6–11

talkback 10–11, 147–58, 162, 169

Tara 63–8, 72–3, 110, 114, 124–5, 128

Tedesco, J. 123

text-oriented discourse analysis 35

textual bias 22–5, 31–2, 34–5

time, access 111–13

transferable skills 23–5, 56

tutor–directive talk 134–8, 143–7, 158

tutors: addressivity 43–5; approaches to student writing 163–5; conferencing 29–30; essay questions 58–72, 169; gendering of text 123–4; grading criteria 57–8; implicit induction 54–6; regulation of student-writers 82–4, 104–5, 161–2; relationship with student-writers 72–5, 120–2; tutor–directive talk 134–8, 143–7, 158; tutor–student collaboration 170; tutor–student talk 132–58, 162; writing to please the 122–5, 129–30

United States of America: 'literacy crises' 21–2; research 26

unity 134–8

utterance: addressivity 43–7; dialogicality 41–2

Villanueva, V. 80

vocabulary: regulation of student-writers 84–5, 86, 90–100, 105; talkback sheet 148; see also wordings

voice-as-experience 46–7

voice-as-language 46–7

WAC see writing across the curriculum

Wenger, E. 133

Wise, S. 80–1

Womack, P. 20

women: see also gender; student numbers 17; subjects 18

wordings: context of culture 145–7; desires 162; regulation of student-writers 161–2

writing: meaning making 27–9; role in higher education 20–3; as social practice 31–2

writing across the curriculum (WAC) 26

writing centres 22

written guidelines 23, 168–9